Ethel Marie:

How a Minnesota Farm Girl
Helped Me to Understand
Life, Love, and Human Destiny

by
Kelly Nicholson

For permission, serialization, condensation, adaptions, or for our catalog of other publications, write to Ozark Mountain Publishing, Inc., P.O. Box 754, Huntsville, AR 72740, ATTN: Permissions Department.

Library of Congress Cataloging-in-Publication Data

Ethel Marie by Kelly Nicholson 1951 -

In this book a long-time academician recalls his life and the shaping influence of his mother, a woman of plain origins who gave him insight, by her example, into the timeless wisdom of the world's great spiritual traditions.

1. Spiritual 2. Traditions 3. Metaphysical

I. Nicholson, Kelly, 1951 - II. Metaphysical III. Spiritual IV. Title

Library of Congress Catalog Card Number: 2025937303

ISBN: 978-1-962858-38-0

Cover Design and Layout: Victoria Cooper Art
Book set in: Times New Roman, Britannic Bold
Book Design: Summer Garr
Published by:

PO Box 754, Huntsville, AR 72740
800-935-0045 or 479-738-2348; fax 479-738-2448
WWW.OZARKMT.COM

Printed in the United States of America

To great souls,
so many of them unsung,
who light our pathways Home

Table of Contents

Foreword

To begin this story, I might say a few words about my livelihood. Most of it has been spent in the academic world, where I have taught courses of many kinds, mostly in philosophy, a "love of wisdom" (*philia, sophia*) rooted in culturally Greek areas of Europe and Asia Minor.

The spark of this enterprise was struck, say historians, in the 6th to 5th centuries before the Common Era when a few bold thinkers in that region began to inquire into the nature of the cosmos—the grand theater of all that is—and their place within it.

To do this, they relied not upon mere tradition, and the time-honored stories, say, of men like Homer and Hesiod. Instead, they struck out upon a venture of abstract reason. The universe, they supposed, had in it a coherent nature that made it accessible to the mind. What was its key substance, its origin and guiding principle? In coming centuries, this inquiry would widen to include concern with *the good life* and how personally to achieve it.

Philosophy, as we think of it today, is an inquiry into life's most basic questions. *What do we make of this mortal journey on which we find ourselves embarked? What do we know, and what ought we to do? Where, in the end, are we headed?*

There was a time when this enterprise enjoyed high status. It was the basis, the queen mother, so to speak, of inquiry altogether. The seminal philosopher Rene Descartes, writing in the seventeenth century, likened it to a great tree, its roots being the endeavor of "first principles," or *metaphysics*, an exploration beginning with his own conscious experience and what he knew with immediate certainty. Its trunk, so to speak, was physical science, its branches, the fields he called ethics, mechanics, and medicine.

Descartes wrote during the rise of "natural philosophy," an enterprise that would spawn, over the course of a few hundred years, the world-transforming activities of science and technology. As this activity took center stage, the discipline otherwise became less of a going concern. While philosophy has a place in the present day college curriculum, its role is a modest one. Few students choose it as a major study—what, after all, does one "do" with it? (Employment prospects within the field, as any *alumnus* can tell you, are daunting.)

I think, even so, that my subject remains essential to life. In fact, everyone down deep is a philosopher of sorts. Or at least, everyone should be. Our most important choices, if one thinks about it—what we want from life, what we require of ourselves and expect from others in turn; the people whom we choose as friends and the way we raise our children; where we imagine this mortal path leads—all proceed from some sense within us of what is good and real and important.

Granted, not everyone has a strong bent in this direction. Many of us are passive, resting satisfied with the doctrines and mindsets we inherit. In which case, the choices that shape our lives owe to nothing more than happenstance. Had we been born into another time and culture—or raised even in the house across the street—our whole outlook might be different.

Philosophy begins for us, as it did for the Greeks, when we step back from this personal setting and seek answers of our own. The mere fact that some viewpoint is in vogue, or was foisted upon us in our formative years, is irrelevant to its truth. (Granted, this may be *how I was raised, but was I raised rightly?* The answer to this question requires some work on my own.)

It could be that we never escape altogether these shaping influences—as will be apparent in coming pages, much of what I believe today was absorbed quite early. But any verdict we reach about such influences, and ultimately about who we are and where we are headed, must be gained by active reflection if it is truly to be our own. Speaking as a longtime instructor, I might add, it is heartening to see a student take hold of life in this fashion, whether it be at eighteen or thirty-eight, or even at seventy.

That said, there is yet something odd about this inquiry into "basic" questions. In most human endeavor there is discernible *progress* from one era to another—mathematics, the physical sciences, military technology, the excavation of human history, and so forth. True, there may be dark ages and periods of stagnation; there may be areas of controversy, and problems that resist solution—such resistance is found even in the field of pure mathematics, where doubt may arise as to an alleged proof, or whether a solution is possible.[1] Yet in most cases we seem to get closer, with time, to a truth that is "out there" waiting.

With philosophy, the situation is less clear. Old questions endure. Problems that engaged Socrates centuries before the Common Era in the marketplace of Athens—the gods, the soul, good and evil, the meaning of life—are still open. Such questions, we imagine, have answers. Yet two "experts" of comparable skill, armed with similar credentials, can arrive at wildly different conclusions.

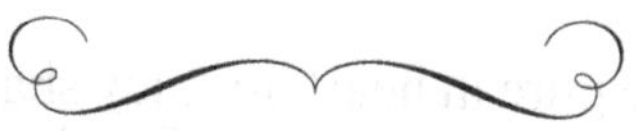

The dominant trend of academic philosophy, within my own lifetime, has been a thoroughgoing *materialism*. This term has a familiar ring, since it is used commonly to describe a certain lifestyle—one that is devoted to material wealth and the status it confers. The materialism I note here, however, is theoretical. It is an intellectual endeavor, one that seeks to reduce all reality to witnessable events in the world of space and matter.

Thus, there is little interest in many of today's programs, in gods, or souls, or things generally of the spirit. Values, obligations, ideals toward which we strive—such things, on this view, are but odd stirrings acquired in our long history of animal struggle. We ourselves are lumps of organic machinery, here by accident with nothing awaiting us beyond this scant brief adventure.

It may be that this view is only natural. Perhaps it does figure that this world, bathing us each waking moment in its image and texture, should provide for many the home ground of what is real. Yet there is another way of seeing reality—one quite old, and present across many cultural settings. It is not so much about things in the world, but how we "take" the world altogether. Life, on this view, is not an accident, but a spiritual event, running deeper than the flow of sight and sound that passes daily before us.

Novelist and religious scholar Aldous Huxley, borrowing a phrase from the philosopher-mathematician Gottfried Wilhelm von Leibniz in the 18th century, calls this outlook *perennial*. It is a vision, rather like an enduring flower, that waxes and wanes,

---

1   For an engaging example, see Sandor Singh, *Fermat's Enigma* (New York: Doubleday, 1997).

and thrives again. It can fade in the chill of cultural seasons, wither even to the brink of death. Yet always it returns.

The substance of *The Perennial Philosophy* can be gleaned from topical headings in the chapters of Huxley's work, which bears that phrase as its title. God, Eternity, Salvation, Good and Evil, Immortality—such things as beckon us away from this visible world toward something higher.

The excerpts in that volume, as Huxley himself notes, do not come solely from "professional men of letters." For this vision finds its greatest expression, at times, not in scholars, but in plain and decent folk who have made themselves "loving, pure in heart, and poor in spirit."[2]

"Blessed are the pure in heart, for they shall see God." Huxley cites Jesus, a First Century *tekton* (a Greek term for a craftsman who works with stone and wood), who proclaimed this message (Matthew 5: 8) in his hallowed Sermon on the Mount. Thus truth, it seems, can be found in humble places.

My mother knew these words well, having absorbed them at a young age and believing them all her life.

"I remember my mother's prayers," once said Abraham Lincoln, "and they have always followed me. They have clung to me all my life."

How well I know. My own mother never stood at a lectern to instruct a class, and left behind little writing, but for a modest diary she kept for a couple of years during her twenties. Yet her impact on me was immeasurable.

It was because of her, I imagine, that I never dove as energetically into mainstream academic philosophy as did some of my classmates. My starting point, my whole sensibility, it often seemed, was different from theirs, and from the dominant outlook of my instructors. It was not until I began teaching that I knew what it meant to be fully engaged with my own subject.

How exactly do we come by our sense of life and what it means? Philosophy, I have come to think, is more than the cataloging of ideas or the acquisition of skill in debate. If we are to understand life, we must open not only our minds, but our hearts,

---

2   Aldous Huxley, *The Perennial Philosophy* (New York: HarperPerennial, 1945), page x.

paying heed to our deepest intuitions and to our encounters with our fellows. In these sources, I believe, are revelations. I think of childhood friends, teachers and students, ministers, gymnasium trainers, hospital nurses, and firefighters, who have given me insight, lent me support, called me up short when I needed it, and provided an occasion for growth.

Need it be said at the outset, this is an odd piece of work—antiquated, some will say, in its outlook—straddling academic discussion and earthy memoir, highbrow discovery mingled with homely episodes of ache and joy. And I guess that Mama was about the last person in the world who ever expected to be mentioned within the pages of a book. Trained from early years to put others before herself, she was rarely a focus of personal attention.

She was born into a world very different from the one we have today. Her life, on the face of it, would not count for much alongside those of high achievers in various arenas of large scale industry. My mother came of age in a time and place where a young woman's obligations were different, on balance, from those of the present time. She rode to school, part of the Minnesota year, in a horse-drawn winter sled, and much of her time was spent tending five siblings, four of them younger. As a hero, I suppose, she is out of fashion. Yet she imparted to me things that have remained all my life.

Heroism indeed has many forms. It arises in each case within its concrete circumstance, shaped by the need at hand. The life of a Minnesota farm girl in the early twentieth century will flourish differently from one that is channeled, say, into the academic arena, the law office, or the world of political activism. Thus I do not hold my mother up as a model of what "women" should be. Still, I say, her life is worth celebration.

As to sources, some readers will recognize names and traditions that appear in this story. Socrates, Immanuel Kant, William James, the Vedic heritage of India; and more recently, individuals like Huston Smith, Brenda Ueland, and John Hick: History, and my own life, are strewn with men and women who have provided inspiration.

A few of its themes—morality, free will, the theological

"problem of evil," religious experience, and the speculative issue of individual human destiny—will be familiar, likewise. I have written about some of these at length elsewhere, along with chapter-length accounts devoted to men like John Hick, Frederick Myers, and Miguel de Unamuno, and will not repeat all of it here. My main intention in these pages is to describe succinctly the people and the works that have influenced me most deeply, and the woman whose presence, in flesh and in spirit, has been with me throughout a lifetime.

In putting together this book I find myself often citing authors of the late 19th to mid-20th centuries, an era overlapping largely with Mama's own lifetime. This was an era, it seems to me, alive with new discovery, revealing to us the immensity of our own physical universe, generating miracles of technology and providing glimpses of a mystery present at the core of the world we inhabit.

By and large, I draw from authors open to truth on every front, ones willing to explore life through every resource they find worthy. These are men and women, in the main, unfitted to old style pictures of a life to come, pictures bound by legalistic notions of reward and punishment that long have weighed heavy in the literature of the spirit.

I might add, while the view outlined in these pages is a broadly spiritual one, I do not insist that human beings can be gauged solely by their receptiveness to it. I have friends who harbor little sense of such things, and who cannot fathom my lifelong interest in a reality beyond the one now vividly in front of them. Such people, it often strikes me, are splendid examples of the philosophy I harbor even if they do not consciously share it.

The first chapter of this book casts a brief look at Northern European migration and settlement in North America, and my related family background in Minnesota and the Pacific Northwest. The next few describe my relationship with my mother and her impact on me over the course of my life. In the process, I share memories of childhood and my time as a philosophy student and classroom teacher, the latter role now approaching half a century. Throughout the story, I recall moments and germinal sources that figured into this journey across roughly my first four decades.

The several chapters remaining offer a miscellany of thought that includes a possible sketch of life hereafter, as inspired by some of my favorite authors, and reflection upon the enterprise of philosophy overall. While this last portion of the book involves material with which Mama was unfamiliar, I believe they will have her blessing. Numerous chapter notes are provided for readers who wish to explore further the topics touched upon throughout.

A novel, said Miguel de Unamuno, is a peculiarly good source of history, as it provides insight into the very soul of the man or woman who crafts it. While this book is not a novel, it does seek to share something of the soul of its author. Yet in the end, I wish to stress, it is not merely about one man's humble life, nor one woman's—rather it is about philosophy, and the challenge it holds out to each of us upon life's way.

I wish to express my thanks, in this effort, to my cousins Marcia Runnberg Valadez, Marissa Dufault, and Kristin Kjarum Schmidt, for their help and encouragement. I am indebted to Kristin and Marissa for images and long-preserved family information I might never have turned up in popular services currently on the market.

Chapter 1
Adventurers

*Over the foaming salt sea spray, the Norse sea-horses took
their way, racing across the ocean plain.*
        Heimskringla: The Lives of the Norse Kings

The Nordic peoples, notes contributor H. Arnold Barton in a recent volume on their movement across the Atlantic, have a long history of migration, their ancestors arriving in Scandinavia many centuries ago from the region of the Black Sea.[3]

Some of the Germanic tribes that overran the Roman Empire in the fifth and sixth centuries A. D. probably hailed from Scandinavia. Several hundred years later, Northern raiders, known as Vikings, conquered and settled territory in Normandy and the British Isles. They moved east, as well, deep into what today are Russia and Ukraine, and down to the shores of Africa.

Scandinavians in the New World

"One doesn't discover new lands," observed the renowned French author Andre Gide, "without consenting to lose sight, for a very long time, of the shore."

Gide's metaphor is an apt one regarding much that is contained in this book. It finds a literal instance in these Nordic voyagers, who twelve hundred years ago amazed their contemporaries, venturing out beyond coastal waters onto the deep and crashing northern seas. The dangers were many, and the chance of going off course in this effort made it perilous even more.

3   *Scandinavian Roots / American Lives* (Copenhagen: The Nordic Council of Ministers, 2000), page 9.

1

Like the men themselves, the ships were resilient: They were of several kinds, including the longboat that was fashioned often of oak, green and pliable, and iron bolts, elegant in its lines and capable of speeds well exceeding those common in that day. Typically their crafts were framed in "clinker" fashion, the wooden strips overlapping slightly down each side and welded with concoctions of tar, hair, and animal grease.

Means of navigation were scant—a plumb bob enabled sailors to test the water's depth in the relatively flat inland river bottoms. Further out, the men made use of a *gnomon*, a simple device protruding from a circle of wood in a water bucket, the sun's rays giving them a rough estimate of their latitude.

In large part, the Vikings employed their immediate senses, keeping track of high hills and odd rocks as they went. An experienced sailor, it is said, can smell land in a sea breeze. Besides which, whales were visible in some currents, providing welcome news, along with the sound of birds calling and waves hitting shore. At times, sailors had the testimony of those prior to give them guidance. Always there was danger. The great currents could be treacherous, and some venturers met their end by sinking or starvation. Those more fortunate, often taxed by now to their limit, caught the joyous sight of land awaiting.

Around the year 1000, Leif Erikson, son of Erik the Red, braved the cold northern water and arrived with a few dozen intrepid companions from Greenland, setting foot upon several sites along the coastland of North America. Their experience is recounted in *The Saga of the Greenlanders*.

While the exact placing of these sites has fueled much speculation, it is a fair guess that the first lay toward the lower east end of Baffin Island. There, it is said, they found no grass. Glaciers covered the highlands, and the land on which they stood was like unto "a single flat slab of rock from the glaciers to the sea."[4] The land was of little use.

Leif called this area *Helluland* after its hard flat appearance. Further south came one that he named *Markland* owing to its forest. Two days south again was a place where "a river flowed into a sea from a lake" with abundant salmon, and land so rich "that livestock would need no fodder." It would be called *Vinland* for its lush grapes. The men built log houses that served them for perhaps three summers and winters, establishing a settlement before returning to Greenland.

---

4   Contained in *The Vinland Sagas* (London: Penguin Books, 1997, Keneva Kunz translator), page 6.

Recent estimates put Markland somewhere on the coast of what is now Labrador or possibly Newfoundland. Vinland has long been a tantalizing mystery, its proposed whereabouts ranging across areas that include Nova Scotia, Rhode Island, and Cape Cod, Massachusetts.

Scholarly divisiveness over these locations, along with the inevitable hoax, now and again, gave rise in time to the thought that the Saga literature was but idle storytelling. Yet in 1965, Helge and Anna Ingstad, a husband and wife archaeology team from Norway, made a stunning find at L'Anse Aux Meadows in Newfoundland. There they encountered remains of several buildings, adequate to house perhaps a hundred people, and similar in style to those current in Erikson's time in Iceland and the Faroe Islands.

The chief activities of the inhabitants, it was clear, had been hunting and fishing. Among the items found were an oil lamp carved from soapstone, a bronze brooch, and a spindle wheel, this last item giving reason to think that the enterprise included women.

Some wondered if it might be Leif's Vinland. More likely, it was decided, this place had been a boat landing and center for repair and refitting. Probably Vinland lay further south, in the Gulf of St. Lawrence. But the discovery was no less significant. Vikings had been in The New World long before the modern age.

Centuries later, this New World would be common knowledge, though it was awhile before Scandinavians gained a foothold in it. *Nya Sverige*—New Sweden—an ambitious enterprise in the lower Delaware River Valley (roughly the southwest edge of today's New Jersey), was overtaken by the Dutch in mid-17th century during conflict in Europe that pitted the two powers against each other. As late as the Declaration of Independence by the American colonies, Scandinavians counted for little in the demographics.

But their time was coming. While New Sweden, on the face of it, was a failure, those who remained in the region succeeded on several fronts. They built the first colony in America, notes Arthur Herman,

> that was free from famine or natural disaster. They also established the first Lutheran church in America, as well as the first flour mills and first shipyard, and they drew the first detailed map of the Delaware Valley. And once they had settled

down to a life of farming and logging, the Swedes were there to stay…[5]

In 1825, emigration from the homeland received a stimulus when a group of fifty-two people of decent means from Stavanger, Norway, purchased a small sloop and sailed for New York, settling in Rochester. Soon many of these "Sloopers" were venturing inland, sending back encouragement to those they had left behind.

Northern Waves

The young nation, says Herman, had a special appeal to Scandinavians, and the same was true in turn.

> Nineteenth century America needed the energy and focus of a people willing to work hard in clearing virgin land, building a farm, and raising a family, often in a barren landscape, in order to create a lasting future for themselves and their posterity. Scandinavians happened to have these qualities in abundance.[6]

Like their Viking forebears, he notes, these immigrants sought new horizons of discovery, and new environments in which to build a home "and shape a way of life that combined individual achievement with a devotion to family, church, and community."

Technology, too, was on the rise. In coming years, the traditional ship's sails were replaced by the steam engine, and railroads were connecting remote parts of the continent. Some 1.25 million Swedish men, women, and children, notes historian Joy Lintelman, came to the United States between the years of 1845 and 1930.[7]

They came primarily in search of land, employment, and freedom from social caste and the rigidity of the Lutheran church. Their experience, says Lintelman, was summed up by one Mina Anderson, an 1890 immigrant, saying simply that she was "tired of hard work and disappointment."

During the 1840s, Swedes were settling in Illinois, and soon

---

5   Arthur Herman, *The Viking Heart: How Scandinavians Conquered the World* (Boston: Houghton Mifflin Harcourt, 2022), page 223.

6   *Ibid.*, page 222.

7   *Ibid.*, page 281.

they were reaching north and west. By 1854,

> a Swede arriving on the East Coast could travel by
> rail to Chicago and the Mississippi River and then
> take a steamboat to St. Paul. This stopping-off point
> in Minnesota Territory (established in 1849) made
> [it] a logical destination for farm seekers. The Pre-
> emption Act of 1841 also encouraged settlement,
> as it enabled migrants to claim government land
> prior to its public sale.[8]

Immigration waned during the American Civil War, but resumed soon after. The American Homestead Act, effected during the Lincoln Administration in 1862, was a powerful impetus, offering 160 acres of land to anyone presently a citizen of the U. S. or intending to become one.

The situation in Denmark was similar, with the population nearly tripling in size from 900,000 to two and a half million between 1800 and 1910. By 1880, jobs were scarce and land expensive. Most Danes were tenant farmers who could not afford to live on plots larger than two acres. As a result, reports of fertile land and plentiful jobs beckoned them westward. Personal letters from friends and relatives in the new land sometimes ran in local papers, sparking hope and ambition.

By 1903, Minneapolis boasted, after Stockholm, the largest Scandinavian population in the world. Author Lincoln Steffens, reflecting on its chemistry and spirit, would describe it as having "a round Puritan head, an open prairie heart, and a great, big Scandinavian body." [9]

---

8   *The Perennial Philosophy,* page viii.
9   Joy K. Lintelman, "Swedish Immigration to Minnesota". Minnesota Historical Society. http://www.mnopedi.org/swedish-immigration-minnesota

Pictured here are the children of Adolph Eberhart (1870–1944), a Swedish immigrant who in 1909 would become Minnesota's 17th governor.

Family Roots

My great-grandparents on each side came amid what Lintelman numbers as the third of several waves of Scandinavian arrivals in the period between 1880 and 1893.

In 1989, after I had finished a program of study in Claremont, California, I visited my mother's relatives in Moose Lake, Minnesota. Aunt Bea and her son Ben gave me a little black hand-bound album containing some very old photos, including these two.

On the left is John Runnberg, stepfather of my grandfather Axel, who was born Nels Axel Johnson. The woman is Carri Johnson Runnberg, Axel's mother. When Nels' father, Chris Johnson, died, Carri married John.

When Carri and John returned home, they sent word as follows:

> Dear children, we are well and hope you are the same. We are on the English Coast today and tomorrow we go to Norway. On Friday morning we get to Sweden. We have a nice trip, all are happy and fine, not hungry and [are] well. We will send you a letter when we get to Sundsvall. A friendly greeting to all of you. From Father and Mother.[10]

The photos in Bea's album, seventy-nine in all, were numbered, with an information key in a small spiral notepad with brief comments. These two were passport photos for the trip back to Sweden. *"Carrie,"* it is said, *"wanted to come back to the U. S.*

---

10   I am indebted to my cousin Kristin Kjarum Schmidt for this item, and for details of family history, and for several precious images, including the ones shown here of Axel and Carrie and of Jensine with her first three children.

@ age 100 but was denied by [her] doctor."

Nels Axel was born in the region of Sundsvall, Medelpad, a couple of hundred miles north of Stockholm, in the nation of Sweden on March 27, 1886. He came to the United States when he was eighteen. Jensine Maria Gram, who would be his wife, entered the world in Dalby, Denmark, on November 27, 1887, setting foot upon the new land with her parents early in childhood in 1891.

Neils Jensen Gram, Jensine's father, was born on April 23, 1848, in Kolding, Denmark. He worked in Cloquet, Minnesota, at one of the sawmills. Neils lived until 1910. His wife, Charlotte Amelie Gram, was born on April 27, 1855, in Kolding and passed in 1934.

On the right is Charlotte Amelie, late in life.

Chapter 2
Mahtowa

Hotter than ever! Washed and ironed some, churned, baked bread, made root beer, milked cows!! Paul took us swimming tonite. Flat tire!
Etta Runnberg, diary entry of July 13, 1936

Axel and Jensine

My grandmother Jensine met Axel when she was tending grill in the Pokegama Hotel in Grand Rapids, Michigan. They married on December 28, 1909, in Deer River, Minnesota. Axel and Jensine—she was called Sena—lived in Mahtowa from 1910 until Axel's passing in 1953. Their union would produce six children. Sena, of whom I have some recollection, lived until 1960.

Axel and Sena, undated, from a very old collection: They seem to embody the image of stoic and reserved folk from the high North.

The Family

The area was largely farm country, snow aplenty during winter months, and home to many Scandinavian immigrants and their offspring. Life was somber and work hours long. Drinking was routine in many families, hard liquor being a staple for the men.

The village, lying about 125 miles north of the Twin Cities and 30 miles from the tip of Lake Superior, was settled in 1875, thirteen years after the outbreak of a deadly conflict to the south called The Great Sioux Uprising. It featured a post office and a station of the Northern Pacific Railroad.

Mahtowa today lies in Carlton County. Its name appears to derive from the Dakota language *mate* and the last syllable of the Ojibwe *makwa*, each word making reference to a bear. On occasion it has been listed in print as *Mah-to-wa*. To date it is unincorporated, with a population of 370.

My mother Ethel Marie Runnberg was born on December 5, 1911. Here, in the lingo of the hobby sports card, is a "rookie" from 1912. (It was contained in Bea's hand-bound album with her name as the sole entry.)

Shown here is Sena with a recent addition to the family, sister Bea, with Raymond, eldest of the siblings, in the back and Ethel Marie on the right. She seems to have her hands full. Three brothers—Gordon, Leonard, and Melvin—would follow.

How often has it been said—"I wish I had *asked* more." I came into this world in the middle of the 20th century, and made the acquaintance, in my youth, of family and friends on each side who had been born well prior. It is a sad paradox that close as we were, my mother and I spoke so little about her life prior to meeting my father. Bea, younger by three years, lived into her late 90s. Neither sister was inclined to speak much of those years. As best I could tell, they were hard ones.

Mahtowa kids, shown here in the winter of 1921-22.

Etta

Ethel Marie—Etta—was a bright and graceful young woman, yet bearing early the marks of mortality with a heart murmur and varicose veins on each leg. Bea, more stout of build, often worked in the fields with the boys while my mother, lacking her stamina, tended house. Her talent in the kitchen was remarkable, and it would enable her, in time, to set a holiday spread that visitors to our home remembered well after.

Etta, they said, was the apple of her father's eye. His resilience and sense of humor in the midst of difficulty, judging from things she would say, was a powerful shaping influence on her own sensibility. Their bond was reciprocal, I sense, with the one she would share with me. If she was special to him, it did not cause animosity with the other siblings. (As Bea once told me, "She was *our* favorite, too.")

Money was scarce. By the time she was out of childhood, Etta's feet would bear sad testament to that scarcity, her toes on each foot bent outward for lack of adequate shoes. It would not be corrected until long after.

Her little diary, which she kept during the years of 1935 and '36, is filled mainly with entries about chores she performed—meals, scrubbing, mending clothes, tending other people's children—and reveals her gratitude for kindnesses with little thought otherwise for herself.

A pastor would say, decades later, that all he had heard of my mother seemed to resonate with her service to others. As to the handwritten record, her modesty keeps her from spilling the beans about much. On the page for January 13th (she typically has two entries on each date, one for each year), for example, she writes, "*Oh dear! What a day. Most terrible blunder I ever pulled. Talk about red neck and embarrassment!*" Still, "*it could have been worse.*"

What was so embarrassing, I will never know—probably it would not make a major episode in any story, though it might reveal something of her daily experience and the development of her young soul.

While in school, Etta had been bumped one grade ahead, but at twelve she had seen the last of formal education. She told me once about how she fretted when seeing in her Confirmation photo (shown below, with her public school certification), in which a smidgen of her slip is showing.

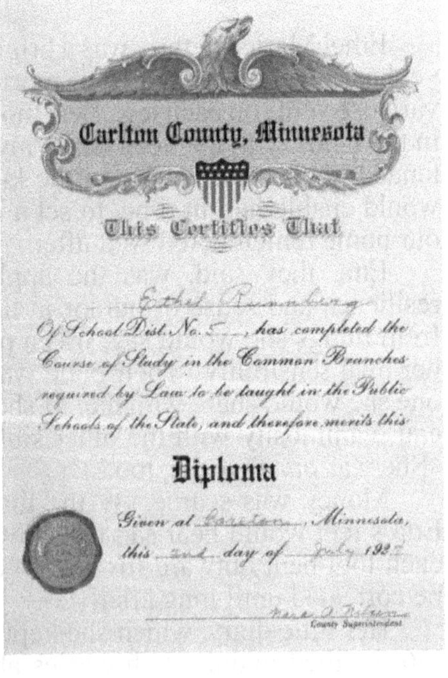

Here is the troubling image, from around the same time she finished public education. In the summer of 1924, Etta entered the work force, rather than "high" school, which today is routine, of course, for young people in this country.

Excerpts from Etta's diary show entries for 1935 and '36 on each page.

This photo was taken in 1933, when she was 21. It captures her ingenuous good will and serenity, which made her a treasure to all who knew her.

Again, I wish I had been more inquisitive. Every so often, she would mention the Hoffman family, with whom she lived for a number of years, helping to raise the children. Now and again, I would do something that reminded her of little Freddie Hoffman. A 1940 census record lists her employment as "Maid" in the Hoffman family residence, employed by Walter and Clara, each in their 40s. There were three children, W. Fredrick at age four being their youngest. (Her work hour total per week was reported as 60, her salary negligible.)

Mama's employment with the Hoffmans lasted for some years, and took her to Massachusetts when they relocated. I imagine that she saw herself, by this time, as essentially a servant, unlikely to have much of a life otherwise.

Etta here is about 23, perhaps a year before the first diary entries.

Mama bore a great affection for her older brother Ray and her younger brother Gordon, shown here during his hitch in the Second World War. The back of this photo reads, *"This is a Jap gun (what is left of it) we captured from them in the invasion. Quite harmless now, I assure you. Taken in New Guinea, August 1944."*

Gordon was perhaps the most gregarious man I ever met. In his later years, when I knew him, he was tall and rotund, like unto a solar center that drew others to him. It was hard to pick up a tab when Gordon was near.

This is Axel together with Bea and Mama, perhaps in the 1930s. If Etta was troubled by that earlier Confirmation photo, I can only wonder what she thought of this one.

Etta stands here with her mother Sena Gram Runnberg and Bea's son Benny, three years of age, in 1942. Ben Kjarum and I had somewhat parallel lives, twelve years apart, each of us raised as an only child by a loving mother, with a father (the two men bore each other some resemblance), named Carl.

Chapter 3
Carl and Ethel

I guess it was kind of a crazy deal from the start.
Ethel Marie Nicholson, when asked one day by
her son what had drawn her to the man she married

My Father

Carl David Nicholson, youngest of four siblings, was born on November 4, 1905, in Tacoma, Washington. A restored photo from an old album shows him here with his father Charles John, a hard sort, I gather, fond of drink and not easy on his wife Mary (*nee* Regina Mariana Rudberg), two years his senior. Born in

Sweden in May of 1871, Charles left school at the end of the eighth grade.

It was a rude existence, judging from any echo that ever sounded from it. Carl—Kelly, as he was called at home—lost Mary at sixteen, an event, it seems, that left him fractured for years after. Though acute and keen-witted, he quit high school following his junior year. I gather that he and Charles had little connection. Near the end of his life, I would see a handwritten commentary that he had kept while receiving counseling from a team of therapists. It recalled the trauma of losing his mother, and his grandmother awhile later.

As to his life before he met my mother, I can only speculate. He did remark to me once, around my mid-teens, that he had journeyed to Alaska in his youth. (A ragged hand-bound album with a few hazy photos depicting wooden sheds and fur parkas is all that remains of the venture.)

On the Sunday morning of December 7, 1941, it was learned that a squadron of Japanese bombers had rained destruction on a US naval base at Pearl Harbor in Hawaii. With this event, America was drawn into the greatest conflict in human history. That coming April, at age thirty-six, my father—to his sour surprise—found himself drafted.

Carl, it seems, did not take well to the Army, nor it to him. Though he would muster out with an Honorable Discharge, he was not well fitted to regimentation.

Owing to his "baby" status in the family and his extended bachelorhood, my cousins on that side of the family were a generation older than I. His niece, Jean, would tell me, in later years, how she used to slip him his flask through the barracks fence late at night. One time he didn't make it, and the drill sergeant happened to see her there waiting.

He asked her what she needed. Holding out the silver container, she said in earnest, "My Uncle Kelly isn't here tonight for his bourbon—can you see that he gets it?"

"Don't worry," replied the sarge. "*Get it*, he will."

Discharged in December of 1944, Carl had risen in his stateside service to the rank of Corporal. Eight months later, an apocalyptic new weapon, harnessing energy in a way the world had never seen, exploded at a calculated height over the city of Hiroshima. Days after came a second detonation over Nagasaki. Soon many draftees were back in the workforce.

Vancouver

Mama met my father when she was living in an apartment on E. 10th Street in downtown Vancouver, Washington, and working at a paper mill. (A 1950 census record lists her as a full-time employee with an annual gross pay of $2,100.) He was employed by the Bonneville Power Administration, a hydroelectric agency that had been signed into existence by Franklin Roosevelt in 1937. He held the position of warehouse storekeeper.

My father's sister, the first of his two elder, married a man named Morgan, by whom she had several children, and after his passing, one named Mike O'Dell, whom I recall from visits in my childhood. She was Ethel Maria Nicholson, sometimes called Ethel Marie, thus bearing in her maiden years a name that might have seemed significant to my father, now well into his 40s.

Mike was very taken with this new Ethel, likening her to Ingrid Bergman, whose angelic features had graced the silver screen in films of the past decade. The relationship came as a surprise to all.

Market Street, San Francisco: Carl David and Ethel Marie Nicholson stepping out smartly on their honeymoon—the original photo bears the hand-penned date *October 23, 1949*. Though he and I would grow apart, with the years, I find myself looking at this photo, admiring the style of that era and thinking of the life juncture each of them now had reached. I wish I could congratulate them, and tell him how lucky he was.

My father had few friends outside the family. Over the years he had developed serious habits of smoking and drinking and was up to three packs a day with his unfiltered cigarettes. When my mother unexpectedly, and to her joy became pregnant, he was none too happy.

When I arrived, however, they both were thrilled. Soon after, a doctor told him that he would not live to see me grow if he did not quit the alcohol. And so he did. I can count on my hands the number of times I saw him drink in years to come, and up to the last few years of his life.

As to smoking, he told me once that he had quit one day when he couldn't stand it any longer. There were no patches or support groups (or CBD *gummies*, on the market of late), to aid this quitting, as would later be commonplace in American culture. He tossed his last pack with a sense of relief, never wanting another.

The Hillside

This is a view from below, looking up toward the street, with the Columbia Gorge visible from the top. I don't remember the planting, but I surely remember the land. About a year before I was born, my father bought this Knob Hill lot on the curving outside rim of East 11th. It was three-quarters of an acre, an elongated Nevada shape stretching down most of the hill. It bordered property below on Mill Plain Boulevard, an arterial running from downtown and rising to our Heights area a couple of miles east.

The lot was part of a WW II veterans' housing project—residences built in small and simple fashion, costing a few thousand dollars. These on the outer row were like the others, but with spectacular views. It was an unusual setting.

1951

The post war era saw a rising economy and optimism regarding the nation and its integrity. Westerns played nightly on the television, a black-and-white device that had its first breakthrough in the 1920s and found some use conveying special events, such as prizefights, in the decade following. Late in the 1940s, that glowing little box would make its way on a massive scale into the American living room.

I came into the world around 7:05 PM on the 22nd of March in 1951. My earliest memories are those of being tended by Mama and Daddy, the center of attention as first-born children generally are.

They took several photos outside our house some time perhaps in spring or early summer, after bringing me home from the old downtown St. Joseph's Hospital. My father's shadow is visible in this one against the right front wheel of the car.

I never thought much in my younger days about this image. Looking at it now, I think he angled it this way very astutely to show a Road of Life that opened out into the distance, curving off into destinations yet unknown.

I recall sitting, in early days, in an inflated pool, Mama lugging buckets of water from the dirt floor cellar to provide my enjoyment. I would ask her to let me stay and sleep there that night, never quite convinced that the water by then would be freezing. Our backyard was a green surrounding haven as I lay in the sun with the great river in the distance. The occasional drone of a small aircraft overhead seemed to say that all was well.

The cellar had a musty wood scent. Now and again, to my great happiness, a frog would find its way into it. How life fascinated me—over the hillside were spiders, grasshoppers, and garter snakes that I might occasionally keep, for a short time, in a cardboard box or glass jar. Though I would not dream of hurting one of these creatures, I loved to catch and observe them.

I would learn one day years later from Aunt Ethel, that Mama had become pregnant a second time, this time by their choice, when I was a couple of years old. She miscarried, and with it went the possibility of a sibling. I have the vague recollection of being without her a couple of times in very early days, standing on the living room floor, wondering why she was not there. Possibly this was one.

Maybe this turn of events made me all the more precious in their eyes. I flowed with affection for each of them, though with her I had a special intimacy, indissoluble from the time she carried me. Another very early memory, which may have presaged things to come, was one of speaking out in her defense when they were fighting. She was sitting and weeping as he bellowed at her.

While he would do more bellowing in the years ahead, this scene did not repeat itself. I do not recall her ever again crying as she did then. Over time, a different pattern emerged, somewhat in the manner of parent and child, him baiting her with slight provocations until being scolded in an outburst.

I suppose, looking back, that we were a haphazard comedy in the making—three people who would spend the coming years in uncertain tension, none of us fully able to express ourselves and trouble never far below the surface. My father seemed to feed off these scoldings, perhaps deriving in some fashion a maternal attention he still craved and had sought elsewhere.

Early Years

My own childhood, though it contained much joy, would unfold in lopsided fashion, an odd paradox of poverty and only-child indulgence, of emotional abuse and unfailing nurture. But my mother's companionship would see me through it all.

It is one of my life axioms that if we are in this world, we are here to *work on something*, our integrity tested in an arena with others like us, and one that does not always bend with our desires. Such was the case with the three people who lived under that roof. None of us, heaven knows, was perfect. But if Mama was not perfect, she was extraordinary, and special to every person who met her.

In the eyes of her child, writes N. K. Jemisin, "a mother is a goddess. She can be glorious or terrible, benevolent or filled with wrath, but she commands love either way." He adds, "I am convinced that this is the greatest power in the universe." On occasion, Mama could be frightening, as when my stern little will collided with her authority and I felt the fire of her hand on the back of my jeans. But most of all, I remember her love.

Down in me somewhere is a sense (stemming maybe from a later event), of this cake, an unearthly good concoction if ever one existed. My mother made it, as she made everything, "from scratch"—the greatest angel food anyone ever tasted, with a pinkish buttercream frosting that put to shame the white sugar paste used in many commercial bakeries.

I look now at this photo, the cake with a single candle, and feel I am gazing out into an as-yet unwritten future. I think, too, of a theme that was prominent in the era of my birth—a mode of philosophy, rooted in the century prior and finding impetus amid catastrophic world conflict. It was called *existentialism*—a movement that described human existence from the inside, as it were, seeking to capture its texture and substance.

Its authors, by and large, resist the view of an iron-clad universe that turns human beings in *cause and effect* fashion into mere objects. Instead, they emphasize our capacity for creative freedom. Often, in place of linear argument, they employ drama—plays, films, short stories, and novels—to convey their ideas, finding such vehicles to be more adequate carriers of the human condition.

Their imagery, at times, is simple and startling. There is a wonderful passage in an essay by the 20th century Spanish philosopher Ortega y Gasset, in which he describes the peculiar situation of a creature endowed with a capacity for choice. We are never quite the same, it seems, from one time to the next, paradoxically shaping our very selves with each new action.

For this reason, says Ortega, our being does not fully coincide with that of the material world. We are made "of such strange stuff as to be partly akin to nature and partly not...a kind of ontological centaur, half immersed in nature, half transcending it."

If this seems mysterious, take, for one, the small act of reading words at this instant that an author has composed: "At each moment of my life there open before me diverse possibilities: I can do this or that. If I do this, I shall be A in the moment after; if I do that, I shall be B. At the present moment the reader may stop reading me or may go on."[11]

Either way, I will be different for having chosen. This self-forging is constant, involving choices of every magnitude, turning a man with time into "what he is going to be."

This way of seeing human existence, which became a staple

---

11   Ortega y Gasset, from "Man Has No Nature", contained in *History as a System* and excerpted by Walter Kaufmann in *Existentialism from Dostoevsky to Sartre* (New York: Penguin Group, 1975), page 155.

of thought in the twentieth century, has a powerful kinship with religious thought, which would become a focus of my own study in later years.

Freely navigating the living room floor.

Chapter 4
East 11th Street

... all I am or can be I owe to my angel mother.
> Abraham Lincoln, as quoted by
> his former law partner William Herndon

I must go down to the seas again, to the lonely sea and the sky,
And all I ask is a tall ship and a star to steer her by.
> John Masefield, "Sea Fever"

And here's the pitch—swung on... and there she goes!
> sportscaster Dizzy Dean, watching Mickey Mantle

"OK, here's the wishbone."

I was maybe seven or eight. It must have been a chicken soup day. She held out the V-shaped piece by one end and I took the other. We pulled.

"Oh, you got it this time, Mama."

*"Well, that's all right. My wish was that you would get **yours**."*

Would that every child know such a moment.

Goodness and Wonder

Sunday School had been a staple of the Mahtowa Covenant Church the Runnberg family attended. Here in the backyard we await my own entrance into tradition. This early training in faith and morals came a few blocks up the road in a mixed venue, African-American and white, at a Methodist community center called The Shack. It would last through my elementary school years.

Mama wrote on the back of this photo, "*All set for Kelly's first trip to Sunday School – Easter Sunday – 1954*," about three weeks after my third birthday. Rarely have I been dressed this well since.

I remember her reading me the Biblical stories in comic strip format we took home from class. One depicted brave young David in his clash with the towering Philistine, Goliath. Another told of the Israelite hero Samson, who declares that he is "not afraid to die" for a righteous cause. How, I wondered, could anyone have it in them to make such a sacrifice? These stories were held as great instruction in human values.

All of life, it seemed, was imbued with a freshness and warmth that gave me a sense of belonging. It was my fortune to be loved unconditionally, to be loved, shielded, doted upon as the only child of a woman who had learned to give of herself to all who came into her orbit.

Honesty, Compassion, Levity, and Vision

Years later I would hear of Socrates, telling his followers of a world beyond this one. Down here, he declared, we behold things that come and go. Yet amid these passing scenes there arises in us a sense of things eternal.

I remember an exchange between my mother and me about stealing. The exact setting is hard to recall—some kid a few blocks away had gotten pinched, it seems like, for shoplifting. I told her about it, saying that taking what was not mine had no appeal to me.

Visibly pleased, she bolstered this thought, saying that I would enjoy nothing gained in that way regardless. The lesson seems as true today as it did then, and through the years that followed—wherever else I might fall down—I would never feel an inclination to theft.

I don't suppose I had the wherewithal, at that age, to articulate a position on the subject—what it was that made stealing wrong, whether circumstance might ever justify some instance of it, and so on. Maybe, in fact, the issue is still a mite hazy. In time, I would realize that the whole issue of property was open to challenge, and that corporate and governmental agencies, great bastions of societal enterprise, could commit theft on a grander scale than any criminal might manage.

Still, this aversion to stealing, like my aversion to lying, would stay with me. I believed then, as I do now, that in this exchange with my mother I was onto a timeless truth. She never lectured me on this subject, never threatened me with punishment, or with guilt that might hang over me if I went astray. There was no need—I knew that taking from someone what they had earned, or had been given, involved a profound violation of the human order.

It would occur to me, in later years, that I was probably one of the few things that Mama ever wanted that she got. In turn, she gave me all that she had to give. My earliest recollections are ones of being lifted with her into magical worlds through reading of every kind. One book told of Rudolph the Red-Nosed Reindeer—on a page near the end, filling me with yearning, was a mad flurry of stars against the night sky. In another was the

Little Mailman of Bayberry Lane, a chipmunk letter-carrier who helps one of his feathered neighbors extend herself to find the friendship she secretly craves.

One day, when I was about four, I spied a comic book—maybe a Halloween special or year's end annual (these were the big ones that ran a full quarter)—high on a cylinder rack at the Fred Meyer store on Interstate Avenue. It was Little Lulu, a children's classic conceived years earlier by Margery Henderson Buell and driven now by the artwork and story lines of the ingenious John Stanley.

This item called to me, and every month, over the next couple of years, the sight of each bright new issue would send its fresh thrill, delivering me into a world of clubhouses and tree-top lookouts, magical dreams and supernatural stories told by Lulu to young Alvin who lived nearby. Stanley's wryness—his microcosm of human life in young children, is a marvel to me even now when I come across it.

As I grew out of *Little Lulu*, Mama gave me a hand with other things. One Christmas, Aunt Ethel gifted us a collection of stories by our kinsman Hans Christian Anderson. We tried a few of them until their grimness (at some point, it began to strike us funny), was too much to take.

Even so, these stories, born of Anderson's own experience, had telling force. One, only a couple of pages in length, describes a forsaken little "match-girl" who stands barefoot, freezing and alone, on a street corner. As darkness comes and her strength ebbs, she strikes matches on a wall, seeing things she longs to have.

She beholds her grandmother, the one person who has ever treated her with kindness. She strikes the last few sticks, wanting to keep the old woman with her.

> And the matches burned with such a glow that it became brighter than daylight. Grandmother had never been so grand and beautiful. She took the little girl in her arms, and both of them flew in brightness and joy above Earth, very, very high, and up there was neither cold, nor hunger, nor fear... [12]

The remains of the girl are left behind, together with burned matches, where passersby pity her, seeing nothing else. The scene remains burned into me even to this day.

––––––––––––––––

12   Hans Christian Andersen, *Complete Fairy Tales* (San Diego: Canterbury Classics, 2014), page 226.

"You were too protected," my father would say to me long afterward, when I told him of pain I had endured years prior. Probably so. It was standard wisdom, in those years, to suppose that a child without siblings suffered in personal development— yet, too, this truism would give way in later years to concern over the "middle" child (and recently too, I have noticed, over the eldest daughter), in families of greater size.

In reality, each situation provides its own challenge and its reciprocal advantage. An only child, in my experience, may have trouble mastering the rhythms of the social arena. But he can also be highly resourceful and self-sufficient. Like first-born children in general, he may find himself well fitted, in time, to a position of influence among his peers.

True, at times I lacked fight. One scene that stands out, looking back, came at the great old amusement park at Jantzen Beach, a sunlit palisade on Hadyn Island in the Columbia River just across the Interstate Bridge on the Oregon side. Opening in May of 1928, an Elysian field of rides and games, hot dogs and cotton candy, it spanned some 123 acres. The Coney Island of the West, as someone dubbed it, Jantzen was the largest amusement park in the country, kindling joy in every soul who entered.

On this occasion a group of kids crowded round a stack of hay thick with pennies for the taking.

My father, cousin Jean would say long afterward, was like

two people. For all his ill temper, he could be generous. All his life, he had a special fondness for young people—in later years, for example, he would admire liberal youth who challenged governmental policy during the US conflict in Southeast Asia.

During my childhood he was also, it seemed, in a kind of time-warp where kids were concerned. One of my earliest memories is seeing him, from a distance, on a flat stretch below the house next to ours, roasting hot dogs with neighborhood youngsters over a small fire. If he'd had his way, I would have looked like kids he had known in 1912, hair waxed straight back (he tried it once, after my mother had done her job with the electric clippers, leaving her speechless), and wearing God knows what. (I somehow imagine coveralls and a newsboy cap, a bullfrog in the front pocket and slingshot in back, with smudge-faced comrades around me named Hodie Finch and Dub Willy.)

This penny-grab, I suppose, was something from his own day. He steered me toward it, and on his urging I stepped forward. Figuring it to be a civil exercise, I readied myself to stoop down and pick casually through the hay with everyone else.

On "go" there sprang, like crazed jaguars, six or seven kids into the dirt. It was over before I collected my wits. My father said nothing, but I could tell that he had hoped to see better. Still, I was not disappointed. Who in their right mind would thrash around in that mess for those little bits of copper?

Through it all, Mama was my center and refuge, the best part of anything life provided. She was there also in times of misery, as when I contracted hellish inflammation from poison oak down the hill from the house. I remember standing naked in the bathroom, being slathered with white cream head to toe, then pink-red calamine, stuff that hardened like plaster of Paris, after which she helped me on with my pajamas and I trudged off, mummified, to bed.

I was in her hands, one way or another, coated with goop and plaster and love. If this utter protection took something from me, in terms of boldness, it gave back other things in turn. I learned what it was to have a wholly honest rapport with another human being, something that has stayed with me all my life.

Were more men loved in this way, it strikes me, there would be less grief in the world, and women would be respected as they should be. Men and women would be less estranged from one another. Men might relate better to each other, as well. Deceit, envy, possessiveness, insecurity—such things would be less common in every quarter. The exploitive attitude of so many men toward women would be unknown.

Old Days—and Indians

Around this time, perhaps a year before I started kindergarten, Mama took a sewing class at Clark College, adding to her skills as a homemaker. I remember my father and me dropping her off, one evening a week, from a side road that ran up to the northeast end of campus. He and I would return home to watch *Jungle Jim,* a Johnny Weissmuller vehicle that had begun as a theater production after the great Olympic swimmer's years as Tarzan starring with Maureen O'Sullivan at Metro Goldwyn Mayer.

In time she would be sewing my shirts, and later fastening labels into my socks when I went away to college (an awkward situation, depending on who chanced to find them). Later she crafted for me a blue velour bathrobe that had a special place in my heart. She gave of herself to all who needed it, a living lesson in generosity, though a lesson that took me time to absorb.

I like to think that America still had in it, when I was born, some taste of its old grit and spirit. This was true, at least, in the media industry, where frontier, Old West, and Native American dramas were a mainstay in what is now called The Golden Age of television.

The eras, for what it is worth, have intriguing overlap. I recall, for example, finding out that I could have conversed in early childhood with the last of the Indians who rode against Lt. Colonel George Armstrong Custer at the Little Big Horn in late June of 1876. Bearing later the name Dewey Beard, he had ridden as Iron Hail at sixteen years of age into the battle. I remember the car trip we made in the summer of 1955 along beaten old roads to visit my mother's family in Minnesota. The ride took us through Dakota territory. (Maybe, I fancy, old Iron Hail and I were momentarily in the same neighborhood.)

Here we sit outside Gordon's Moose Lake tavern—Mama, him, and me. Here with me, to this day, is a pendant depicting American Indians that hung on one of his walls. I still remember being inside the place, even if kids, as I was told, were not supposed to be there—it was an honor.

We visited the old house where the Runnberg children grew up—a hollowed shell of a place by that time. I recall being strangely spooked when we looked around inside.

And these Native people—how they fascinated me.

The day after Labor Day each September brought the start of the year at Harney Elementary, its buildings and playgrounds visible from our house on the hill. I remember looking down there, knowing that a challenge lay ahead. Mama accompanied me on the first day of kindergarten. As summer approached, that coming June, our teacher, Barbara Parrot, would write, "Everything Kelly has drawn this year has been about *Indians*."

In coming decades, they would be called *Native Americans*, and more recently *indigenous*. But then they were known by this name, and indeed most indigenous folk in my own acquaintance have worn it with pride. By any name, I admired them. (The only ungrammatical thing I ever said, from the time I could speak, judging from what Mama told me, was regarding a television show: "It gots Indians.")

In the summer of 1957, we drove to eastern Oregon for the annual Pendleton Roundup. One highlight during our stay was a lengthy parade of native riders down the main street of town. I watched from the back seat of the car as mounted warriors strode past, terrifying and beautiful.

I was leaning, in awe, out the back window, eyes wide as they got closer. Finally, I drew back, and back again, until—as Mama would remember to her amusement ever after—they were next to us, and she looked back to see me still as stone, face-down on the floor. (They had seemed peaceable up to that moment, but I had seen them spring surprises before, and you never knew when things might go south.)

The Weekly Fights and the Portland Armory

My early interests veered strongly into the world of sports, with an odd affection, despite my shyness, for prizefighting, a prime feature each week in the television network schedule.

My father's job did not afford a lot of time off, but once or twice a year we would get to the coast, often to Seaside, Oregon. The coastal strip that lies about fifty miles north and south of the great Columbia seemed to me each time, as it does still, like a foretaste of heaven. (Judging from the sparseness of this image, I am guessing we were on the Washington side in the vicinity of Long Beach.)

I remember being very young, a few years before this shot was taken, when after the weekly fights I would dance frantically, boxing an imaginary opponent on Big Blanket, an oblong ply quilt that had been stitched by someone back on the Minnesota farm.

One time I got my footwork crossed and landed flat, my head taking a rude whack when it hit the pad. My mother, laughing so hard she nearly fell herself, got up and sounded the count over me as I lay wailing. (It felt like there was a lesson in this mishap somewhere, involving maybe pride and carelessness. Yet it didn't keep me from seething the rest of the night.)

The first grade: 1957-58, a joyous time of year with the class picture taken in the last days before summer break, which seemed to last forever. Mrs. Sherman was a kind soul, a mother hen who took joy in our success and provided us, late in the spring, with a wonderful reading venture about rural life in place of the endless cadence of "Run, Dick, Run" we had endured for months prior.

The end of the school year brought a day of recreation prior to our departure. In the afternoon the 1941 Walt Disney classic *Dumbo* played in the cafeteria, a film that captured the bond of mother and child as few ever have. Though in coming years I would see fun poked at its sentimentality, the message of sorrow and victory in this story made my young heart soar.

Our first graded reports came in the year following, and all went well in Mrs. Ehrle's class, handwritten A's standing out in each column. I made acquaintances that year that remain with me six and a half decades later.

At around this time, up very late one Friday night, I discovered on a local channel, to my amazement, the weekly pro wrestling matches staged at the old Portland Armory. Coiffed young heroes and barrel-gutted bad guys with names like Bill Savage and Kurt Von Poppenheim (for some reason, and despite his post-war stock German villainy, Kurt would become my favorite)—I drifted off that night with their acrobatics bright on the screen of my closed eyes.

The highlight of that year came when my father and I sat at ringside to see the action live. The place was smaller than I had imagined, and the Crow's Nest, home to two broadcasters who called the action and did the interviews, quite sizeable. The ring, I discovered, was square, not oblong like it appeared on the screen at home, and like the one I had fashioned—a short plaque of painted wood, sturdy headless nails for ringposts and tiny rubber bands for turnbuckles, with white string ropes inside which I staged matches with plastic figurines.

This up-close action was explosive, far more than one realized when watching from the living room. The event was raucous, its impact jarring—at one point a floor-shaking body slam, to my stunned dismay, sent the chocolate on my ice cream bar shooting to the floor. Sucking up nerve, I got autographs during the evening from a few of these men that I kept ever after. Now and again, over the next few years, we would attend bouts here and at the annual Clark County Fairgrounds. Always it was great fun, yet this first show would remain forever an experience unto itself.

Although I was becoming abler in reading on my own, wrestling now became a brief part of the joint venture when Mama and I tackled an article or two in one of the pulp monthlies on the newsstand market. How we both laughed when she got to a part in an interview where some arch-villain called one of his nemeses a no-good *sonofabitch*. (The word, at least, was not new to us, having ridden in the car with my father.)

Sorrow and Triumph

Third grade brought an odd mix of fortune. A few weeks into the fall, I had trouble concentrating, and could not follow what was happening in the arithmetic sessions. Day upon day, when the chalkboard lesson ended, I would stand in line at the teacher's desk, seeking explanation.

Soon her look was telling me what a nuisance I had become. One day, seeing what I had attempted on paper, she exploded, telling me I had worked problems on the wrong page. Confused and exhausted, I turned and started away. Heading to my seat, I nearly lost consciousness.

Shortly afterward my parents learned that I had suffered for some time with anemia. I spent several days at home, tended as only a mother knows how, able to do little but receive her attention. She wondered once if I needed anything—I said I'd like to have my water paint set. She asked if I felt strong enough to use it. (Strong enough to use *water paints*—was I dying? Yet even then, I could not feel fear while in her care.) In a few days, I was on my feet, and the rest of the year brought flourishing on every front. And while I still loved combat sports, baseball was becoming my first passion.

Some of us lived for softball at recess and the noon hour. My own skills were developing, thanks also to weekend go-rounds with the "California" ball (baseball sized, with softball texture), drawing together a few of us in the neighborhood. Though I would always be on the quiet side, everyone in class seemed to be my friend, and I theirs. Even the seating arrangement changed for the better. My fleeting crushes on girls, which had begun the year prior, now reached an apex with Carol, a precocious little cherub one desk ahead who enthralled me with each stray glance and giggle.

Our Social Life

I did get a jolt once or twice during this time, when crossing Mill Plain Boulevard to visit the Southcliff hillside palaces where lawyers and oral surgeons resided. I still remember the look from one mother in response to my hand-sewn shirt and Mama haircut, which together with my backwardness in new company did not make for a great encounter.

My father no doubt did the best he could during these years, rising early each morning and heading to Bonneville. Like a lot of the Vets in that hillside project, he found little satisfaction in his employment. Afflicted now with diabetes and hemorrhoids, he was becoming more irascible and harder to please.

Our circle of contacts was small, social activity limited mainly to impromptu visits with Melvin "Curly" Stovall and his wife Evelyn, wonderful Texan folk he had known many years. They lived in one of the small units on the outskirts of that hillside venue, mid-way up the rise of Grand Avenue near East 11th. A couple of times a year we would make the humongous drive on old Highway 99 to Tacoma to visit my father's two sisters. Later, after Uncle Mike passed away, Ethel lived with an occasional boarder in a stately white house built in the 1920s, her sister, Theresa, across town in an apartment.

Each was a Gold Star Mother, having lost a son in the war. They'd suffered a falling-out some years prior, refusing to cross paths ever after. Our visits meant always a ritual stop at the house and then a drive to the apartment. Invariably each sister would say something to set my father off, prompting a fit that had Mama and me cringing. We never knew exactly what generated these tantrums, or why the women put up with it. Had they seen him traumatized, I would wonder later, in his early years? This was not an era when people talked about their problems, especially ones with backgrounds like theirs. Still, the two of us could always find a bit of fun in hashing it over later.

Now and again his outbursts would come, it seemed, for no reason at all. I remember a couple of times when he pulled up to an ice cream stand and told me to go and get something. I went to the window counter, waiting with two or three buyers in front of me. When at last I laid down my dime, I heard a scream from behind, seeing him out of the car and telling me, in a cursing fit, to get out of there if they weren't going to wait on me.

The second time this thing happened, I remember one young fellow, who I sense might have contended with such problems of his own, intoning in my ear as I shot past, *"That guy is out of his mind."* He wanted me to know that it was not my fault.

I was extremely wary, by now, of having classmates near me when he was around. One day at Jantzen he wanted me to get on a ride, a small Merry-Go-Round contraption with closed metal cars that rocked as they made their run. Though I was a mite big for such a thing, there seemed to be no harm in giving it a try.

The cars started around, and there was no way to make mine

rock.

"Step on the pedal," called the guy running the thing. The next time around my father was yelling the same thing. There was no way to fix the problem, and with each orbit I worked frantically to put the thing in motion, stepping everywhere, straining and pressing. The last couple of rounds had him up on the landing, screaming into the window at me to step on that goddamned pedal.

Finally it was done. I walked away with him in silence, my eyes frozen wide and fixed on the ground in front of me, afraid to look elsewhere, praying that no one I knew had seen this thing happen.

So it went, in years that followed, in "father and son" situations at a rifle range, and later when I was learning to drive. I might have the gun pointed upward after firing a shot, which would set him to yelling. When I pointed it down, he went berserk.

It was hard to know what to make of this. Maybe he had inherited these demons, or perhaps he had been damaged early on; maybe, too, he envied my mother for her innate bond with me. Looking back, I think that she might have held me so close, he found it hard to relate to me as he wanted. And again, it might not have made much difference. As years passed and his condition hardened, I became too inhibited to discuss anything with him and so never gained much insight regardless. In time, his unhappiness—with his job, his lack of education, his alienation from each of us—would congeal into a sadism and passive aggression that made home life a constant tension.

To this day, I know not what to make of some of those episodes, but I did come away with a modest resolution. When hearing how children repeat, in cyclical fashion, the abuses of their parents, I determined that these things would not happen with me. When a child has endured difficulty of this kind, he should know, better than anyone, how wrong it will be to inflict it now upon the son or daughter he may raise.

Diz and Pee Wee, Bill and Jerry

East 12th was a curving inner stretch, concentric with ours, on which lived the Riedlers, Walt being a WW II veteran like my father. His wife Marge was a schoolteacher who had been raised, somewhat like my own mother, with a midwestern religious sensibility.

I entered into baseball, and veritable reverence for Mickey Mantle, by way of Jerry, a year ahead of me, and his brother Bill, older by another four. The NBC Saturday *Game of the Week*, hosted by Hall of Fame veterans Dizzy Dean and Pee Wee Reese, featured New York's Bronx Bombers to the thrill of every Yankee fan in America.

A flawed young Hercules, tow-haired and boyish of smile, Mantle had suffered in his adolescence from osteomyelitis, a bone disease that nearly cost him a leg. He came to Gotham at ninteen by way of Spavinaw, Oklahoma, in the spring of 1951. Despite repeated injuries, starting with damage to his right knee in a freak accident that October in the World Series, Mick would remain one of the fastest men in the game. A switch-hitter with arms that would have done proud the fabled Greek Hephaestus, he launched balls from each side of the plate that seemed headed for the stratosphere. For a few years, before leg ailments and after-hours hard living took their toll, he was arguably the best player in the game.

We on the hill did not fall into any neat category as to social status—some of us, though modest of means, were steered with a strong hand, given to reflection and instilled with a modest dignity. While not fitting with the affluent crowd, we were immune to delinquency. And though we would never be "rednecks," we were immune, as well, to trends of thought and fashion engendered, in later years, by liberal mass media. If wealth to us was a pleasant thought, it would never be our driving concern. We did not envy the kids who lived across that Mill Plain divide.

Spring and summer were glorious. Around mid-March, baseball cards—nickel packs holding a half dozen of the prized items with a stern slab of pink gum (they could have used the stuff, I think, to gird armored vehicles)—came to Mac's—The Little Store—an old Mom and Pop grocery up 13th. The place sat alone across from a large area still vacant amid residential growth moving east during those years across the Heights.

Our neighborhood season started in ritual fashion each spring when the boys came to the door with mitts and bats. When we wanted a game, nothing could stop us. If we had enough players, we could fashion one like we saw on television. More often, if we were four, we played two-on-two "double or nothing" using half the field. Otherwise, it was rotating three-man "workup", batter, pitcher, and left fielder, each man getting his turn at the plate. Sometimes Jerry and I would practice on that little East 12th lane in front of his house with a tennis ball, mimicking "grounder to short and the throw to first." (Now and again I took my swings alone, using a wiffle ball or the makeshift lump I had devised out of crumpled paper and rubber bands.)

The summer of 1961, which still lives in the hearts of those who saw it, saw an epic home run contest between The Mick and newcomer Roger Maris, an acquisition from Kansas City the year prior. And the year following would have our sacred Yankees still ruling the roost.

Classroom Lessons for Life

Teachers at Harney, of course, did not have the classroom technology that is taken for granted today. Still, equipped with little more than chalkboard and imagination, they could probe our hearts and minds.

Upper classes—grades 4 through 6—met in an old multi-story building that may have been part of the layout when Harney was established in the 1890s. I was now apprehensive about fifth grade after learning that my instructor would be a man, bracing myself for a rough time.

But young John Lindblom, new at Harney that Fall, turned out to be a surprise.   John taught us about history and arithmetic—and civility. He also sparked creative effort, as when he assigned us to review a book or write a story and share it at the head of the class. (How I loved crafting a tale, or writing an alternative ending to one we had read, and explaining the advantage of Mantle's switch-hitting against an opposing pitcher's curve.)

He asked us what things were important in life, and how we might best govern ourselves toward other people. Never being asked this in a classroom before, I had to think. I raised my hand, after a few responses had been voiced, saying that the Golden Rule—something I had received veritably in my mother's milk— served as the best guide of all.

While I didn't excel grade-wise this year (my preponderance of Bs and Cs giving my father massive cause for the condemnation he secretly enjoyed), and chafed under the homework that was now routine in evenings, John's impact on me would last. He got us thinking along lines of self-examination, as for example the day he asked a few of us what "chores" we did at home.

"Kelly, how about you?"

"Well, I feed the dog…take out the garbage. And mow the, uh…"

"In other words, *nothing*."

We all laughed, our answers one after another reminding us of how easy we had it.

On another occasion, when his son was born, he handed out ice cream bars, a pleasant occasion, even if he did remark later that scarcely one of us had said *thank you*.

Gratitude, I was coming to see, was crucial to human interaction. More than rote acknowledgement, it expressed a condition of the soul. My notes of appreciation, duly ordered by Mama after each Christmas and birthday, had always seemed like a minor pain to be gotten out of the way. But she was instilling in me something more. So was John.

I remember him, too, admitting on the first day of class that he had a temper. "I hope," he said by way of warning, "that you never see me *mad*." I did get a glimpse of it one day, late in the year, when we were heading down the spongy old first-floor rampway to an exit onto a blacktop *en route* to the cafeteria.

One kid happened to lose hold of his lunch sack on the ramp. When the one behind him gave it a derisive kick, John sped down. Taking the smart-aleck by collar and belt, he hurled him an alarming distance back up.

While I can hardly imagine the uproar (the offender, I heard, had suffered a fractured wrist), it would cause today, the incident was smoothed over and the year ended with everyone on good terms. While this act might have seemed like an error on John's part, it struck me in a positive way, saying something about basic human respect.

This man, about fifteen years our senior, bridged a certain gap in my mind, bringing study together with recreation. One morning before class, a large workup game got going on a nearby field. Minutes later, John arrived and sportingly took a place in left field. Then, as if by fate, a fly ball was lifted straight at him, which he caught barehanded, entitling him to a turn at the plate. On the first pitch, he drove a wicked shot into the gap in left field, tearing like a comet around first, never breaking his stride all the way to the plate. In that moment he became more than a classroom authoritarian. He was a teacher and a friend.

One day I needed something and approached his desk. My thumb strayed under its edge, and a splinter buried itself clear down the length of the nail. I stopped what I was saying to show him what had happened. He managed to lay hands somewhere on a small pair of pliers, pulling carefully and extracting the thing (teeth clenched, I bore it like a Spartan), without drawing blood.

When I told Mama about it after getting home, she hoped that I had said something to express my appreciation. I honestly could not remember if I had. It still pains me to think not. I wonder also about the day I went up, during a study session, and asked him how to figure a player's *batting average*—the ratio of his base hits to his official at-bats. He happily obliged, giving me a new level of understanding of the sport by which I lived.

John was fascinated by a catalogue I had come by through the mail, listing prices for baseball cards available through a supplier. Some were quite old—a Honus Wagner, from before the First World War, went for the whopping sum of five dollars.

"So," he mused, "these things are like *stamps*." While the card industry was nothing like it would be in coming decades, older specimens were now gaining status as collectibles. A few of us in the neighborhood had speculated about the long-term value of the ones we were getting around town, reasoning that unfortunately they were too plentiful to gain worth. In time, of course, we would find out otherwise. (And I do wonder about that five-dollar Wagner item—might it have been the one that later auctioned for more than a million?)

One of the greatest moments I would have at Harney came on Play Day, that day next-to-last devoted each year to games and recreation. Jerry and I entered the contests—he in the sixth grade 50-yard dash and I in our class softball throw.

We fifth graders, five or six of us, lined up behind the mark, one a towering kid named Jay who scaled upward of six feet. At the call, I lingered for a second as the others let fly. A couple of them threw on a line, each ball hitting quickly and rolling a way further. Jay launched a veritable moon shot, an amazing heave through his trajectory left him about even with the others.

I took a couple of steps forward, firing at a natural angle, the ball rising like an artillery shell and prompting John, who stood nearby, to say "Kelly's got this!" (*Damned straight* I did—that throw must have doubled the distance of the others.)

The dash was a foregone conclusion to those who drew close to watch. Ron and Robert—two lithe competitors from the Shack cloister—figured neck-and-neck as favorites in a race that would determine who was the fastest kid in the school. All eyes, including mine, were on them until the last ten yards or so, when Jerry, in the side lane right in front of us, came streaking to the line nicking the two of them. So Knob Hill got its second winner, each of us sporting a blue ribbon the rest of the afternoon.

I have a special feeling, too, looking back on the year that followed.

Mr. May

In September of 1962, there arrived at Harney another new face. Etched in memory is my first look at Daryl May, young and slender in suit and tie with dark hair and glasses.

He stood next to our class doorway, one of the first-floor rooms in that multi-story building from the old layout where our grades had met upstairs the two years prior.

He folded his arms, waiting for the troupe to make its appearance.

At that moment he looked fiercely *hard*. Little did I know that it would turn out to be one of the best years of my life.

The Diamond, the Stage, a Wounded Bull, and the Greek Hill

The baseball season ended on a glorious note. While the old Yankee Dynasty was nearing its end, the final month of the '62 season saw them again clinching the AL pennant. I played ball often before class started, and again at recess—and at noon, and in PE.

And the classroom, once more, was an adventure.

Mr. May, as we would forever call him, stirred and humanized us, introducing us to classic artists, allowing us to be swept away by the recent sounds of *West Side Story*, *antebellum* Southern spirituals, and Caribbean *calypso*, the last of which had us rapping the metal flanks of our seats in sync with the LP.

A few of us volunteers did stints at the front, reciting poems and miniature biographies of classic authors and great canvas artists. Now and then the class trooped down to the basement piano room and lent its voice to music from every era. (On one occasion some of us would long remember, our maverick hipster Steve, beige trousers snug and high on his calves above dark slip-ons, was moved to stand on a table, Daryl accompanying him on the keys, breaking into a solo of the down-home classic "Mammy's Little Baby Loves Shortnin' Bread".)

John Masefield's "Sea Fever", Harry Belafonte, a sweeping masterpiece from the New York City stage, or the grim *pathos* of a bullfight that Daryl had once seen under a Spanish sky—the year was soaked with revelation. I remember him describing also, with admiration, a girl in his class who had stayed inside during recess reading a book, her eyes welling from the power of its narrative. (Several years ago, I read Masefield's poem and marveled again at its power.)

Mama helped me rehearse each week as I recited poems, read aloud my bios of classical painters, and assembled a notebook devoted to the history and commerce of Canada—all of it enriching both her and me. She got quite a workout when exploring with me math problems assigned to the clique that met with Daryl once a week to cover extra material.

At the close of the day ending Fall quarter, he handed out our report cards. I sat looking over the front sheet, suddenly realizing that there were typed three A's and a B down the length of it. I sat aglow until the bell rang.

By now I could do nothing to please my father, though I thought that this might turn the trick. Instead, he looked at the page, then turned it over with a critical eye, as if perusing a delinquency report. He tried to point out a defect in my performance, but I showed him otherwise. He said nothing.

Either way, I would never again seek his approval of anything I had done. Nor would I want it.

At this point, though he had encountered Daryl but once or twice, my father detested him. My mother went alone to the quarter's end consultation, recounting to me later what a worthwhile experience it had been.

In fall and spring, we played softball, Mr. May occasionally taking his turn at the plate. (While no John Lindblom, he was a decent spray hitter who could line shots to either side of the field.) Over that year, our minds were set afire and our souls lifted. Places like Athens and Rome became real, their legacy being essential, in his mind, to a young person's education.

This time in America, of course, had problems like every other. During these years we were deep in the Cold War, and nuclear threat was ever present. Now and again came school-wide drills, three distinct alarms piped at random into every class, each requiring its own response. The most dire of these had us on the floor beneath our desks, one arm cushioning the face and the other shielding the head.

That October the Russians sought to establish a missile base just 90 miles from our Florida mainland. For a couple of days, we walked around waiting to hear, at any moment, the daily awful city-wide wail, this time not as a test, and with destruction upon us.

No doubt every generation has its joys and crises and breeds its own nostalgia. Just how good were anyone's *good old days*, of course, depends on who remembers them. Still, I cannot help but feel there was something special in this era, a cultural stretch of roughly the mid-1950s to early 60s that would inspire in coming decades the film *American Graffiti* and a television show called *Happy Days*, and would spawn a fantastic range of musical output. With more than 60 years now passed, moments from that time seem ever more powerful, their echoes carrying in my heart not just remembrance, but a harbinger of destiny.

It was my deep regret to never meet Daryl again in later years. One rumor had him perishing during a viral contagion of the 1980s—I don't know, and have never been able to unearth much about his life beyond our time with him. (Several years ago, when at last I stood atop the hill of the Parthenon, I looked skyward and told him I'd finally made it.)

Chapter 5
A Changing World

*"Clay, with a left and a right, attacks! A left and a right,
and another left and a right by Clay...and here is Liston
taking a right on the ear...Clay with his eyes open wide—
they look like doorknobs, they're so wide open.*
Live Radio Broadcast February 25, 1964 – Miami Beach

Summer was waning. About a week before my start in junior
high school, engaging in horseplay with Jerry and Bill, I went
down the basement stairs in a hurry, laughing all the way. Turning
at the bottom, I stumbled, going hard onto the concrete floor.

A dark 4 x 4 propped at the side came down with killing
force, crashing inches from my head. It seemed, for one startling
moment, like nothing more than a close call. But my right hand
had taken a sharp impact with that fall, and lifting myself up I
saw, next to the thumb, a gash an inch deep into the dark muscle.
It looked like a hatchet wound.

One of the guys called out to know what had happened.
Stunned, I could only say "I'm hurt," then shot back up the stairs,
blood spilling through the kitchen and into the bathroom. Trying
to keep everyone calm while standing at the sink, I said, "I don't
think it's an artery." It wasn't—but when Bill saw it, he was
horrified. (He would say later, "I thought *half your hand* was
off.")

Blood now had been flung floor to ceiling. I called out
something from the bathroom about the cut and Jerry yelled,
"Run cold water on it!" That I did, blood now gushing crazily
down the drain.

Mr. Beaker, an old fellow next door with a gruff yet amiable
manner, seemed to appear out of nowhere. (Bill had summoned
him, possibly figuring we ought not to wait even for an ambulance.)
He had a quick glance at the wound—I sense, in looking back,

that he had seen many a wound in his day—and said cheerfully, "Well, come on, you'll have to go and get that sewed up." He hauled me to the hospital as I gave him desperate thanks.

Shortly after, Mama was there next to me as I lay on the hospital bed and the nurse went on with an interminable scrubbing. Wanting to ease my concern and theirs, I struck up a conversation, asking about the makeup of blood and what made it stop flowing.

Though my mother had proverbial nerves of steel when needed, she admitted later she had been woozy through most of it, as she had when seeing blood shed by a family member a time or two on the farm. In a couple of hours, I came home with ten stiches. The boys had stayed behind to clean up the mess. (No, they politely told my father when leaving, they did not care to stick around for ice cream.)

Junior High

The photo was taken by my mother as I set off for my first day at McLoughlin Junior High School—Mac Hi—that first morning. I am heading down to East 13th and up toward the bus stop.

The world, it seemed, was shifting beneath my feet as the

day-long Harney classroom gave way to a new bustle where one session ended and we headed fast to another. A few days into the term I was seized with an anxiety unlike any I had ever felt, or would again. It did not have an exact object, and oddly it seemed to dissipate once our bus pulled into the lot and business began. Yet it was a grim and killing sense, one that did not belong in the mind of a twelve-year-old.

Seventh graders were the youngest and generally smallest of the crowd that filled the hallways. Yet soon classmates were shooting up before my eyes, adding half a foot to their stature, it seemed, in scant weeks, and moving into social territory I had no idea how to enter.

Chemistry, it felt like, was changing everywhere. My beloved Yankees went down to defeat in the October Classic at the hands of the Los Angeles Dodgers in four games straight. Popular music would soon see a transforming new wave, one I did enjoy even if I did not accompany the more forward and agile types who were learning to dance to it.

Our curriculum that year, someone said, reflected a feeling among the nation's leaders that American youth were not competitive with that of communist nations (principally "Red China" and the gigantic Soviet bloc) and needed to be pushed harder. There was instituted at Mac Hi a massive social studies program, along with a hard-as-nails science class that had us working each week with a *do or die* test on Friday. Failure to ace it meant hand-logging answers to the chapter questions next time around. Of seven classes, six had homework. Those of us in "New Math" confronted issues in algebra, geometry, and number theory that took hours each evening and on the weekend.

The actual work, though like unto a *tsunami*, was not itself painful. But something inside was tearing me apart. A few times, in the Common Learnings session of English, reading, and social studies, the details of a lesson had me confused. I sat in a panic, head down, tears welling. The same had happened in other classes—a couple of times, in class and in the hallway, I wept outright. By now, some of the people there might have wondered if I should be institutionalized.

On it went, through that messy autumn—if it wasn't a homework assignment, it was my physical state—I confessed to Mama one morning before heading to the bus stop my terror at not having "wet dreams" the PE teacher told us about in Health class.

She was there always, whether putting me at ease about

my physical maturation or pondering with me insights that had shaped mathematics from Euclid to Carl Gauss. Though I was getting a handle on it, and my second quarter grades would end up mostly at 'A' level, I could not, for now, escape the worry. Mama listened, seeing me vomit breakfast cereal, on occasion, into the kitchen sink before heading to the bus stop.

Her care never ceased, nor did our shared attention to duty. I never let down, no matter how hard the assignments, even when the math consumed, as it occasionally did, four or five hours before there came, at day's end, the welcome peace of sleep. I never arrived late for school that year, or any other, in fact, submitting each piece of work when due.

November 22nd

The world at large was changing, as well. Active war was brewing in a place called Viet Nam. And there was turmoil on the home front. One morning in Miss Van Valkenburg's science class we heard over the wall speaker the voice of our principal, telling us that an emergency had arisen.

"We understand," he said in a disturbing tone, "that there has been an attempt on the life of *President Kennedy*." Details were not yet known.

For the next couple of hours tragedy hung in the air. In the afternoon, two students outside the building were arguing about whether the worst had happened. The one, at last, pointing across the road to the Methodist Church and looking around at the rest of us, said "*Yes*, he's dead. Why do you think the flag is at half-mast?"

Shortly after, Kennedy's death was known. One girl in Common Learnings sat in a panic, crying as I had, a few weeks earlier over the English lesson, fearing we would now be attacked by enemies who knew we were without a leader.

Perspective

For all its sorrow, this crisis did not affect me as did the one at Mac Hi. Soon the nation's trouble passed as my own continued. Mama did what she could. I talked to her incessantly, returning to the worry even after she had done her best.

One time she upbraided me for bringing up the subject of school after I had agreed to strike it from my mind for the next hour.

"Well," I said dejectedly, "if someone told you not to think of *elephants* for the next five minutes, I'll bet you would." We could always find humor in a situation, no matter how dire. And during this time, our bond became all the stronger.

On one occasion, hearing me bewail some new difficulty, she took me aback with the idea that I should focus instead on things I could be thankful for, such as "a nice warm school bus." I was incredulous. Many years later, I saw a photo in Aunt Bea's little album.

A snowy day in Mahtowa: The wooden sled has a canvas sheet, faintly visible on the right, serving as a windbreak. Maybe Etta had a point.

A New Champion

Toward the end of Fall semester, which extended into late January, my anxiety was fading. In the Spring, a new schedule, replacing a couple of the high-stress classes with more agreeable ones, provided relief. But I would never work as hard in academics—not in high school, university, or grad school—as I did that year at Mac Hi.

The whole of American culture, it seemed, was in metamorphosis. In late February, I hovered over our little Motorola radio, the long silver sweep-hand set to an AM broadcast out of Miami, where a 22-year-old Louisville upstart named Cassius Clay was taking on heavyweight champion Sonny Liston.

A few years after this, author and activist Eldridge Cleaver would note, in his best-selling book *Soul on Ice,* white America's curious affection for the *supermasculine menial*—a black man of prodigious physicality who remained loyal, in field-servant fashion, to the going power structure. Maybe this was an example. Liston, a sharecropper's son with a prison record, had a hold on much of conservative society. In truth, had more been known about Sonny's off-track recreation, sentiment might have been different. At any rate, he was a mystery. No one knew Sonny's age—though listed at thirty-two, he was said by some to be closer to forty. By either reckoning, he seemed invincible.

This new kid, a sing-song embodiment of brag and sass, promised incredibly that he would stop Liston in eight rounds. I myself wavered in feeling, seeing in Sonny the irresistible force *Sports Illustrated* recently had made of him, yet admiring young Clay's spirit in the face of odds (Las Vegas reportedly had it 7-1), that had him doomed.

Fast as a tan bullet, the youngster cut through Liston, slashing him under the left eye, beating him to the punch until the older man, sitting tired in his corner, spit out his mouthpiece in resignation at the bell for the seventh round. The next day, the new champion declared his allegiance to the Nation of Islam. He no longer was *Clay*, that name being rooted in slave ancestry, but Muhammad Ali. While it would take America time to digest it, he would be known by this name in the decades that followed. He would also be a hero to those of us who rode with him in spirit on his journey.

Eighth Grade

In the coming fall, my parents finally had me checked for allergies—a *scratch test* matrix of injections on my back, loaded with elements that might be causing a wretched annual spring misery.

In recent years I had sat in class, rubbing my eyes until abrasion on the whites of each one was visible, Kleenex pack exhausted and nose still running. There were mornings when I woke up with eyes welded shut from seepage.

The injections now turned my back red, burning white welts showing that I was averse to every strain of pollen known to God. A program of shots, initially three a week, was begun. By spring I was free of the problem.

Meanwhile, autumn brought another development.

What is its origin, this deep wellspring that can turn us into scholars, prizefighters, actors, and artists—that can make us love Indians or live and die by the exploits of one athlete rather than another? One finds intriguing examples in memoirs of many kinds, from the sporting world to the fine arts, to the field of aviation: The young Cassius Clay would marvel, in later years, at his intoxication with the sound and scent of the boxing gym when he first came upon it. He knew that he belonged here. "As soon as we left the ground," writes the irrepressible Amelia Earhart, recalling her first ride in an airplane, "I knew I myself had to fly."[13] In time she would become a groundbreaking hero of aviation, setting multiple records and becoming the first woman to fly solo across the Atlantic Ocean.

And whence this magnetism that draws us with impossible force to some young man or woman? Some people say that they have experienced the feeling at first sight. If this did not happen to me, it was near to it.

Early that autumn a flaxen blonde classmate, one I had noticed but little in days prior, entered into my world at day's end when Mr. Grace was out of the room. I don't remember just what started it, but it seems like a few of us were trading wisecracks, the trade escalating into a long-distance assault in several directions with wads of crumpled notebook paper.

Picking up an errant missile coming to rest at her feet, she hurled it back, hitting me, to the enjoyment of everyone, from across the room squarely between the eyes. Seconds later, when she duplicated the feat, I was struck as well by the shaft of Cupid. A few days after, a change in seating put her near me beside the windows looking out onto the boulevard. Soon the afternoon English—Social Studies block was aglow with magic.

She lived a couple of blocks away in a shining white house in Braewood, the high-end area of the Heights, about one mile and a light year removed from the curving lane on Nob Hill. During class, when we could manage it, several of us would trade quips,

---

13   Amelia Earhart, *The Fun of It* (Chicago: Academy Chicago Publishers, 1977, reprinted in original format of 1932), page 25.

she and I sometimes exchanging *faux* insults in the bargain. I would say or do anything to get her attention, her laughter being the most madly wonderful sound I had ever heard.

Now, too, I was finding out that such banter came with a risk. A sour note was struck one day when she made a self-conscious remark about the new perfume she was wearing. "That's OK," I dryly answered, "You don't smell half as bad as you did yesterday." I was only being silly, yet unbeknownst to me, she had come to class from PE the day prior in a hurry without showering. (Not until long after would I know what now fueled her ire toward me for what seemed like a month.)

My enthrallment would last all through our teens and until she left Vancouver behind at the end of a year at the local community college. Following this year, however, most of her classes were remote from mine. For the most part I would look on from the sidelines, a delayed puberty and twisted home life making social activity impossible.

Onto the Sidelines

Soon my introversion was setting, hard as pavement. Despite this, I did not lose my interest in athletics, nor my interest in ideas. A young readers' volume in our school library called *Knockout* described the journey of a mild-mannered kid from the tenements who finds himself by learning to box. I began delving into instruction manuals and into the history of the sport.

In the quiet of my room, around the middle of ninth grade, I developed a dice game—an idea spurred by the APBA Baseball table game that a few of us on the hill played—by which I could match boxers against mock-up nameless "opponents" and against each other, across eras, each man getting a rating on things like elusiveness, punching power, and durability. (Though the game had its limits, it was appreciably better than one along similar lines that would hit the market a couple of years later.)

I began to work out at the Vancouver Boxing Club, a little shed of a gym that sat next to The Shack, developing talent that few of my classmates imagined I had. But I lost my nerve in the coming fall, discouraged by creeping weight gain, and so—the last thing I should have done—stayed away most of the year.

Meanwhile, as I retreated from outside contact, there began to stir in me a reflective sense that reached down into basic issues of life. I found myself wondering, in odd moments, if life was worth the care that most people took to preserve it.

Now and again, too, in unlikely situations, I would find some cause for amazement. During the summer of 1966 I labored in the fields—strawberries, raspberries, and beans—each requiring a rise before dawn and a shift of roughly nine hours. Pole beans were the most worthwhile, yielding two and a half cents a pound. (A good day might get you six dollars.)

One day in the August bean season, soiled and sweating, I began to feel something happen—a melding of my mind with these hanging green clusters that brought an inner hum shutting out all else around. I marveled later at how this labor, outwardly dreadful, might bring about a state so agreeable. A wedge, as it seems now, was being driven into my thinking between material surroundings, on the one hand, and genuine well-being.

I entered Hudson's Bay High that autumn a stout 15-year-old duckling, weight continuing to grow with the coming months. Weight, but little height—the "love-handles" that had appeared a year earlier became unsightly, and my chest sagged. "Hey, Fat Lady," yelled one student that spring, relaying to me an inquiry from across the locker room. (As Sylvester Stallone's franchise hero Rocky Balboa says, in a later installment, to a woman who thirty years ago had distained his brotherly advice with "*Screw you*, Creepo," great insults last a long time.)

Some young people find a niche in situations like this, a misfit counterculture, of sorts, with others of the same stripe. I could not. There was a man inside that sad little carcass that wanted to come out. I held in my hopes and fears through high school, anguish growing until it nearly took my life.

The Reverend Peale

Some time during that year, I came onto Norman Vincent Peale's 1952 inspirational classic *The Power of Positive Thinking*. It was alive with an optimism that spoke to many, and does still, more than seven decades after its first issue.

I was struck by certain passages in the book, one of my favorites being, "You can become strongest in your weakest area." While this reading did not bring about any magical transformation, it planted ideas in me that would germinate, a little at a time, over coming decades.

Toward the end, Peale describes his attachment to his mother Anna—a precious soul whose influence upon him outweighed every other.

Mrs. Peale was a conversationalist "keen and alert," her sense of humor infallible. She had traveled the world, her life rich in friendship and adventure that stemmed from her mission activity. Whatever challenge life might bring, thought Norman, losing her would be the one thing he could never endure. But for now, she was the center of his life. In later years, he would sometimes journey home, where family gatherings—"everyone [talking] at once as we sat around the breakfast table"—were filled with joy.

Then one summer came her passing. Anna DeLaney Peale's remains were laid to rest in a small cemetery in Lynchburg, Ohio, where she had lived as a girl. A few months later Norman felt drawn to Lynchburg again. "All night long on the train," he recalls, "I thought sadly of the happy days now gone and how things were utterly changed and would never be the same again."

At last the train made its stop. Soon Peale arrived at the cemetery, the air cold and sky overcast. He pushed open the iron gates and trudged to the gravesite where he sat alone.

"Of a sudden," he writes, "the clouds parted and the sun came through," lighting up the southern Ohio hills where Norman had played as a boy, and she before him.

Then, by inward ear, he heard it.

The message was clear and distinct, "stated in her beloved old-time tone."

"Why seek ye the living among the dead? I am not here. Do you think that I would stay in this dark and dismal place? I am with you and my loved ones always."

"In a burst of inner light," says Peale, "I became wondrously happy. I knew that what I had heard was the truth."

He stood, reaching out and putting his hand on the tombstone, seeing it for what it was, "only a place where mortal remains lay."[14] The famous Reverend, whose books would inspire generations ever after, never again felt the sadness he had carried into that cemetery.

Their chemistry, mother and son, was much like ours. While Mama was less forward in social company, owing to her circumstance, she was no less radiant. Her benevolence was present in every encounter, and she managed always, with family or out in the wider world, to be a comfort to those around her.

Every so often came moments that brought it home. One time, we were in a department store, about to leave, when she

---

14   Norman Vincent Peale, *The Power of Positive Thinking* (New York: Touchstone Books, 2015), page 207

caught sight, a ways off, of two people starting down an escalator. It was a woman struggling with what might have been a family member having an epileptic seizure. In a flash she was there, helping this distraught stranger keep control of the situation until they got to the bottom. A moment later, she was back, as if nothing had happened.

Maybe this tendency owed to her rearing, and to the influence of the surrounding community and Mahtowa church. Mama, to an extent, was a product of her surroundings, reared in a time and place where women were geared to service, and were largely confined to home and subservience to their husbands. (At the weddings of two young men on our street, as I recall, "to love, honor, and obey" was part of the bride's sacred vow.)

A product, I say, but not a passive one. There was no rigidity in her outlook. She never insisted, for example, that her own lot be shared by women in general. She would not dream of criticizing a woman in different circumstance with another inclination—one, say, who sought out an unusual career path or chose to forgo marriage for life of another kind.

The Weekly Rally

High school was like unto a gauntlet, flashes of light, as it were, amid slaps and jibes that seemed to blindside me as I made my way down a night-black corridor. Now and again came a crushing reminder of how little place I had left in the world around me.

The end-of-week highlight at Bay was a thundering pride-fest known as Pep Assembly. The star of this show was our Boy's Dean, a striding platinum figure whose look and demeanor were pure Hollywood. Now and again he would let slip a *hell* or *damn* with a side chuckle in his Friday monologue, prompting even the hoods, edgy types who smoked in the "can," to think he was extraordinary.

Granted, I only saw the man from a distance, a quarter of a century removed in age and life experience. No doubt there was more to his story than I will ever know. But whatever the case, one thing was clear the two times that our paths actually crossed—he detested me on sight.

My horror over campus life reached its climax late that year when students improvised an episode of an ABC hit TV show called *The Dating Game*. My Braewood love had been one of the three rounded up as "Bachelorette" contestants, now seated behind a divider, each receiving questions from the young suitor who would choose among them.

Sitting with our Sophomore Advisory class far up in the bleachers, I watched with a sense of doom. Sure enough, our gymnasium Bachelor chose her at the end. Out she came across that bright wooden court, happy and shimmering, kiss-greeting him like a pro as the crowd roared. Yet high in that cavern darkness, the universe was crashing down, forcing me to watch as it left me behind, taking her with it.

Value and Literature

"Oh," said Mama one night coming back from a PTA event, "your *English teacher* is pretty!" A thin ray shone that year and in the one following when I discovered writing with the encouragement of Ann Hartley, a slender young brunette who saw something in me she admired.

Ann was vibrant, her classes provocative, even if she and her audience could feel at times like a mesh of satin and burlap. Each class, Sophomore and Junior, had in it a wide scatter of types, some acute and some vulgar, a few older *ne'er-do-wells* coming from auto shop to struggle (as no doubt I would have struggled in their venue, as well), a second time with the mechanics of literacy. Added to this, in the latter year, was a self-styled young visionary who had spent time in the San Francisco Haight-Ashbury scene, along with a swarthy brooding rebel, a would-be voice of his generation who (to the amusement of all), liked to call things *groovy*.

Ann never pulled rank, letting our comments spill as they would and moving us with an elegance of soul beyond her years. In covering Jack London's *Sea Wolf* or Edmond Rostand's *Cyrano de Bergerac*, we soon found ourselves confronting challenges present in our own day.

I struggled, the first time through, with London's novel. Then we watched the film, a 1941 mist-drenched sepia gem with John Garfield and Ida Lupino, and Edward G. Robinson as the amoral Captain Wolf Larsen. Though by now we had turned in our copies of the book, I headed straight for the school library that afternoon, grabbed their volume off the shelf, and devoured it over the coming weekend.

The story has in it a resounding moment where poor Louie—

Doctor Louis J. Prescott, an aging drinker now clean by his own effort with hands steady—is tripped by Larsen as he descends the deck stairs to the enjoyment of all on board. Humiliated, Louie pulls himself to his feet. Salvaging a last moment of dignity, he climbs the ship's mast and plunges to his death after crying out that there is a price no man will pay, even for life itself. Larsen refuses to believe what he has seen, for what, in a man, can be stronger than his animal will to survive?

Value was at the heart of what Ann taught. On one occasion she mentioned her time in college, and how a co-ed student might leave her purse under a tree, walk away for a short time, and know that it would be untouched when she got back.

"You're talking about morals that went out twenty years ago," retorted one jaded young adversary who found the discussion ridiculous.

Such cynicism, I would learn in time, was nothing new. The Greeks had debated these things more than two thousand years earlier with a power and imagination to rival any generation after. The Sophists—professional teachers who made their chief trade in *rhetoric*—had little use for ideals, calling morality a device of the great average "many" to inhibit men naturally stronger. Socrates, hero of Plato and the central figure in his young friend's undying portrayals, would confront these types in the city marketplace, upholding the reality of truths eternal.

Amid these sessions I found myself voicing my own fledgling convictions, insisting that morality did not go *in* and *out* like fashions. Its truth was unchanging.

Still, my social life was dwindling, even within our small band on the hill. Any effort to branch out into activity at school would have turned into a crucifixion had my father gotten hold of it. Any new presence within his territory—a wrong number call, say, or someone at the door, or anything outside that looked odd to him—could set him off. Once the glare came into his eye, there was no salvaging the situation. Phone calls, incoming or outgoing, triggered crazy anger.

At the same time, my failure to flourish as a teenager had him incensed, prompting the warning that I would become a "freak" if I did not start doing what *other kids* did. Long after, flipping through a copy of our '68 Class *Aquila*, I had to smile, even if sadly, when seeing bonfires that celebrated the fall '67 Homecoming. That must have been the night, I thought, when the two of them returned from a shopping trip, and I heard him yell as they came through the door. There was something "going on" down there—why the hell wasn't I part of it?

Maybe my fondest memory of that year was finding a simple way to slip out, on those Friday afternoons, as the great student trek went south to the gymnasium. This escape, I might note, involved no ill will toward students and faculty who enjoyed this event. Had things been different, I would have been there, spring-loaded for each standing ovation and yelling loud as anyone. But as it was, I had no yells to offer. As I strode, head down against the current, to the north end, the sound of the gym-bound wave grew fainter until I found myself in blessed quiet and washed free of pain.

Getting home early, I could share a quiet hour with my mother and watch a show produced by an organization called the Homestead, which delivered selections from composers like Bach, Beethoven, and Tchaikovsky accompanied by images of fine oil painting. While these works would never replace my love of British rock and Detroit *Motown* or the wondrous lilt of classic *doo-wop* (all sounds that enliven me still), it was an unadulterated blessing through this spring and the year to follow.

A Slugfest—and a Taste of the Teaching Business

In the fall of 1968, I decided at last to lose my bulk and returned to the boxing gym, willing to absorb a bloody nose or two in the process, if need be. In time, the weight fell off, and I approached graduation four inches taller and twenty pounds lighter than two years before. On March 12th, I climbed into the ring on a "smoker" staged by the Eagles Club at a meeting hall downtown.

The other guy was older than I and vastly more experienced. By now, Bill Connors, a Vancouver police officer who had worked with me for the past couple of months, had been put off by my erratic ways. Owing maybe to some inner conflict, I could look both great and terrible in the same session. He now decided, I think, to throw me into deep water and be rid of the problem one way or another.

The two of us slugged toe-to-toe for three rounds, the crowd going wild for the first time all night. At the final bell, there were cheers. For an instant I started to black out, then recovered and went to my corner. The guy with the mic noted that it had been my first fight. When the scores were read, I had lost on a split decision.

On the urging of old Tom Connors, the deacon of our club, I went over and shook the other fellow's hand. As our hands clasped, he said, "Thought you had it." When we spoke later in the dressing room, and he learned that I had only been training a short while, he was incredulous. Tom, too, was amazed, saying he wished I had gotten into the gym sooner—"You could've won ten fights for us this year easy," he said, "fighting like that."

I found also, on a very different front, a new interest at about that time, revealing in me a bent I could not have foreseen. Many of us in the graduating class were enrolled in a year-long elective course in psychology, a recent addition to the Bay curriculum, taught by Bill Bleakney, a pleasant fellow, about twenty-five, who obviously enjoyed his students and his subject.

Through our unit on parapsychology, I came onto the alleged phenomenon of *out-of-body experiences*, which fired my imagination. When that section of study was done, we submitted research papers on our topics and gave a solo talk to the class.

I chose this one—*astral projection*, as it was called, a thing that stirred in me a sense of freedom, resonating with the euphoria I had felt years earlier in dreams of flying. I found myself coming alive when describing the experience and its significance, and how, if at all, its reality might be confirmed.

Students and instructor were equally intrigued. How I loved exploring this idea with them, thinking on my feet as I replied to their questions. Bill invited me to present this talk to other sections of the class, and I accepted, though maybe the idea was rejected by the Admin. But how strange, after these past several years of alienation, to find myself once more in this role and enjoying it as I had at Harney.

The Strain of Home

Around this time, Mama went to work doing a night shift at a nursing home that lay in a gully along the road going north from town. Though rugged work, it brought in a few extra dollars, and she was, even at her advanced age, one of the most valuable employees they had seen. How nice it was to drive out in the early morning to bring her home, trading thought and laughter all the way.

All the while my father's mental state was causing strain. After a blowup one day, she told me that she might rent one of the units that sat in a row along that road within walking distance of the job. They were rough little places, she said after looking at one, but cost next to nothing. She seemed to think that I would want to stay in the house on the hill, but the idea made me sick at heart.

The difficulty blew over, my father no doubt realizing that he would be lost—not to mention filthy—without her care. Though the time was coming when I would be out of the house, had it been a forced choice here and now, I would have stayed with her. In truth, she was my home. Had it come down to living with him in a castle, or with her on the side of that road (or in a dank basement, or a tin storage shed), the choice would have been easy.

A Brief Career in the Restaurant Industry

Toward the end of that year, I happened onto a job at Waddle's Restaurant, a clattering joint with a bit of old swank feel on Haydn Island just across the I-5 Bridge spanning the Columbia River. High overhead was a clock and a hungry-looking duck (decked out, if memory is right, with bib, knife, and fork), that area residents may remember.

I was brought on board, I would soon learn, to bus tables. But this first night—maybe as an introductory gauntlet—I was assigned to wash dishes in a chamber thick with stench where plates and silverware, arriving in a stream, got tending on their way to the washer. It was a nine-hour shift, five hours without break, thirty minutes for a meal, and four more before punching out.

No two convicted men, says Russian novelist Feodor Dostoevsky in *The House of the Dead*, do a stretch of prison time in quite the same way. The same might be said about certain occupations. This job at the conveyer may have been a minor chore to some who did it. For me it was mental agony.

No meld, no soft inner hum, came with this. A back sprain I had suffered, carting around a friend on my shoulders in his back yard a few years earlier, had created a pressure point in a middle vertebra.   Owing to the height of the conveyor, this point got continual stress as I stood there, reaching out and scrubbing with time all but frozen.

The clock on the other side of the wall, it seemed, where I passed back and forth every so often, was scarcely moving. I set to work in earnest, somehow thinking that focused aggression would speed the process. Finally I leaned out to check again, figuring that thirty minutes or forty-five had passed.

The hour hand was where it had been, and the minute hand had gone from the six to the seven. By 2:30 AM I was all but destroyed.

In following days came two miserable shifts of busing tables, exacerbated by my failure to grasp the system (it was not complex, one ding for this side of the floor, two for that) tipping us off to a table that needed clearing. After that, the phone at home stopped ringing. Maybe they didn't figure I was worth firing.

A New Connection

A few months earlier, I had taken a Civil Service exam to qualify for federal employment. One day now came a phone call about a job in Estacada, Oregon, a logging town near Mt. Hood National Forest, 25 miles southeast of Portland.

There was an opening based at the Forest Service station there in town. I wavered, unsure of my worth to anyone after that eatery debacle. My mother was standing nearby. I turned to her and quickly indicated the situation. Her urgent yes settled it, and though I didn't know it, Estacada would be my summer home for the next several years.

Mama, *circa* 1969: It was around the time I was graduating from Hudson's Bay and leaving for Estacada. She said one afternoon, seemingly out of the blue, that she wanted me to take her picture in the back yard.

I think that she wanted this for posterity, knowing I would value it one day. She was right. Though I frown when seeing how it is clipped at the bottom, I treasure the image.

It was also around this time that we learned my father's recent EEG had turned up an irregularity in his brain waves.

"Well," I mused, "we could have told them that."

Chapter 6
What to Make of This Life?

I don't belong in this hum-drumming world
I want leather bound books with the pages all curled.
A heart full of quiet, and seedlings to grow,
and one love that's always the color of snow ...
                         Ed Ames, "The Color of Snow"

No one is ever a hopeless case. There are always those
who care for one, if not on this plane, on another.
                         Lobsang Rampa, personal correspondence

...the fight could only be decided by who could take the
steepest pitch of the hill. So Frazier, trying to drive the
heart out of Ali, put the pitch of that hill up and up, until
they were ascending an unendurable slope.
                         Norman Mailer, "*King of the Hill*"

During this senior year and for a few years following, I was drawn to anything that offered an escape from life as I knew it.

Escape, in one respect, was always there at hand. A .22 rimfire rifle and 20-gauge shotgun, picked up by my father through *Nickel* Ads a few years earlier, stood in a mahogany gun case at the foot of my bed. Around the middle of the Spring semester I took out one and loaded it, pressing its iron bore to the side of my head, finger on the trigger, wavering a few seconds on that mortal precipice.

This scene would repeat itself a time or two, over the next couple of years. But I would reach out also for solutions of other kinds—Christian devotional books, Buddhist chanting, yoga meditation, Jehovah's Witnesses, the Astara Foundation and Herbert Armstrong's Worldwide Church of God. Psychic phenomena, Eckankar soul-travel, the Church of Scientology, born-again evangelism, Hugh Hefner's *Playboy Advisor* and psychological counseling—looking back, I must have been a walking sandwich-sign invite to sellers of every stripe.

An Odd Glimpse of Light

Thus unfolded, in these years, an incongruous development, an adolescent with deep interests, lacking social tools and ridden with confusion, entertaining choices of cosmic proportion.

That restaurant go-round might stand out in my mind as nothing but a misfortune, albeit a comic one (at one point, failing to grasp the system, I had resorted to going in circles around the central lunch counter, prompting stares from the audience), but for one moment my last day there. As I wandered the floor that afternoon in the gold cloth Nehru jacket of a Waddle's busboy, there descended on me, for no obvious reason, a sheer euphoria.

The feeling seemed connected, when I thought about it later, with devotional prayer books I had picked up one night at the NE Portland Lloyd Center mall. It was brief and free-floating—I was not happy *about* anything, whether something I owned, or planned to obtain, or some thing that was to happen. But this moment would stay with me forever.

Such a moment, of course, elicits little response from doubters who hear of it second-hand. Should any reader dismiss it, say, as a mere fluctuation of young brain chemistry, I would attempt no reply. Maybe, in fact, it was nothing more. But I will never think so. It seemed to me then, as it does now, to be a glimpse of truth, an insight into my own nature and a harbinger of its realization. Here and there, I was coming to feel, life is tinged with the sense of another reality.

Boots and a Hard Hat

The Forest Service job began on June 16th, several days after graduation. Estacada, a strongly blue-collar town where logging, mill work, and forestry provided work for many, numbered around eleven hundred.

And what a departure—until now, I had known mainly Portland and my own neighborhood on the north side of the river. My employment had been yardwork around the neighborhood and a couple of summers in the bean and berry fields. Now, pulling down a respectable teen wage, $2.03 an hour, I resided in a bunkhouse trailer on the compound at a cost of six dollars' deduction each pay period. I was assigned to Trail Crew, four of us in total.

After a week of orientation and odd jobs, the crews dispersed to their tasks. Over the next month, with a few technicians and FS veterans spearheading the effort, we fashioned a log bridge, felling three gigantic firs and moving them with pulleys (I would not have believed this were it explained beforehand), high on the Clackamas River near Bagby Hot Springs.

Noseums, voracious specks swirling like a cloud over rushing water, attacked every inch of my exposed skin the first week we were there. I took to using spray repellants on the local shelves, soon finding that their alcohol drew the creatures closer. In defense I lacquered myself wet and glistening, the blood-suckers now meeting their end in droves like tiny hell-bent *kamikazes*.

The rest of the summer was spent away from the water maintaining public hiking paths. In mid-September, the thirteen-week stretch was done, and a choice awaited.   By now an undeclared war in Viet Nam was raging. College deferments were available to those who maintained a full courseload. Since I had shown promise, now and again, as a student, my parents were anxious for me to have every ounce of the education possible. (Had the conflict made more sense to me, I might have gone. But as it stood, the choice between an Asian jungle and the local campus was not hard.)

There at Clark College I made the acquaintance of two people who would become close friends in succeeding years. One was Chuck Epton, who had graduated with his MA in Philosophy from the University of Washington in Seattle shortly before arriving in Vancouver. The other was Lee Partain, a world-wise English Comp and Literature instructor in his mid-30s, blue collar to his core, who loved my boxing stories and whose English 101 Composition fed the flame that had risen in Ann Hartley's class.

My Curious Encounter with T. Lobsang Rampa

Meanwhile, during that summer in the woods, I was making the 90-minute drive home at quitting time each Friday to Mama and a platter of battered salmon and potatoes (the greatest fish and fries in the Western Hemisphere, it seemed, and I was not alone in the opinion). Later in the evening I would head across the river to Portland and explore the heart of the city.

One night, roaming the 6th floor book department of Meier and Frank's, I saw something on the shelf called The *Rampa Story*. It was authored by a self-alleged Tibetan, Dr. Tuesday Lobsang Rampa, whose name I recognized from a blurb in one of the monthly "paranormal" reads currently on the market.

Rampa had made quite a splash, I would learn, with a bestseller that appeared in print back in 1956, a purported autobiographical work called *The Third Eye*. A year or so after, he was declared a charlatan, though his books would sell for decades after. Most are available for purchase to this day.

Eying the back cover, I saw that this fellow was versed in all sorts of hidden subjects, among them, out-of-body travel. I turned, newfound treasure in hand, and bolted straight for the cash register.

Over the next couple of years, I would pore through everything Rampa had to offer, finding a few titles in mainstream outlets and then one night a trove of others at the charming little Green Dolphin Bookshop in a cobblestone sector north of downtown.

Auras, *chakras*, and ethereal bodies, a hollow Earth and secret ways of divination—Rampa knew how to stoke a reader who craved the extraordinary. Unfortunately, much of what he described was out of reach—ancient items stored in crevices of the Himalayas or buried under Antarctic ice; events of long ago, or on distant planets or higher realms of vibration. Some of his ideas, I would find, had been around awhile, as they are now.

What did one make of this fellow? A volume of the hardbound *Readers Guide* had in it a story from a 1957 issue of a weekly news magazine declaring that Rampa had been found out: Far from being a Himalayan, he was an English native with little to identify him, save that he was Cyril Henry Hoskin, son of a Devon plumber, and had worked odd jobs in plumbing, manufacturing, and photography. He had never been within a thousand miles of Lhasa.

One account, available still on-line, describes a scene in which the putative sage presents his *Third Eye* manuscript to a publisher. His credentials, it is said, are comically ungenuine. During their acquaintance, the fellow one day offers a test greeting to Hoskin-Rampa in Tibetan, which the lama does not recognize. On being told that the phrase is Tibetan, he collapses to the floor in a writhing fit, explaining afterward that years earlier he had blocked his own knowledge of Asiatic languages as a safeguard against "information" falling into the wrong hands.

I should probably have dismissed Lobsang after seeing the news article, except that by now he had made an impression on me, not just through his books, but by two letters he sent in response to my own. Each was single-spaced, running upward of a page and a half, humble in its phrase and powerful in its sincerity.

One, in June of 1970, dealt with my encounter with evangelical religion and my crisis over the Braewood girl. Another, a year later, had to do with my wider failure to find direction in life. Each, though it was earthier in tone than I expected, penetrated my psyche as few things ever had.

"Do not let anyone push you or terrorise you," he said," into becoming something you don't want to be." I was dissatisfied with myself, not with my religion or lack of one. If it was religion I was after, it was best to wait until convinced, but he added, "you will be on your way Home in any case."

In truth, religious ultimatums had not made much of a dent in me, anyway—I'd never had much sense of being lost forever owing to things I had done, or left undone, or what I had failed to believe, in this world. Yet some things we know, I would come to see with time, are still worth hearing. I was bolstered by what Rampa wrote, his words in some places curiously isomorphic with those of my mother.

Whatever really happened, this Hoskin fellow, by the accounts of those who knew him, *had* undergone a radical change in demeanor before *The Third Eye* made its appearance. Was he, after all, a genuine seer who had taken over the body of this Englishman? To some, of course, the notion will be ludicrous. Yet to those close by, such as Sheelagh Rouse, who lived under his roof for some years, he was far more than his critics fathomed. (In one of her books, she describes their first meeting, which occasioned an out-of-body experience and a realization that she was entering into another dimension of life.)

As he himself said, in his late years, what difference did it make, in the end, whether he really had come from Tibet, or had taken on a new incarnation in the latter part of his life? What mattered was the substance of his outlook, which could be verified by anyone who took the time.

From his books, I must say, I gained new perspective, saner in some respects than religious dogma to be found elsewhere. And I cannot square the comic scenario (the tacky credentials, his falling down screaming, and the rest), of that publisher with the communication I received from the man himself.

"Thank You, Jesus"

In my senior year at Bay, at the urging of a classmate, I attended services for a couple of months, as graduation approached, at a Pentecostal church in a well-worn section of downtown Portland. Called Lighthouse Mission, it abounded in song, testimonial, and praying in tongues, a phenomenon unlike any I had seen before.

There was a rub, however, in this situation, owing to my inability to share the founding vantage point of the ministry. Added to which was my unending concern with the girl in the white house, something my young mentor did not comprehend.

One Sunday after the morning service, I repaired to one of the prayer rooms, on his instruction, dropping to my knees in hope of finding truth. Hovering over me, he tried to summon divine power that would yield the light. When his own words did not bring this about, he beckoned to a comrade, a plump and addled looking fellow about our age, prone to sobbing over congregational songs and his own impending spiritual martyrdom. (It was not going to be easy, he wept, when he was crucified.) The fellow began with a wrenching call to God. He then went into a quasi-oracular state, calling upon the powers that be, finally gripping my head and (the Holy Spirit ostensibly speaking through him), declaring, "Yea, my child, let me *crruu-sify* you!"

Unmoved, and a little confounded, I could manage no

response. My young proselytizer, looking on, seemed to regard this failure as a willful one on my part, a squandering of this moment that had been offered for my sake.

He later fixed me, as he was wont to do, with an even stare.

"You know what the problem is, I don't."

He sensed, I think, that my departure from this place was fast approaching. He was right.

I should say, in fairness, that most of the members there were not like these two. Even if I did not feel altogether at home in this place, I would always remember it as one of genuine worship. But the smugness of this young fellow, and the bullying impulse that seemed to underlie it, pushed me in a different direction.

As to the girl, my efforts to approach her had faltered— awkward conversation, stammering hellos on the phone, broken engagements to meet, always to no end. How would I resolve this problem?

My most meaningful moment under the roof of that church came one night when a guest minister bid us, at the end of his sermon, to go off and kneel, and to say without ceasing "Thank you, Jesus" if anything in our lives needed remedy. I went to one of the back rooms, got down on my knees at the edge of a couch, and began to vent as instructed. Shortly, there rose within me a wave of assurance letting me know that this problem would be solved. I left feeling emptied of all anxiety.

Departure

Still, it came as a shock when I learned now, in the spring of 1970, that she was heading to Los Angeles to join her family near the aluminum plant to which her father had been given an executive transfer. I told Mama that I did not think I could bear it.

Days prior to that departure she read the letter I would soon give her, pouring out what had been in me now for six years. She marveled at it, wishing she had known what her son had been going through all this time and could have provided him with encouragement.

She understood the situation, in fact, from each side. She told me of a suitor she had when about my age, an ungainly fellow with indigenous Indian blood would bear the mark afterward of an attempt to end his life when she refused his advances. She herself had suffered a failed romance years later when living in southern California.

Poor Etta could not have cared less whether she lived or died when making the train journey, in the wake of that disaster, to the Pacific Northwest.

"She's been hurt a lot," one of my cousins would remark to me some years later. I will never know, in this world, exactly what transpired during that stretch of her life—Mama was about thirty-seven when she left California, probably feeling she had missed her one chance at having family of her own. She was at that point, I imagine, more receptive to my father, himself lonely, wry, and pleasant though "crabby" when he'd had too much to drink, than she would have been prior. And so a new chapter of her life unfolded.

"I don't think she'd make you very *happy*," she told me now about the object of my own crisis. But seeing me distraught, she said, "Well, Kelly, ask her to marry you."

Of course, it was an absurd situation. I doubt that Mama expected to hear that she had said yes, or that she hoped for it. And not many a young man, I suppose, has proposed marriage to a girl without dating her (or anyone else, for that matter) at least once. Maybe if some gridiron team has attempted a field goal, deep in its own territory, into a high wind with seconds left on the clock, they have an inkling of how it felt. That night I knocked on the door where she was staying with one of her Bay girlfriends. I related to her the conversation with my mother.

She smiled as she stood in the doorway, exuding a kindness I had not seen when talking to her in recent days, telling me that she was too young to make such a decision.

I realize, looking back, how very odd this whole encounter must have seemed to her. A few days prior, we had talked a couple of times as I fumbled to explain myself. She felt bad that she had caused me such grief, even if she had not intended it. But how could this thing, and she herself, she wondered, have assumed such mythic proportions in my innocent mind? A cavernous horror opened as we spoke, each exchange telling me how far apart we had drifted over the past several years.

A failure for her, in this arena, was nothing traumatic—a date, maybe, that did not pan out as well as she had hoped. If these guys (her use of that word, it seemed, distinguished them as a species separate from me), were sometimes a let-down, but it was not cause for anguish. (Maybe, as I look back, a misfortune like this was for her like a day I played ball and had a so-so day at bat. A disappointment, yes, but the next game would be different.) So what, she wondered, was the big deal?

I myself had some glimmer of the absurdity of this situation. But it did not enable me to shake free of what I felt. Soon she would be on that plane. A week from now, guys at the other end, sanguine and fluent in the ways of the world—full-fledged *guys* who did not even know at this moment she existed—would be carrying on with her in ways I could scarcely imagine. The thought of it made me insane.

Her flight the next day, a Sunday, was an early one. I thought that I might sleep through it, but awoke sharply before sunrise. Without knowing what more to say, I drove back to that house anyway, walking down the sloping driveway and waiting for her to appear.

Getting a sharp response from the woman of the house, when she saw me hovering outside (and maybe thinking I was dangerous), I retreated up to the road's edge. Minutes later, the young traveler was in her car, heading out and pausing at the top. When she rolled down the window, I told her that I would always be there if needed.

I returned home with some measure of relief, feeling that my life might never be right, figuring never to see her again, but knowing at least that there was nothing more to be said.

Some people, I sense, are with us in this life for a reason. Perhaps somehow they and we share a connection before entering the world. Now and then, in coming months, I took slight comfort in the thought that she and I could be linked in this way, however little it seemed so on the face of it.

Summer—and Firefighting

Around dawn the next day—probably it was a good thing—I was loading items into my little brown stick-shift Rambler and hustling across the river bound for Estacada. This time, I was on *BD*, a brush disposal crew of fifteen or twenty that existed mainly for round-the-clock fire duty.

The man who oversaw this operation was Benny Parmele, then a few months shy of thirty-five (though he had us convinced he was fifty-two), a lean and craggy soul whose devotion to duty was as pure as any I would ever encounter. He was affable, seemingly devoid of ego, with a benevolence that he retained through the toughest jobs we would see.

Much like Mama, in that time of her own life, I was lost. When I left, she handed me her Bible, a black leather Revised

Standard Version, copyrighted in 1901, she had received when joining the local Covenant Church. I read through it now and again during off-hours, finding passages she had marked with pencil many years before.

The world offers revelation of many kinds, sometimes in unexpected places. I made new acquaintances that first day piling brush, several of which I would long remember. One was Al, the assistant crew foreman, a thin fellow possessed of wiry strength despite his withered arm. At twenty-eight, he could have passed for forty.

Though few around him knew it, Al was a veteran of much of the counter-culture that flourished in those years—hard drugs, commune life, and exploration of occult realities. Early on, he sensed something unusual in me, and we began to trade ideas. One day my copy of a book by Rampa caught his eye—a fellow he knew about and respected. He asked what I thought of him.

He also asked if I had a girl—I told him about the one who had just flown to California. I explained to him that I was in a difficult place—for unlike most guys there, I imagined, I had *problems*.

"We *all* have problems, Kelly"—with those words, which a hundred other people could have uttered to no effect, he changed my vantage point. He too, in fact, had suffered a loss of what he supposed was the love of his life. He lifted the cuffs on his plaid work-shirt to show scars on each wrist left by a razor blade.

Al, to outward appearances, was an easy-going sort who showed up each morning and logged his time. But in private conversation he was a conduit into another world. He still had minor flashbacks, he confided to me, from his escapades in earlier years. One day, we were heading up the Clackamas River Road to one of our job sites. My head was drifting, as it often did, to things far removed from the task at hand. He turned to me, his hands on the wheel, with a startled look.

"What are you thinking about?"

"I was just wondering," I said obligingly, "what I would do if I thought I was possessed by an evil spirit." (Need it be said, even though I was friendly with people around the compound, no one there ever took me for a Forest Service *lifer*.) We traded thoughts on this topic, which must have widened some eyes in the back seat.

Al, I was beginning to realize, had seen things in his time that most of us never would. ("All you have to do," he apprised me later that day, seeming to remember his own narrow escape from a place very dark, "is ask Satan to come into your heart.")

How amazing, the reservoirs of kindness and insight we find in places we did not expect. Though the war inside me would flare up, now and again, in the coming year, Al helped me get through this part of it. In a summer thick with mud and ash, with bugs and scripture and Lobsang Rampa, he and I talked about women and life and out-of-body travel, and the need to persevere even when all seemed against us.

It was odd how these influences—my mother, a scandalous best-selling author, and a fellow firefighter—converged so powerfully in their spirit. Al was staying, at that time, with his grandfather on the outskirts of town. He would leave for parts unknown at the end of the summer. Our paths did not cross again.

Safety Harbor

Fires could erupt at any time of day or night. Around July and August, the heat was up, and drying east winds, when they came, turned each clear-cut unit into a tinderbox. Now and then, at any hour, might come a lightning strike. Negligent campers posed a constant danger.

While I will not try to equate our job with armed combat, it was arduous enough, fraught with enough hazard, to draw that comparison from men who had spent time in the military. Most of our work was "digging line," a trench that would (if winds allowed), *contain* the fire as a step toward controlling it. Sometimes we lugged "piss bags," black neoprene bladders held with a shoulder strap and filled with yellow spray fluid. The rest of the task was hitting the flames with dirt and water to give us a foothold. On major "project" operations we rode to the action in helicopters—their maneuverability was astounding—our labor augmented by planes and copters dropping crimson retardant.

I would see plenty of firefighting in that summer and the next few that followed. But none will I remember like the one we encountered late that July taking us into the rugged Wenatchee terrain of central Washington. Our camp lay near the shore of a long deep sliver of water called Lake Chelan.

Shooting over a rise, heading to our base at Safety Harbor, we beheld across the divide flames rising high as the trees. Our shift, for most of that two-week stay, had us up at 4 AM in bone-chilling cold, slinging a tool and heading back to camp (in this case, a harrowing climb out of a canyon testing us to the brink) where the chore ended between nine and ten at night. With lunch a momentary event, it was a seventeen-hour day.

Safety Harbor tested us as nothing had. Even multi-year veterans would say later it was the toughest assignment they had seen. The first two or three mornings, I slid out of my paper-ply sleeping bag to greet the cold air, feeling as if I were walking chin-deep in a freezing sea, wondering if I had what it took to see this task through. But sitting down moments later to a breakfast of meat and eggs boiled in a plastic bag, I said nothing, keeping a wry spirit and managing a wisecrack if one crossed my mind.

By the end of the first week, Benny had heard one outcry more than he could bear about "going home"—calling us together, he said that we might be doing work like this for the rest of the summer. Each one of us was free to stay or leave, but either way, he was staying, and he was done hearing us complain. I was glad beyond words, at that moment, that I had been one of the few who had kept his distress to himself.

(And here again, was a curious discovery: Tough as it was, never once did this day seem as long as those nine hours at the conveyer belt that terrible night at the restaurant.)

Late that summer I was called out of my bunk in the wee

hours and sent with a few other round-ups to join a crew en route to the Chelan area. I hastily packed, then dropped to my knees by the bunk, praying for the strength to do this job a second time.

As it turned out, the shift this time was mostly night crew, putting us on the line at 5 PM and off at ten in the morning. While my GS 3 grade salary was modest, something like $2.43 an hour, the extra 25 percent hazard pay, compounded with time and a half after eight hours, added up. Each time on these Wenatchee ventures, I made enough on a two-week paycheck to cover a year's tuition at the University of Washington. (Times have changed.)

In later summers the fire workday would become standardized to run six to six, whether day or night. All told, despite the stress and difficulty, I remember these times with good feeling. The contrast of this open air labor with the classroom was a healthy one, and it taught me something. Standing up to a task of this kind made a man different in mind and body. Many an employee in the field of education, I say with certainty, would be changed for the better by such a break, be it firefighting, construction work, or full-on exertion in a gymnasium.

Another Evangelism

For all of this, I could not loose myself from the trauma of that romantic failure. Through that coming year, my sophomore term at Clark, I dwelled on it, ground it practically with my teeth, feeling a rage and a confusion that would not let go of me—or was it I who would not let go of it? Seen in hindsight, it was an embarrassing failure regarding the lessons of Reverend Peale— and what Mama was telling me.

She knew, all the while, that a turning outward, an interest in others on my part, could change the situation. Yet to my inverted understanding, this seemed like sacrifice, a hand dealt to people who could not win at life's game. My density kept me locked in this condition, confounded by a universe that for some reason had turned against me.

One evening that fall, wandering the streets of Portland, I encountered young adherents pushing an atypically forward Buddhism, an offshoot that had begun in Japan in the 13th century. Founded by the priest Nichiren, this "True Buddhism" was centered, day and night, in chanting, with emphasis on a classic scripture known as the *Lotus Sutra*.

Once more, as with the Pentecostal engagement, I found

myself in the tow of a young fellow about my age, a year older "in the spirit," who wanted to see me achieve salvation. Feeling lost, my back to the wall, I chanted doggedly through the better part of that year, seven days a week, attending meetings and tagging along with members on their treks around town.

I never experienced the "benefits," inward or outward, described by so many in rousing testimonials. Still, I was getting out of the house and into circulation. These meetings held at homes across the area, heavy with rhythmic sound and pungent incense, provided stimulation. I was gleaning something of life though this mix, even if I never underwent the inner "Revolution" they raved about.

"Tolerance"—and More Words from Dr. Rampa

I think naturally of my mother when recalling this time. Here was a woman, raised in an outlying hamlet of Minnesota, knowing little of religion outside it, now with a miniature Buddhist shrine in the bedroom next to hers, a round of Japanese *Sutra* recitation—*gongyo*—sounding through the door each morning. She admitted later that she had been given a scare, when first hearing it, though taken a little with its musical tone.

The word "tolerance" comes to mind when reflecting on the problem of multiple religions. I am hesitant to use it, given the place it has had within mainstream politics of recent decades. It is one of those words—along with "inclusion", "diversity", and others—that purports to signify moral virtue.

Yet such words, it seems to me, denote nothing that is inherently positive or negative; their objects (unlike, say, justice or kindness or honesty), take on value only in relation to their context. Often as not, their value is negative. There is nothing admirable, for instance, about *tolerating* a willful imposition. The forced inclusion of incompetent people in a project of any kind is destructive. Diversity, heralded time and again as "our strength," is nothing of the kind when it dilutes the talent pool of an industrial workforce or compromises a graduate program in academia.

And conversely, these things can be good. Tolerance can have positive value, as when Mama encouraged me during this period to find my way, as she had done in her youth. Her deep Christian faith, in fact, made a mockery of the out-loud brand found in some quarters. Yet she also knew, with her rare understanding, that the soul might flourish within a tradition other than her own. Had I found fulfillment in Nichiren Buddhism, she would have respected my choice. Though she thought it just as well, I imagine, when my foray into that scene did not pan out, she never spoke against it.

At the end of that year, around June, I wrote Rampa a frantic letter, enclosing money once again to pay for his time. What I got back, in addition to his thanks, was a veritable scolding, words not easy to read yet more valuable than others in which I might have invested.

His reply was blunt, shocking me, sentence upon sentence, out of my self-enclosure. My mother, reading it later, marveled at how his letter had given articulation to what she had been thinking for the past year.

As to my frustration with chanting, I could not make progress, in this world or out of it, until I let go of the self-pity that had shut down my existence. "No one," he added, after deriding me for my immaturity, "is ever a hopeless case." We are not alone in this struggle, no matter how it may seem to us in times of difficulty. Our connections extend to things unseen.

I kept his letters for years afterward, and have never forgotten some of their sentences, which pierced my soul. His books, over time, would alter the way in which I absorbed all that life handed to me. Though it is hard to find words to describe it, the change was profound. Rampa's outlook, strange as it seemed, was at some deep level in harmony with that of my mother.

Justice, reconciliation, the fulfillment of aspirations not realized here; misunderstandings here in this world made aright hereafter; our fate in the hands not of the vengeful, but the just and compassionate; the reality of joys awaiting, joys of which we have as yet only a faint intimation—while I did not believe everything he said (a time or time or two, in reading his later books, I wondered if he were falling prey to deterioration), his essential outlook made more sense to me than did others. His message in time would seep into all I experienced.

Again, how interesting that a world-famous (albeit controversial) author and my mother should tell me the same thing. From this experience I gained perspective, and something else I had not had before: Hope. I was not lost.

Hospitality

Now and again, Mama and I would listen together to a few of the cassette tapes in my fledgling collection—she enjoyed hearing things that were current in the industry, like Isaac Hayes' *Hot Buttered Soul* and the breakout album (far eclipsing his effort a couple of years prior), of young English pianist Elton John. To my surprise, she liked some of the material on recent sets by the Rolling Stones.

We shared a great fondness, as well, for the marvelous sound of veteran Ed Ames, who had performed on stage with his brothers, years earlier, and had done an engaging turn as the half-Cherokee Mingo in the weekly *Daniel Boone* television series. Ames was enjoying great success now with his solo career on the popular charts. I was moved, when hearing a song on a collection called "The Color of Snow", a masterful piece both wistful and uplifting that gave expression to a yearning I felt deep inside.

Around this time, too, I began to see my mother not just through my own eyes, but as others did. As the center of her attention, my sense of her had long been grounded in myself, but increasingly I was seeing how her kindness radiated in every direction.

Her skills in that homely kitchen were legend. The families of my father's two nieces, Mills and Kesinger, who resided in Southern California, were at the house now and again for feasts they remembered. Our meals, on these occasions, were nothing exotic—pot roast and mashed potatoes (she peeled, I pounded), candied yams, and *hors d'oeuvres* from a jar. But what she could do with an average cut of meat was extraordinary.

During these years my father was advised by his doctor to have steak with breakfast each morning. Often I had a slab, as well. What we purchased, on my father's salary, was low-end "round"—I can remember her pounding it dutifully with a wooden mallet at night, and how succulent it was the next day. Rarely have I found beef in an eatery to match its flavor.

Visitors who were around for breakfast might get her Swedish pancakes. As with all else produced by her hands on that red-tile floor, they came from basic ingredients, not devices that speeded the process. These were a soft thin crepe, either rolled or stacked flat in the usual manner. We had them with maple syrup, or better still with lingonberries and whipped cream. (My parents years ago had found an import store on the east side of the Willamette

River that sold the berries by the jar. This was not the tepid jam that one sometimes finds in the market, or in cafes that profess to offer Scandinavian cuisine. Once you've had the real thing, you know.)

But most of all, I remember her ability to make others feel needed, no matter their mind-set or walk of life. She could bolster them in time of difficulty and dissolve hard feelings they sometimes carried. I remember one member of the California crowd, eldest of three towering brothers, an acute and hard-driven engineer who was often sharp with his wife, his voice shaking the walls when his temper flared. Yet I would see his attitude melt when he was at our house and he and Mama spoke with each other.

I remember, too, one friend of my father, a co-worker from the post-war years, whom I first met at a July 4th outing provided annually by the Bonneville administration at the Jantzen park on Haydn Island. This was around 1956, when I was maybe five. I remember my father introducing us, a large hand, dark as coal, reaching out for mine as Bob Freeman issued his deep earnest greeting.

In the years to come, Bob would be a frequent visitor to our house, providing me with more encouragement, in my schoolwork and athletic ventures, than my own father ever had. Every so often he would stop by after they got off work for a drink, something my father always had on hand, though he rarely would partake. One time, as Bob unwound with a couple of shots of bourbon, he let loose his anger over something that had happened at work. He obviously was upset, but he could also forgive a man, he said, for a slight when the occasion called for it. My mother praised him for his ability to rise above provocation. Her effect on him was always visible.

He would remember her fondly long after when he and I reconnected and resumed our friendship, which lasted until he passed away in his 90s at a Veterans' facility in The Dalles. I would never know firsthand either side of that situation at Bonneville, but I in thinking of it, I always wished I could have done something to change what had happened.

A Clash of Titans

Bob always got a kick out of my interest in boxing, and in his own ring exploits, of which he told me a time or two when he visited. Like me, he had followed Muhammad Ali during Ali's three-year reign as heavyweight champion before being exiled from the sport in 1967 owing to his refusal to be inducted into the Armed Forces.

After three and a half years away (the best fighting years he would have had, figured some, had he been able), Ali got the green light for a return to the ring. Two rousing victories in the fall of 1970 set up a showdown with heavyweight champion Joe Frazier in a 15-round battle at Madison Square Garden early in the following spring. I went to the Memorial Coliseum closed circuit telecast with Gene and Marty, affable Bay comrades from a few of years earlier, Gene being a classmate intermittently since the days at Harney and a sixth grade "Mr. May" *alumnus*.

Ali–Frazier was something that boxing fans may see once in a generation, a high noon collision of supermen, each at his peak, their combined records totaling fifty-seven wins without a loss. Each man was an Olympic champion, the eighteen-year-old Cassius Clay winning gold as a light-heavyweight in Rome in 1960 and Frazier, a heavyweight at twenty, winning in Tokyo four years later.

Plain and thick-legged, the twelfth child born to a rural couple on the outskirts of Beaufort, South Carolina, Joe was a straight-ahead banger in contrast with this glib dancer who had preceded him. Squat and dark alongside Ali, he had been the butt of his jibes now for more than a year. It was a politically charged drama, the two men cast in roles that cleaved public sentiment.

Frazier, said Ali somewhat ironically, was a *white man's champion.* (In one interview, asked about this label, Joe extended his left hand and pointed, as if to say, "What the hell is *this*?) Like it or not, the Beaufort man had the support of conservative America, much like other black opponents who had suffered from Ali the same slight. I couldn't wait to see this fight, even if I dreaded seeing either man lose.

On the night of March 8th, the bell released them, months of tension exploding onto the screen. Ali struck from long range, Frazier darting and bobbing—he was quite adept at this, despite his image as a plodder—seeking to close the distance. When Frazier surprised him with a left hand over the top, his signature punch, Ali held on and turned to all the world, shaking his head, making that bright canvas stage for just a moment his own playground.

The rounds passed, ebb and flow, Frazier taking hard shots to the head to bury his fists into Ali's middle, then shifting upstairs as the fight approached its mid-point. In the eleventh, Joe caught him with maybe his best so far, a left hook on the chin that nearly floored him, making it seem for a frightening moment that Ali was finished.

Incredibly, each man stayed upright until mid-way through the fifteenth, when finally Frazier landed a blow he perhaps had yearned to land all his life, a sweeping Sunday-best left hand that sent Ali to the floor. Rising gamely, the fallen fighter lasted out the round.

I remember this fight as more than an athletic contest. It was a testament to human endurance, Frazier walking through fire, pounded and bloodied at the end, yelling defiantly in Ali's face at the bell.

Tension now rose as the scores were tallied. Argument would continue long after as to which man (Gene, to this day swears it was Ali) had prevailed. The scores favored Frazier, referee Arthur Mercante's "8–6 and one round even" being the closest—and, I thought, the most apt—of the three.

While the two men would never like each other, each had won the other's respect. Their rivalry, in the ring and out, would continue, producing a trilogy of fights that would have its final act in the fall of 1975 in Manila.

Chapter 7

The University of Washington

There is in the minds of men, I know not how, a certain presage... of a future existence, and this takes deepest root in the greatest geniuses and the most exalted souls.
Cicero, *The Tusculan Disputations*

Every day we have been ready to start for our depot 11 miles away, but outside the door of the tent remains a scene of whirling drift. I do not think we can hope for any better things now. We shall stick it out to the end, but we are getting weaker...and the end cannot be far. It seems a pity, but I do not think I can write more.
Robert Falcon Scott, 1912, facing immanent
death in the Antarctic

Sometimes dreams are wiser than waking.
Black Elk, Lakota visionary

"When it's time to leave your home and your loved ones," crooned Perry Como in a 45-vinyl homage to Seattle, "it's the hardest thing a boy can ever do."

The approach of autumn 1971 brought a sense of dread as I faced a long-term departure from the only home I had known. Looking back, this apprehension seems a mite odd—I had been away, after all, much of that summer and the two prior. On the Lake Chelan fires, and recently again in the rich-earth forest of New Mexico, I also had worked harder, with shovel and Pulaski, than ever I would on a college campus.

That September I wavered on my entrance into the University of Washington, deciding instead to enroll at The Evergreen State College, a bold new experiment in Olympia. Slightly eccentric, politically *avant-garde*, TESC offered independent projects and free-wheeling seminars in place of the standard lecture. There some students would find a niche and flourish as they might not have in a traditional setting. For others, it was a bust, and by mid-quarter I was making arrangements to attend UW. As the calendar year drew to a close, I readied to head north again, this time to the town Como's song had celebrated.

Arrival

In early January I set foot on the campus. After a short stay in an apartment a few miles west, I spotted an ad for a room on 17th Avenue NE, walking distance from the U., in a house owned by an eighty-year-old Russian woman named Ludmilla Reifschneider.

Certain people, certain moments in life, stand out ever after. Ludmilla—Mrs. Reifschneider—was such a one. Charmed by her soft voice and gentle manner as she showed me around, I could feel the rightness of this choice. I saw, too, that I had lucked out—the room was large, also quiet and comfortable as promised, for $55 a month, looking out onto the lane.

Ludmilla, who bore the surname of her late second husband, had come of age during the 1917 Bolshevik Revolution. She and her young Russian love imagined, as did many at the time, that this event would usher in a great new era for the masses. Not long after, however, a different and mortifying reality would take hold. It was amazing now to sit with her at the kitchen table late at night, sharing her recollections.

The Philosophy Department

Shall the seen world or the unseen, asks William James in a monumental work called The Varieties of Religious Experience, "be our chief sphere of adaptation?"[15] Our outlook will form as a result.

By now, of course, I had developed certain convictions about life and what it was about. At the same time, I had little sense of

---

15   William James, *The Varieties of Religious Experience* (New York: Penguin Group, Inc., 1982), page 373. This volume, which represents James' Gifford Lectures at the University of Edinburgh, was first published by Longmans, Green, and Co. in 1902.

the going tenor of academic philosophy in most US universities. The UW department and I made an odd mesh—an earnest young believer saturated with auras and astral bodies brought together with a program had no use for things outside of mainstream science.

The personal side of this situation was friendly enough. I got along, by and large, with the faculty, strong scholars and splendid technicians who had distinguished themselves at places like Yale, Harvard, and the University of Chicago. While they and I lived in different worlds, my time there was not wasted. Even if I was not fully "with" the curriculum, the coursework would sharpen my faculties and acquaint me with fascinating chapters in the history of human thought.

Basic Doubt

To provide some sense of the prevailing tone in this program and many similar, it might be worthwhile to offer a brief word on events that had given it shape.

Around the mid-18th century, a wonderfully irreverent young author named David Hume undertook to challenge basic precepts of common sense that had long dominated European tradition. His conclusions were so odd that established scholars at first refused to acknowledge them. His first major work, *A Treatise Concerning Human Nature*, he would say later, thus had fallen "still-born from the press." Today, this book is hailed as a staple in the history of thought.

Hume's doubt was radical, prying at the foundations of human understanding. Take, for one, *inductive* reasoning, by which we use limited information to infer truths of wider scope about the world in which we live.

At the heart of this enterprise is our notion of causality. To take an instance, I see one billiard ball strike another: The latter ball moves, leading me to say that the motion of the first imparts motion to the second. I imagine, in Hume's parlance, that the first motion *necessitates* the one after.

Granted, I see the balls move, but where, he asks, do I find this necessity—the thing that "makes" them behave this way? Even should I witness the succession time and again, how can I know what is to come the time after? This notion of cause, Hume argues, owes not to any observed fact, but to my own peculiar nature: I acquire it, by what means I cannot say, through the repeated conjunction of events I witness. Yet my belief that it must be this way—that this conjunction owes to some governing natural law—lacks any real warrant.

Hume expressed puzzlement likewise over moral judgments, and how this whole business of good and evil long had been treated by philosophers preceding him. Typically, a writer tells his audience what is the case, then proceeds, as if by inference, to tell them what *ought* to be. On what basis can one make this logical leap?

He offers, as an example, the act of willful murder. Seeing it, if I am like most, I am horrified. I declare the act to be evil. But where in this event (containing, say, blood, noise, and the expiration of human life) do I find this actual vice or villainy? The answer, as with causality, lies not in the object, but in the *subject*—not in the world, in other words, but in ourselves. The action gives rise in me to certain feelings—"sentiments"—of loathing and condemnation. And there, he imagines, the analysis ends. Such feelings, however powerful, provide no objective basis for any judgment concerning the act itself. The judgement describes merely my own oddity.

But surely, one would think, there was some bedrock of certainty, even should the whole world before us be called into question. *Cogito, ergo sum*, as Rene Descartes had put it in the century prior—"I think, therefore I am." My own conscious selfhood, known with immediacy, furnishes a starting point for inquiry of any kind.

Yet Hume, when he looked within, did not find an enduring *self*—he found only "perceptions," discrete momentary episodes of thought, mood, will, and sensation, in constant succession. Could it be, then, that we do not exist, at least in the way we commonly imagine? Thus even "personal identity," as we commonly think of it, was called into question.

How does this notion of selfhood arise in the first place? As in the other cases, Hume's explanation is psychological. We harbor trust in the future because we are (for who knows what reason) structured in that way; we hold moral views groundlessly, owing to our makeup. Our purported selfhood arises out of fleeting experiences, one after another, that give rise to it.

An Evolving Skepticism

Hume, of course, did not have the last word on these subjects. No philosopher, so far as I am aware, was moved by his writing to doubt that the sun would rise tomorrow, or that something brand new would happen the next time one billiard ball struck another. (Such faith, of course, is essential to scientific enterprise, not to mention our daily survival, even if we cannot devise a basis for it.) But his broader skepticism, and its implications for knowledge, value, and selfhood, would inform much of philosophy to come.

A strong tendency was developing, in this age of scientific advancement, away from concern with any world apart from this one. Our hope of reliable knowledge, said some, lay not on high, but in what we find before us here and now. While some of the men involved in this great rise—Galileo, for one, and Isaac Newton—still harbored religious faith, its overall effect was taking philosophy elsewhere.

The emerging picture was both materialist and mechanistic: The universe, declared Galileo according to his observations, was a great book written in the language of numbers. Human beings, many now supposed, were but one more part of this scheme. The French theorist Pierre-Simon Laplace, a stellar intellect versed in physics, engineering, and mathematics, provided late in his career a classic statement of the thesis that would be known in time as causal *determinism*: An outside intelligence, armed with knowledge of what the universe contained and forces acting therein, could deduce by causal inference the exact state of things everywhere, past or future.

Soon after, his countryman August Comte put forth a related thesis called positivism. Human understanding, Comte maintained, has three stages, the first religious, the second *metaphysical*, and the last *scientific*. The first of these stages sees in natural events a force or will that lies behind them. The second, deductive in its thrust, employs reason in a vain effort to reach past observed events to an invisible truth that resides beyond.

The third and *positive* stage, which concerned only these events and the patterns they exhibited, yields at last something reliable. While Comte doubted that a perfect and comprehensive science was in the offing—the human mind, he gauged, is too feeble and the universe too vast—he believed that all knowledge lay in principle within this arena. In time, he supposed, a *social physics* would absorb the human element into its scheme.

On a political front was voiced kindred feeling. Religion, declared Karl Marx famously in mid-century, was *the opiate of the people*—the cheap goods, as it were, that salved the great many who lived out their lives in poverty and alienation. His devotee Vladimir Lenin, writing seventy-five years later, would call it "a spiritual vodka in which the slaves of capital drown their human shape and their claims to any decent human life."[16]

Related thought arose from the fledgling enterprise of human psychology. "The apparent permanency of the ego," wrote Ernst Mach in an anti-metaphysical vein, "consists chiefly in the single fact of its continuity, in the slowness of its changes." Given time, this gradual process brings about a self fundamentally different from the one that existed at an earlier stage of development. Indeed what most people fear more than anything—their own extinction—comes about naturally within the span of an average life.[17]

Our belief in God, claimed pioneering psychoanalyst Sigmund Freud, is best understood as a reiteration of our encounter, from earliest childhood, with a towering figure who dispenses love and protection. For this reason, he says, such a belief is *illusory* (*i. e.*, even did it turn out to be true, its truth would owe to coincidence rather than to insight). Though historically religion has provided a basis for our ethics, we must now find a reason to conduct ourselves responsibly toward others without the hope it provided.

As to ethics, Hume's skepticism would see a revival cast in the terms of modern biology. Our moral experience, supposed some, is essentially an accident, born of *natural selection* amid struggle in every quarter, reflecting some feature of human makeup that tends toward the survival of the individual or the group to which he or she belongs. (Thus our deep respect for *justice*, to cite one case, is grounded in a retaliatory impulse aiding in the preservation—and so the reproductive success—of the organism that has it. An animal that *fights back* when attacked fares better on average than one that fails to stand its ground. As a result, this impulse in time becomes common in the species.)

In line with this trend came a 20th century "logical" positivism holding that longstanding problems of philosophy could be

---

16   This quote, contained in a multi-volume collection of Lenin material, is cited by Robert Klark Graham in *The Future of Man* (Escondido, CA, 1981: Foundation for the Advancement of Man), page 46.

17   Ernst Mach, *The Analysis of Sensations* (Pantianos Classics, C. M. Williams, translator). This book had several editions in the late 19th and early 20th centuries, and had it first English edition in 1914.

solved—or perhaps *dissolved*—did we pay more attention to our use of language. There exist limits, maintained these advocates, to what makes for a genuine *assertion.*

We use words, if one thinks about it, in varied ways—to issue a command, for example, or ask a question, recite poetry, urge someone to rise to an occasion, curse our fate, or sing from our inner depths. But if we are to assert something, to make some claim about *how things are* in reality, what we say must remain within certain bounds: It must be either *analytic*—a statement true (as with *All squares are rectangles* or *7 + 5 = 12*) according to relations between ideas—or capable of public verification by means of the senses. When language strays outside this limit, its utterance, even if it has subject and predicate and appears to say something important, it is but hollow noise serving to vent our emotion.

And so, to put it bluntly, a great deal of traditional philosophy across twenty-five hundred years, uttered in full sincerity, was literal nonsense. Such issues as God, the soul, radical "freedom of the will," or an "absolute" morality, however urgent they seemed to be, had no place in serious inquiry. This essentially materialist outlook, while not shared by every member of the UW department, infused the bulk of its curriculum.

A Moment of Realization

Another thing that I remember from this time concerned something outside the classroom.

It came near the end of the Spring '72 quarter when I was walking across Red Square, a rose tinted, fashionably *contra*-named plaza in the center of campus. All at once I stopped. Was this situation what I had feared? I looked around, all but laughing at my own foolishness.

This crystallized for me a lesson. I saw how human beings multiply their difficulty in life by taking on mental burdens as I had. Never again would I fear taking up residence anywhere— even, in later years, on the far side of the earth. (Yet again, if only I had trusted my mother.)

Paul

Fortunately, not everyone in that department shared its skeptical leaning. In my senior year, I took a course from Paul Dietrichson, a Yale alumnus from Bergen, Norway, who taught largely in the areas of existentialism and religious philosophy.

Paul taught with an urgency and a seriousness I had rarely seen in a classroom. It was through him that I found spirituality cast in a positive light, one example of being the work of German scholar Rudolph Otto.

A student of religion East and West, Otto had become dissatisfied with the way in which spirituality was treated in academic circles. His best known work, *The Idea of the Holy*, sought to awaken readers to the primal force of religion, to its depth and unearthly terror, something that had been obscured, of late, even in theological circles. The very term 'God', grown flat from use, had come to designate merely an abstract set of properties providing scholars with a contemplative pastime. Religious thought, believed Otto, needed to recapture something of the primal force contained in the thing it studied. Ultimate Reality was not an abstraction, but a *Mysterium Tremendum*, a "Wholly Other" that evoked something unique in human encounter.

Holiness is not something we absorb with our eyes and ears. It is a *priori*, a "category" of experience underlying sense perception. I cannot lay hold of it with my senses, yet still is it available to me, much like a moral truth that impresses itself upon me, now and again, in daily life. (I can see, of course, what society bids me to do, what it alleges is my obligation to those around me. But the real substance of morality I discover within.) Without this capacity, religion is merely a branch of social science. Yet for those awake to it, religion is a whole new dimension of reality. Religious folk, however they may falter in describing it, swim in a reality richer and wider than the one our senses disclose.

Not a Single Word

Here was an author to which I could fully relate. Meanwhile, as I broadened my exploration of books and ideas, I continued to realize how unusual my mother was, not merely in my own eyes, but in the eyes of all who knew her.

In September of 1973, after finishing a hard summer in Estacada (our "weekends" were now at mid-week to have us available on days of high risk, and often as not we worked straight through), I flew to California to see a fight between Muhammad Ali and a new face on the heavyweight front, free-swinging ex-Marine Ken Norton.

This was a rematch. After that epic 1971 bout with Joe Frazier in Madison Garden, Ali had set himself to getting another crack at the title. In January of 1973, however, the heavyweight picture was scrambled when Frazier was demolished in Kingston, Jamaica, by George Foreman, a young dreadnaught in the mode of Sonny Liston and bigger. It appeared that Ali was headed for a shot at Foreman, yet another surprise came two months after. His effort was derailed when he received an unexpected beating from Norton, one of Kenny's looping right hands fracturing his jaw in the early going.

Cousin Jean and her husband Carl (yet another one in our family) hosted me for a few days in Alhambra. A former Marine himself, Carl had served in the Pacific during World War II. He had no use for the pop liberalism that was flourishing in America of late, which made for a family politically divided, mother and father being staunch conservatives and their two sons and daughter leaning the other way.

Carl, seeing how excited I was about the coming battle and the boyish enthusiasm of the former champion when interviewed from his training camp, hoped that Ali would regain his old form despite the ex-champion's polarizing anti-war stance. Seeking, at thirty-one, to regain his old flash and form, Ali came through, though struggling again with Norton, whose movements seemed always out of rhythm with his own. A decision win put him back in the running for a bout with George.

About five years earlier, when my parents and I were there, Carl and I had talked at length about things that were tearing apart the nation. Though I shared some of the liberal mindset, he and I had common ground and a strong rapport. He was intrigued also by my interest in books celebrating human potential, such as Peale's volume and Claude Bristol's *The Magic of Believing.*

Now, on this visit, there were more talks. As Jean and I chewed the fat one day, the subject turned to my mother. I will never forget the admiration in her voice when she told me how amazing Mama was in her eyes, saying that in all the years she had known my mother, she had heard not a word said against her.

John Haynes Holmes

Around the time I was finishing my Bachelor's credits in Seattle, I came onto an Easter morning sermon delivered decades prior by the renowned orator and social activist John Haynes Holmes. It was entitled "Ten Reasons for Believing in Immortality".

Born in 1879 in Philadelphia, Holmes graduated high school in Massachusetts and entered Harvard College in 1898. He graduated in 1902 and completed a degree from the Divinity School two years after. His inclination toward the ministry emerged when he began teaching Sunday School at a Unitarian church in Cambridge in the year following.

After serving in this capacity in Dorchester, Massachusetts, he was called in 1907 to the Unitarian Church of the Messiah in New York City. His pacifist stand, in coming years, against American entry into European combat went contrary to a Unitarian pledge in support of the effort. As a result, his church became non-denominational and (though it managed to retain its Unitarian ties), took the name Community Church of New York.

Throughout his career Holmes was active in social causes, championing an interfaith alliance with Jewish colleagues and supporting Civil Rights activity in America. He was a founding member in 1909 of the National Association for the Advancement of Colored People and the American Civil Liberties Union in 1920. He would serve as chairman of the ACLU from 1940 to 1950.

While he is remembered largely for his interest in another world, Holmes' day to day ministry centered upon this one. The true concern of the Community Church, as he saw it, was not religious doctrine, "but...the community as a whole." He had little wish to debate differences between denominations, being more interested in bringing together members of these groups in recognition of their common humanity.

He decried, as well, the tendency of some religious types to remain complacent about injustice in this world, expecting disadvantaged citizens to console themselves with faith in a world to come. In his 1915 work *Is Death the End?*, though the book affirms the reality of a future life, he mentions with sympathy the old story of a saint who was seen one day running through the streets, torch in one hand and pail in the other. When asked the meaning of this, the fellow said, "With the water I am going to extinguish the fires of hell, and with the torch I am going to burn the ramparts of heaven, that men may see this world alone and do good for no other reason than the love of God!"[18]

A responsible church, Holmes insists, "substitutes for restrictions of creed, ritual, or ecclesiastical organization, the free spirit. It relegates all matters of theology and worship [to] where they belong—to the unfettered thought and conviction of the individual."[19] It substitutes for conventional Christianity something universal, seeing the religious impulse as "inherent in human nature, and all religions as contributions to the fulfillment of man's higher life."

At the same time, an otherworldly conviction burned bright within him. For in this free human spirit, he found an undying reality. During the Great War, when life across Europe had taken on the cast of tragedy, he found cause for hope. His anthology *The Grail of Life*, co-edited with Lillian Browne-Olf and published in 1919, is divided into two sections of quotation, one honoring heroism in this world, the other focusing on the life to come.

In the words of those young men most traumatized, he found something that gave strength to his own faith. He describes "the testimony which had been coming to us from brave young hearts, in the filth of the trenches, in the icy wastes of the sea, even in the vast spaces of the air, during these years of the world's blackest tragedy and most awful agony."[20]

"Something there is within man, or above him,"

> that makes him greater than himself, stronger than the universe, mightier than the mysteries which always challenge, and sometimes beat him downward, to despair. Man, in his fronting of death and his dream of immortality, is all that we need after all, to teach us of God. The soul is its own best testimony to the everlasting reality of religion.[21]

---

18   John Haynes Holmes, *Is Death the End?* (New York: G. P. Putnam's Sons, 1925), page 317.

19   This passage, from Holmes' 1958 autobiography *I Speak for Myself,* is contained also in Carl Hermann Voss, ed., *A Summons Unto Men* (New York: Simon and Schuster, 1972), page 40

20   John Haynes Holmes, Preface to Holmes and Lillian Browne-Olf, eds., *The Grail of Life*, pp. xiv – xv. The passage is quoted also by Voss, page 111.

21   *Ibid.*

His worldly commitment, said his son Roger Wellington Holmes, professor of philosophy at Mount Holyoke College, had in it the same fire. John, noted Roger, was deeply influenced by men like Socrates and Plato and the Roman stoics, and by the 18th century philosopher Immanuel Kant. His sense of moral rightness and his unwavering belief a life to come were the fundamental driving forces within him to the end.

The immortality sermon was first delivered on Easter morning at Holmes' Community Church in 1929. I came across it in a large anthology used at UW in many of the introductory classes, contained with other pieces in a section headed "Body, Mind and Death". Probably it was ignored by most instructors in the department, or was passed over quickly as the relic of a naïve time and culture.

Inclined as I was toward other worlds and future life, I read it with interest, albeit with the healthy resistance instilled in me by my mentors. I was not moved by its opening paragraphs, which declared that belief in immortality is encouraged first by the fact that "there is no evidence against it." (Surely the intimate tie of consciousness with the brain, I thought, made it fair to suppose that the former is dependent for its existence on the latter.)

Still, there was something here. As the sermon progressed, I found myself reading in another way, awakened to something that listeners might have felt that morning at the church in New York City.

What, after all, is a human being? We have in us a depth and a potential, Holmes believes, that cannot be understood in terms of material accident.

"What shall we think," he asks rhetorically, "when we see a [Percy] Shelley drowned in his thirtieth year by the heedless sea, a Phillips Brooks stricken in the prime of his manhood by a diptheric sore throat, a Captain Scott frozen in mid-career by an accident of weather?"[22]

Can it be, in the end,

> that these lives of ours are dependent upon a fall of snow, a grain of dust, a passing breeze upon the sea? Is it conceivable that our personalities, with all their potencies of spirit, can be destroyed, as our bodies can be broken, by the material forces of the world? Are we to believe that eternal powers

---

22   "Ten Reasons for Believing in Immortality", contained in Payl Edwards and Arthur Pap, eds., *A Modern Introduction to Philosophy*, page 243

can be annihilated by transient accidents? I cannot
think so![23]

Rather, he says,

must I think, as Professor George Herbert Palmer
thought, as he looked upon the dead body of
his wife, one of the greatest and most beautiful
women of her time, stricken ere her years were ripe.
"Though no regrets are proper for the manner of
her death," said this noble husband, "…who can
contemplate the fact of it and not call the world
irrational if, out of deference to a few particles of
disorder matter, it excludes so fair a spirit?"[24]

Our souls, insists Holmes, "have promises and potentialities
which should not, as indeed they cannot, be subject to the chance
vicissitudes of earthly fortune."

As I chewed this notion, something came over me. Palmer's
words concerning his deceased wife demanded not a knee-jerk
reply, but a prolonged meditation.

These "particles of disordered matter"… I thought of men
and women of the kind mentioned in Holmes' sermon, some
within my own acquaintance. As I pondered this question there
flashed before me in mind's eye the image of my mother, bright
against the darkness, and I asked myself what manner of reality
she could be. Had accidents of molecules brought her into being,
giving rise to her life venture and to all she was as a human being,
only to extinguish it a few decades after?

This mortal hypothesis, I supposed, was possible. It would
have the endorsement, no doubt, of most of the people who were
teaching these classes. But I could not embrace it. As I pondered
this question—a question about love, about kindness and heroism
in daily life—I saw that I could not reconcile my experience with
the attitude that prevailed in this campus venue. This conviction
was not dampened by anything I read or heard while in the
program, and even if I would have moments of doubt, in coming
years, it remained with me. Ironically, Holmes' statement, found
by chance amid my training in skepticism, would be the single
most powerful shaping influence of my career.

During that senior year, I learned that I needed a few
distribution credits owing in part to lack of a third year of foreign

23   *Ibid.*
24   *Ibid*, page 244.

language on my high school transcript. I came back in the fall of
'73 to take care of this problem, finishing without difficulty. With
this, I imagined, I was done with formal education, even if I did
not know where things went from here.

Pushing Further

"We didn't want you to be drag-ass poor people like we
were," my father would say to me years later, in one of the rare
moments when we exchanged meaningful words of any kind.

Maybe that was why they wanted me to stay in school. I
myself had no intention, by now, of going on with it—a university
degree was the most I had ever expected, and beyond what
anyone of the older generation on either family side had acquired.
(A high school diploma, in fact, had been a rarity.) I took more
philosophy, and a couple of "methods" courses that preceded the
public teaching practicum offered through the UW Department
of Education.

Through these years Mama and I continued to bolster one
another. Our relationship was a curious one, never abounding in
kisses or loving declarations. Yet it ran deep, a tacit connection
of two souls present to each other on a shared path. In December
of 1975, we were beset with various troubles as she sat in the
hospital, having been hurried one night in an ambulance to an
emergency room at St. Joseph's—it was now a few miles east
on Mill Plain—with food poisoning. She had contracted it from
something in a damaged can on our basement stairway shelf. I
sat at her bedside, relieved beyond words to find her recovering.
"I'm going to be well," she informed me, her face bright as she
sat reclined there on the bed.

"We've been through *so many* things like this."

There was marvel in her voice, and I thought about it, too,
going back in my mind to all we had seen over the span of a
quarter century. I sat with tears in my eyes watching a scene from
the 1961 *King of Kings* story of Christ on a TV screen suspended
a few feet away.

Our rapport had begun early—she once told me how startled
she had been, one day when I was a few months old, as she tended
me and happened to clear her throat. Whereupon, looking at her,
I did the same. She never told anyone, since she was not prone
to share such things, and didn't think she would be believed,
anyway.

This connection, I think, made it easy for me, all my life, to speak one-on-one with nearly anyone and win their trust without conscious effort. (How many times would I hear someone say, "I've never said this to anyone before, but…") As the two of us sat together now, we never felt closer.

An Odd Friendship

Though my time in the program had been amicable and my work passably good, I wondered now and again if my exploration of ideas might be better served elsewhere.

I remember, for example, a bit of chatter after class one afternoon, when fun was poked by one student at how little his family understood what we were doing there. "Oh," smiled the prof, "we get phone calls every now and again from some housewife wondering how to find a new *philosophy of life*." While we found this amusing, I wondered. "Maybe," I ventured, "what's odd is that we *think* this is funny."

It was around this time that I made the acquaintance by phone late one night with Silver while working nights at a volunteer crisis hotline in Seattle in the mid-70s. She was half-Chinese (maybe, she said, the first Chinese-Icelander ever), about fifteen years older than I, and had grown up in a tough borough south of city center.

Keen and incisive, possessed of a mystical leaning, she had the aptitude of someone highly educated, though her circumstance—she had given birth to a daughter at fifteen—had not allowed her to go that way. While she and I came from far ends of life, our rapport was immediate. By now she was divorced a second time, her three children in the custody of their father, a dynamic and highly successful salesman who had ruled her with an iron hand. I, in turn, was stumbling through my early twenties, all but done with my efforts in the social arena that I still viewed largely from the outside.

Hour upon hour, we talked on the phone or in venues of the city, recounting absurd situations we had encountered in this life, feeling often like misfits, and enjoying now our strange commonality of experience.

"Maybe we didn't get the *instructions*," she would say, "when we came here." (I once said to her in turn, "We started on this life at a great disadvantage, didn't we? When people say something to us, we think they actually *mean* it.")

Feeling we had each found a sibling, we would see each other through much in the coming years. She altered my sense of things, starting with myself. "You have more going for you," she once said, "than any man I have ever known." With these words she took me from the far end of despair, regarding my place in the world, to a place where I belonged. In time, with her prompting, I found myself breaking free of old trauma and entering into the dating world, which had seemed up to now like a blood-letting thicket denying me entrance. Silver and I, though we would lose touch a time or two, would continue to share this curious tie until her passing some forty years later.

The photo of my father is taken, I believe, at a Nicholson family gathering around 1975. At about this time he was retiring after many years with Bonneville Power. Uncle Carl, Cousin Jean once said to me, had a likeable side, but she knew how difficult he could be, and she did not envy me for having him as a father. A difficult creature he was indeed, though I always liked this photo, which conveyed to me something of his humanity.

Grad School—and a Return to Clark

I completed requirements for a public teaching certificate in the spring of 1976 with a one-quarter practicum at Issaquah High School east of Seattle. In the fall, I entered the Master's philosophy program, thinking now that I might emulate the career of my friend Chuck, who like me had dual-majored in philosophy and psychology before starting his MA.

While I had reservations about its going outlook, the UW program by now was familiar, and it seemed like a better track than some, where employment was concerned. Well acquainted with faculty and curriculum, I managed the coursework without difficulty. One day in the latter part of that year, when I was home from Seattle, Chuck called. He asked if I would be interested in teaching at Clark that summer. I was stunned—and elated.

That June, mid-way through the MA, I was given five-credit sections of Intro and Ethics. The condensed eight-week schedule meant I was in the class 14 hours a week, a *bona fide* full-time load.

Full-time and then some, as it was my first time teaching at a college level—there is a great difference, I had learned in the Public Ed program, between absorbing a one-hour lesson and standing up to deliver one. Apart from that torrid first semester of the seventh grade, I had never worked so hard at an academic task.

The summer term had me teaching morning and afternoon, and working long into the night to be ready for the next round. This, however, was a labor of joy, a quantum leap giving me strength in whole new areas of the discipline. In coming years, I would piece together adjunct employment around the Portland area, getting a green light from the Clark admin to develop courses as my own yen and popular demand would warrant.

Some of these we listed as Philosophy 100 "Topics"—a new designation that allowed the two of us to offer special interest courses with new content making them repeatable for credit each time around. The problem of evil, freedom and causality, psychical research, near-death experiences, philosophy and personal growth—I myself was getting a workout in the process, and much of what I taught was on a par with material I would offer at an advanced level in years ahead.

All proceeded well with the MA program into the spring of 1978. Still, now and again, I was reminded of how alien, at times, this department and I were to each other. One of my last seminars was taught by a portly and bearded little Ivy League gun heading fast, it was plain to see, up the industry ladder. Week upon week, we sat listening as he demolished, so he imagined, any hope we might have along religious lines.

Belief in God, he argued, was irrational. For one, the problem of evil—how to reconcile belief in a loving Providence with suffering in this world—had no answer. Indeed, was not God itself an incoherent idea—if He transcended time, he observed in a jovial moment, did He know *what time* it was? Mysticism, too—striking intuitive visions that seem to enlighten their human subjects and sometimes change the course of their lives—was a blind avenue. The deliverances of various renowned seers concerning such things as Being and Existence and Union, which sometimes exceed the bounds of logical discourse, were indicative not of insight, but of pathology.

By now I was beginning to see another side to this story, and would learn, in time, that there was more to be said about religion than we were getting in most of these classes. I would find sources that spoke meaningfully to the problem of evil. I would find material, as well, that was sympathetic with religious visions. Renowned mystics, by most accounts, did not lack for common sense. Their feet were on solid ground, even if their otherworldly flights made them extraordinary.

Such flights, as William James would note in his momentous work on religious experience, are *ineffable*, resisting description of an ordinary kind. Yet also they are life-changing: They make their subjects sounder, more alive, more deeply human, than before, even if strange utterances arise at times out of this interaction of the human with the boundless Divine.[25]

We arrived, near the end of that seminar, at the issue of a future life—"By now," he intoned with satisfaction in briefing us for the final class session, "you can probably imagine what is coming…another negative conclusion."

Now and again, I would wonder—might a hyper-analyst like this one be right? Maybe I was the one, young and ingenuous, in need of correction. But with time, I came to think, what separated men like these from religious folk was not aptitude or intellectual maturity. It was a fundamental difference in constitution. Scholars like this one were grounded in a way that did not allow them (for now, at least), to understand the things of the spirit. The

---

25   See, for example, W. T. Stace, *Mysticism and Philosophy* (J. B. Lippincott Company, 1960).

outlook that pervaded the department, I sensed, expressed not the greatest cutting-edge insight to be found, but the way in which the academic hiring system here currently operated. In another time this system, according to prevailing cultural mood, might be very different.

For the most part, the outlook of people there was not conscious denial of the spirit, but lack of interest. This was not cause, I thought, for criticism—I could not blame them, or blame myself, for this gulf that separated us. But now and again, I saw the limits of some, their human depth inversely proportionate, it seemed, to their academic talent. Had nothing in their lives ever moved them to explore their own spirituality? (In one or two cases, I wondered, had they ever been *loved*?)

On occasion, I was tempted to agree with Silver, who had gleaned the impression from me, and from one other degree aspirant in her acquaintance, that some of these types were but "over-learned idiots." While she and I did find amusement, on occasion, in the gamesmanship that went on there, I saw an integrity in this enterprise even if I was not entirely in step with it.

The analysis of texts carried out in these classes was a good corrective to careless thought that resides in many life venues. Still, at the end of the day, this habitual splintering and re-splintering of ideas produced little in the way of genuine life direction. (Certainly I was not alone in this thought—I remember, for example, a couple of us talking after class one day with Dipankar, an Indian fellow who offered courses in his native tradition. He confided to us his amazement that anyone would want to major in philosophy as it was taught there.)

Wrapping Up the Degree Program

I decided to include, against the going tide, a paper on the Holmes immortality sermon as part of my MA portfolio. It was actually well received by the readers, including Dietrichson, who admired my nerve, given how "some of these guys" were. He gave me high praise in addition for one he read on the Buddhist philosopher Nagarjuna. As to Holmes, he said, "You are onto something very exciting."

He also pointed out a thing that perhaps I knew, but needed to hear again. Holmes' notion of deep human "promises and potentialities" could be extended to include people of every stripe, even ones whom we presently find disagreeable. In each of us resides possibility far beyond what even we ourselves may see at present.

In fact, it strikes me, our estimates of individuals here and now requires more effort than we often give it. We sometimes think of people as being loving, or generous, or the opposite, not stopping to realize the limits of these words as they apply to human makeup.

The individual who is self-centered today may be far more generous down the road. Moreover, such things as generosity and self-centeredness, however contrary they be to each other, may exist at present in the extreme within a single personality. A man who stands aloof from his own children may go to great lengths to aid someone outside that circle. The woman who lives alone, thinking and speaking habitually in the first person, may seem to be devoid of concern for anyone else. Yet she may be giving without end when shown an avenue for it.

Maybe a case in point was my father. By the time I was ten, he had become incapable of saying a positive word about anything I did. In fact, by now, when returning on occasion from Seattle and coming through the front door, I would get a comically divided response. ("Oh, you're *home!*" said Mama from one side of the room. "What *happened?*" came from the other.) Yet when it came down to it, this man helped me to have more than he'd had in his own life.

As to instructors, each has his own method and sensibility. Each, if he makes the effort, can bring something unique to the classroom in his time there. In looking back on a career that has spanned most of five decades, there is only one instructor of whom I would say, "If I were to do it just as he did, I would be happy." That was Paul Dietrichson.

Crossroads

There come moments early in life when a given form of entertainment ceases to have worth. A child may look at a text aimed at young readers, or watch a cartoon program, or an episode of a situation comedy, and see that it would not be hard to write something better.

I was beginning to have this feeling on several fronts, including sports publications I had enjoyed for the past fifteen years. Around late summer, when getting ready to start the MA program in Seattle, I had written up one of the Portland area boxing cards for *The Ring* magazine and sent it to Nat Loubet and Dan Daniel in New York. Not long after, I was perusing the "Rings Around the World" section in the current issue and my eyes hit words that were familiar. When I saw the by-line, my heart nearly stopped—here was the story and my name with it.

I continued to write articles throughout the two years in the program, seeing my accounts in print with some regularity, including a feature story in the May 1978 issue on Carlos Monzon, the great middleweight champion from Argentina. A couple of months later, *Boxing Illustrated* ran my piece on lightweight immortal Roberto Duran.

At this point I was divided between sportswriting (by now I had Loubet's encouragement and his invite to visit), and education. While I ended up going the latter route, I would publish two books on boxing, centering upon the era of the late 1890s to early 1900s, and would contribute a dozen extended stories to the quarterly journal of the International Boxing Research Organization years after.

Seattle, Washington, 1978, shortly after graduation: Mama and I have a sip of champagne to celebrate my completion of the MA degree in philosophy.

Glimpses of Eternity

A religious experience, says William James in the *Varieties*, cannot be evaluated by the "medical" conditions that accompany it.

A putative vision or visitation, in other words, must be gauged by its content—by *what it says* to the subject, and its impact upon his life thereafter—rather than, say, the accompanying stress, body temperature, or general mind-frame at the time he has it.

One day Mama mentioned to me a program she had seen on television, in which several people were discussing their purported glimpses of life on the other side.

"Really wonderful, if they are true," she said, impressed with these stories and the sincerity of those who told them.

Such experiences had captured my attention, as well. Not long after, I would put together a course for the Clark curriculum on this phenomenon. I had learned by now, in fact, that this was quite an old topic, acknowledged even in ancient times. It had enjoyed a huge revival with the publication in 1975 of Raymond Moody's *Life After Life*.

This was an interesting development: Moody, who had earned an MD years earlier, had been also a philosophy professor. One semester, when several of his students showed an interest in the idea of a future life, he was reminded of his experiences with dying patients, and with a few who had come near death and briefly had "crossed over". Death, if one believed what they said, was not a cessation of life, but a reunion with loved ones and an entrance into a life exceeding this one beyond description.

This led him to do research on the prospect of human survival. The investigation turned up interesting parallels. The experiences of his subjects, men and women of diverse backgrounds and outlooks, seemed to resonate with sources across a range of traditions. In Book X of Plato's *Republic*, for example, is a story that sounds like those told by some of them. Paul's letters to members of the church at Corinth, canonized in the New Testament, speak of a higher "heaven" to which he has momentarily been raised, and a glorified body unlike the one he now occupies. What awaits believers on the other side, he declares, defies all earthly description. The experiences of these NDE subjects, notes Moody, has ties also to *The Tibetan Book of the Dead* and accounts provided by the mystic writer Emmanuel Swedenborg.

Near-death survivors speak of leaving their bodies, in some cases entering into a place where they are met by close friends and family members who have left this world before them.   In this state these subjects find themselves to be not mere phantoms, but embodied still, yet free of limitations—those, say, or illness or injury—they bear in this world. The impact of these experiences is decisive, freeing them from fear of death and giving meaning to a life that hitherto, in some cases, has been without kindness or imagination.

I think again of Mama's reaction to this phenomenon, and her willingness to entertain it as part of her outlook even if it did not fit neatly into the doctrine she had absorbed in her youth. She had no need to twist these accounts to accord with conventional belief, as some types would do in the years that followed.

Regarding this conservative tendency, I remember one talk show broadcast that included an evangelist with his subject, a nervous-looking sort whose near-death glimpse of the fires of hell made him an apt specimen for the minister's own message. Though asked repeatedly, the survivor could offer little description of his experience, insisting only that he had *s'pressed* (suppressed) it. I have no idea whether this fellow actually did experience the thing he claimed—perhaps such a vision did occur, and it served to provide him with a *bona fide* warning as to the life he was living. But either way, two less impressive individuals would be hard to find.

What was said about these near-death experiences, in Moody's book, and in books and film elsewhere, resonated not only with these older sources, but with experiences I'd had going back to early childhood. In reading of them, I was reminded of dreams in which I was free to soar out over that hillside at home and float to the ground below. The last time it happened I found myself standing on that ground, the sun above, and knowing a rightness of being that haunts me to this day.

There are some, again, who will dismiss such an episode, however pleasant, as neural accident. But in its warmth and light was an inkling of truth, an insight into the true order of things. I was where I belonged, and all was well—all the love and satisfaction I might ever want, at the end of this life's effort, was contained in this dream life moment. Now, as I began to read these near-death accounts, and heard subjects describe their glimpse of Homecoming, I knew what they yearned to say.

Chapter 8
Teaching and Discovery—and a Sudden End of Life as I Knew It

> When a Roman father told his son that it was a sweet and
> seemly thing to die for his country, he believed what he
> said. He was communicating to the son an emotion which
> he himself shared, and which he believed to be in accord
> with the value…his judgment discerned in noble death.
> C. S. Lewis, *The Abolition of Man*

After completing the MA, I continued to enjoy freedom and academic discovery, the new courses at Clark bringing constant challenge and a veritable landslide of new ideas.

I was entrusted also with the full range of our standard offerings, which included formal logic and comparative religion. This latter course put me onto Huston Smith's classic *The Religions of Man* (later *The World's Religions*), first published in 1958 and revised in years after. A work of depth and genius, it captures each faith tradition from the vantage point of a believer.

Team Teaching with a Great Audience

During this time my English Comp professor Lee Partain and I became reacquainted and team-taught several classes there, each with a wonderfully diverse crowd that might see, along with the usual mix of young students, a military person, an ex-convict, a law officer, a homemaker, and a couple of retirees. All the better, we knew, when teaching philosophy.

Lee had no use for pretension, a thing not hard to find in our profession. He himself had grown up in humble circumstance, born to Depression-era farmers in the Ozark Mountain region of Arkansas who in time ventured to Washington. The first in his family to go beyond the seventh grade, he later dropped out of high school and sought adventure in Alaska before doing a tour in the U. S. Coast Guard.

In time, he attended the University of Washington, working briefly in Public Ed before obtaining his MA in English at Duquesne University in Pittsburgh. While working at Clark, he spent summers piloting charter boats out of Ilwaco, Washington. (He once mentioned to me his disdain for colleagues who would pick up a few dollars teaching added sections of composition when they might instead learn to do things that paid far better.)

Lee's boldness drove us to craft projects I would not have tried on my own, exploring such topics as philosophy in art and literature. Together we pooled our backgrounds and offered courses that spanned aesthetics, existentialism, classical philosophy, novels, and short stories, a lively exercise that generated many a returnee—it was a time that he would call, years later, his favorite in the teaching business. Surely it was one of mine.

Spirit breathed in each hour of these classes, whatever the topic—I would always remember the time, for example, Lee invited a friend of his, an accomplished painter, to speak with our class on the arts and their place in human endeavor. After that session, the visitor and I talked about his creative activity, and he confided to me—the first time, he said, he had ever mentioned it—that when starting a project he prayed for guidance.

Teaching logic, the favorite course of my philosophy comrade Chuck, would prove invaluable in my own coursework in California a few years later. Each Friday night now became a sweet and strenuous ceremony of preparation as I would ensconce myself in an nook at La Patisserie, a wonderful second floor café in Old Town Portland where I bathed in Classical sound while working through material for the coming week. At some point, the play list would hit the Pachelbel Canon, a haunting piece that made me marvel (as I would also, at times, in hearing Gregorian Chant and the sound of Southern-rooted gospel) at the truth that music conveyed.

> *"Beauty is truth, truth beauty—that is all*
> *Ye know on earth, and all ye need to know."*

So ends John Keats' "Ode on a Grecian Urn", a poem that fascinated Lee and inspired, I think, a good deal of his teaching.

One term we devoted an entire course to Robert Pirsig's intoxicating tale of the road in *Zen and the Art of Motorcycle Maintenance*, a book that had recently captured his fancy. In the tradition of writers like Ernest Hemingway and Jack Kerouac, Pirsig gave voice to an American generation. Something of Keats' Ode, I think, lives in this story, a fantastic bestseller, albeit one that got him, Pirsig admitted, some 121 rejections before striking the right chord with a publisher.

What was life really about—and how might this reality find expression in the care of a motorcycle? Page after page, Pirsig's insight blended with bikes and cold beer, and warm winding roads (squiggles on a map, he noted, are good news, suggesting rugged terrain), he traveled with his young son across the land. Maybe the most powerful theme in this story was his discovery of *quality*—value—and its primacy in the quest for understanding. To know life, said Pirsig, you had to accept this element as a real constituent of the universe. He also warned of *gumption traps*— ways in which we defeat ourselves by making a problem more difficult than it need be.

It was around this time that Mama cut out a birthday horoscope message for me from the local *Columbian* newspaper—

ARIES (March 21 – April 19th) You could spend so much time worrying about things that you won't even attempt to accomplish anything. It's needless, because all will work out better than you think.

Items like these, of course, get cranked out daily in cities across the country to provide novelty for morning readers. Typically, one must think, these birth-sign messages on any given day could be interchanged and the results would be as apt, or not. Still, this message was meant for me, a message that gained meaning from the one who was giving it. The assurance that all would work out better than I imagined, I would realize in time, pertained not just to that day, but to something more. Mama was telling me something about where my life was headed.

Truth and Opinion: Teaching Philosophy

My tendency in philosophy classes, which often covered sensitive and highly provocative issues, was never to push a single view as had been the case with some of my own mentors. There is much to admire in the work of authors who hold views contrary to one's own, and to one other. I found it best, with each new topic, to include sources on either side—say, atheism and belief in God, or the pros and cons of capital punishment—and present each in its best light.

While students might have detected, at times, my own leaning, they never felt the need to side with it. The result of this *yes* and *no* exercise, I believed then as now, is that students became more judicious, better able to appreciate insight no matter its vantage point.

At no time, however, did I encourage the notion that truth itself is relative to the perceiver. Here, again, the Greeks had broken ground more than two millennia prior. Whether a thing was good or bad, claimed the Sophist teacher Parmenides, was a matter of individual perception, each man being unto himself an individual "measure" of all things. Socrates, on the other hand, insisted that truth was real and vital, and that it had to be sought out by active inquiry. The difference between good and evil exceeded all others in its importance.

Students no doubt saw that I favored this latter view as the one by which to live. The notion that "we each have our own truth"—something they had heard plenty—ignores the real challenge that life poses. Opinions, conceptions, attitudes, assumptions—these may vary with the observer. But not reality. (Here again, of course, they were free to choose, provided they understood what each author had said.)

Even so, philosophy takes shape differently in the minds of those who study it, according to differences in the individuals themselves. The mainstream tendency is to imagine that it solves problems much in the way of history, mathematics, and physical science. Yet here, I would come to believe, the situation is different. For each man and woman has a unique life and constitution; each has a different foundational sense of what is real, of what is evident and important. For this reason, I came to think, philosophy provides not so much *solution* as personal *resolution*, each man or woman forging the view (open to amendment with new experience), that gives voice to his or her deepest intuitions.

I also found that abstract ideas, if they were to have any value in a class setting, needed connection with real life. If one can do this, two things happen in the minds and hearts of both teacher and student. One is that philosophy becomes more accessible. The other is that it becomes far and away more interesting.

C. S. Lewis

Puritanism, H. L. Mencken once slyly observed, is "the haunting fear that someone, somewhere, is having a good time."

There are some who feel this way about morality altogether, seeing in it mere rule-framing crafted by stodgy types bent upon limiting life's enjoyment. In my experience, however, the real thrust of moral philosophy is not inhibitive, but adventurous. It provides essentially an enrichment of life, not limitation upon it.

Pirsig's narrative, set to the tune of cross-country ventures with his son, echoed something of my own experience, and with things I had learned at my mother's knee. Another discovery soon followed. A Clark colleague, knowing of my interests, recommended C. S. Lewis' book *The Abolition of Man*, which Lewis had written during the time of the second World War.

I knew a little about Lewis from my time in the grad program at UW—not so much from classes, where he was out of fashion, but from conservative religious types around campus, some of whom had been left cold by the atmosphere in certain quarters there. Though I understood their dissatisfaction, I doubted that Lewis could have much to offer as a philosopher. How wrong I was.

There is a truth, he observes, expressed from ancient times across the spectrum of human experience. For the sake of abbreviation, he borrows from the Chinese sage Lao Tzu, who speaks of the *Tao*.

The Tao, says Lewis, is the doctrine of *objective value*.

"It is the reality," he writes,

> beyond all predicates, the abyss that was before the Creator Himself. It is Nature, it is The Way, the Road. It is the Way in which the universe goes on, the Way in which things everlastingly emerge, stilly and tranquilly, into space and time.[26]

---

26   C. S. Lewis, *The Abolition of Man*, New York: Touchstone, 1996), page 30.

As with the Holmes sermon, I wavered the first time through. Still, I sensed, there was something here that demanded my attention.

This notion of a truth underlying our daily drama lies deep in human experience, and it spans cultures, varying with the tradition and conceptual scheme of which it is a part. Heraclitus, a Greek contemporary of Lao Tzu, speaks of the *logos*, a truth invisible yet real and undying that makes for right understanding—Plato, likewise, and so too the Hebrew prophets who declare the righteous will of God.

In Book VII of *The Republic*, Socrates tells the tale of a slave held captive with others in a cave. He is released one day from his chains, and turns to see at last the things, enduring and substantial, that have cast shadows upon the inner wall. He thus sees, for the first time, that the world he has known until now is fleeting by comparison. So it is with we ourselves, who must turn from the things of this world to the things of eternity.

Soon after, he is allowed out of the cave into the brisk clean air to behold all manner of amazing things, such as the moon and stars, and finally the sun. This last thing, seen only with difficulty, represents what is ultimate in the realm of things known. It is the eternal Good, "universal cause of all that is right and beautiful," shining down, as it were, and bestowing meaning upon all that lies below.

In other cultural settings, this idea may find different expression, yet in each case it reveals to us something that is absolute. Let justice, says the unheralded sheep herder Amos (5: 24) to the Israelites, "roll down as waters, and righteousness as a mighty stream." No ritual sacrifice, he insists, can make up for wrongdoing elsewhere.

Again, there was little encouragement to think along such lines in the program I chose as my major. Our will, said some, was bound by the accidents of the material world, which had given rise to consciousness in blind and haphazard fashion. Our moral sense was an evolutionary quirk that made us feel we ought to act in certain ways, but it was a feeling with no basis in fact.

Few in the UW program, whether student or instructor, could imagine otherwise. (I remember once being asked, in an ethics seminar, if anyone present imagined that good and evil were anything more, at bottom, than a subjective accident—out of perhaps a dozen people, two of us raised our hands.) But with time, as I pondered Lewis' discussion and shared it in my classes, I came to think that he spoke more deeply on this topic than most.

I saw a connection, of course, between biology and ethics—moral experience, one must think, is a rather late arrival in the history of life on this planet, coming only with development of the relevant brain structure. And yet, so is much else that we experience—mathematical insight, for one, which also has a neurological prerequisite. Such experience, we believe, connects us with truth that is independent of feeling.

Of course, we can accept the dictates of numerical reasoning without accepting those of conscience. But conscience, it seemed to me, was not rendered meaningless merely by its relation to biology. Good and evil, I continued to believe, not some chimera sprung from nature by chance. It was what gave life its rightful direction.

Ordo Amoris

Lewis recalls, at the start, two "modest practicing schoolmasters" who sent him a copy of what he calls anonymously *The Green Book*. It is a volume that purports to train adolescent students in the arts of reading and writing. No doubt anxious to win his praise, "Gaius and Titius" believed that they had written something that would provide inspiration to people in their industry.

In the second chapter, they recount a story told by Samuel Coleridge about two observers who behold a waterfall. One calls the phenomenon *sublime* while the other calls it *pretty*. Coleridge himself thought the first reaction the more apt, since it was better fitted to the object it described. But the *Green Book* authors glean from this episode only that the observers differ in their reactions.

"When the man said, '*That is sublime*'," they explain, "he appeared to be making a remark about the waterfall." But in fact, they say—reiterating an idea of skeptics ancient and modern—he was simply expressing his emotional reaction to it. The object before them had no worth unto itself, even should it happen to excite pleasant feeling in those who beheld it.

"This confusion," add Gaius and Titius, "is continually present in language as we use it. We appear to be saying something very important…and actually we are only saying something about our own feelings."[27]

The young reader who absorbs this passage, says Lewis, will believe as a result essentially two things: First, sentences

27   *Ibid.*, page 18.

that contain "a predicate of value" express nothing more than the ungrounded emotional states of the speaker; second, all such statements are likewise unimportant.

The lesson thus undercuts not just talk about waterfalls. If Gaius and Titius are right, all statements of value—statements that proclaim a thing to be good or evil, or beautiful, noble or ignoble, righteous or unrighteous, tell us nothing about the objects, but only about each observer's own baseless feeling.

The superficiality of this *Green Book* is apparent again when its authors try to analyze, for the reader's benefit, an advertisement that seeks buyers for a cruise on the high seas. Those who come on board, promise the sellers, will venture across the Western Ocean where Drake of Devon sailed, "adventuring after the treasures of the Indies," bringing home afterward a treasure of "golden hours" and "glowing colors."

Gaius and Titius use this passage to caution the reader against being swayed by his own emotions. The traveler, after all, won't really sail where Francis Drake did, or have adventures on that scale. The treasures he or she brings home will be only of a metaphorical kind. A trip on a smaller scale, they say, might give the buyer comparable enjoyment.

Granted, says Lewis, the ad is a bad piece of writing, "a venal and bathetic exploitation" of emotions that men rightly feel when visiting places imbued with history and legend. Yet the task of an educator is not merely to create shrewd readers, but to cultivate in these readers right feelings—ones that are appropriate to the objects that give rise to them. "For every one pupil," he notes, "who needs to be guarded from a weak excess of sensibility, there are three who need to be awakened from the slumber of cold vulgarity." Thus the real task at hand "is not to cut down jungles but to irrigate deserts."

Had Gaius and Titius wanted to do something truly valuable, they might instead put such writing side by side with passages from great writers who seek to kindle feeling in their readers toward a worthy object. They might have used, for example, Samuel Johnson's account from *The Western Islands,* which concludes, "That man is little to be envied whose patriotism would not gain force upon the plain of Marathon, or whose piety would not grow warmer among the ruins of Iona." Or they might cite that place in *The Prelude* where Wordsworth describes how the antiquity of London descended on his mind with "Weight and power, power growing under weight."

This, of course, would have been a more difficult lesson, both for student and instructor. Yet the effort would have been worth it. Such a lesson, says Lewis,

> would have…some blood and sap in it—the trees of knowledge and of life growing together. It would also have had the merit of being a lesson in literature: a subject of which Gaius and Titius, despite their professed purpose, are uncommonly shy.[28]

As Coleridge realized, the two responses—*pretty* and *sublime*—were not merely different. They were vertically related, one being higher, more adequate, than the other with respect to its object. This idea, in fact, has deep roots. It is found, for one, in the phrase of St. Augustine, who summarizes human virtue as *ordo amoris*, a love for each thing according to that thing's real value. Genuine education, believes Lewis, thus aims not only at the head, but at the heart. To do this, it must realize that some things, some courses of action, some qualities of character, are truly better than others. And in battle, he notes, "it is not syllogisms that will keep the reluctant nerves and muscles to their post in the third hour of the bombardment."

Until quite recent times, people found it natural to think that values were real—that *beauty*, for example, was not merely in the eye of the beholder, but a real thing to be discovered and appreciated. They believed the universe "to be such that certain emotional reactions on our part could be either congruous or incongruous to it"—believed, in other words, that an object (be it a phenomenon of nature, a work of art, or a quality of character), did not merely receive, but *merited* "our approval or disapproval, our reverence, or our contempt." Nowhere were these judgments more important than in the realm of our own behavior. Thus real education, following this wisdom, does not just inform— it inspires. It kindles in a student an understanding of what is worth his allegiance.

The *Innovator*, says Lewis, using this term to represent authors like Gaius and Titius, seeks to give ethics a new ground by abandoning the *Tao* and explaining our moral sense in terms of an instinct. We care about others, according to this view, and act for their sake, even at our own expense, because of some accident deep in our chemistry that tells us to do it. Thus ethics, they imagine, lies within the province of empirical study. It is

---

28   *Ibid.*, page 22.

essentially a branch of human science.

Such a view, as Lewis realizes, is theoretically possible. But if so, we must do away altogether—something that Gaius and Titius themselves seem reluctant to do—with the notion that we ought to do anything. For an instinct by itself cannot tell us whether it should be obeyed. To assess its worth, we look at it from the outside, abiding not by feeling itself, but by principle.

Perhaps it will be said by the Innovator that the first one serves some higher purpose—say, that it "furthers human interests"—and so is the more rational of the two. But why, in principle, should I be concerned about any interests other than my own?

Suppose, too, that I have conflicting instincts: One tells me to stand my ground, and to defend, say, the cause of liberty, or to defend the lives of the innocent. Another tells me to run. If I say that the former course is the higher and nobler, I must judge again from outside, discerning that one instinct is *more worthy of my allegiance* than the other. This judgment cannot be derived from any empirical fact, but from a source that is ideal.

The result of education in the way of *The Green Book*, says Lewis, is a race of men *without chests*—men, in other words, so atrophied in spirit that they no longer understand things like courage, beauty, and magnanimity. While such men may have some degree of intellectual talent, they are distinguished not by their aptitude, but by their deficiency—their heads, figuratively speaking, are not large, but may seem so owing to their lack elsewhere.

Wrongdoing as "Neurosis"

With the advance of science, as noted earlier, came the expectation that human agency would be swallowed up in its comprehensive picture. It was thought accordingly that old ideas like sin and moral failure might go by the way as the causes of human behavior became better understood.

In one chapter of his great work *Irrational Man*, William Barrett describes the legacy of the 19th century philosopher Soren Kierkegaard, whose insight he contrasts with that of modern psychology. A central feature of human life, says Kierkegaard in works such as *The Sickness Unto Death*, is despair, a sickness, as Barrett puts it, "in which we long to die but cannot."

This despair, believes Kierkegaard, has no remedy but one that is provided by religion. In this, maintains Barrett, he is onto something that social science has yet to see. We cannot understand human behavior in purely clinical terms. There is a place for hard and uncompromising value judgment in its arena.

The condition called *sickness* in modern psychology, Barrett explains, is at its core a form of *sinfulness*.

> We are in the habit nowadays of labeling morally deficient people as sick, mentally sick, or neurotic. This is true, if we look at the neurotic from the outside: his neurosis is indeed a sickness, for it prevents him from functioning as he should, either totally or in some particular area of life.[29]

But the closer we get to this so-called neurotic,

> the more we are assailed by the sheer human perverseness, the willfulness, of his attitude. If he is a friend, we can up to a point deal with him as an object who does not function well, but only up to a point; beyond that if a personal relationship exists between us we have to deal with him as a subject, and as such we must find him morally perverse or willfully disagreeable; and we have to make these judgments to his face if the friendship is to retain its human content...[30]

At the center of this clinical sickness is "a sickness of the spirit."

A good many academicians, says Barrett, might learn something from Socrates, who taught by example, his life being inseparable from his philosophy. A scholar, however much he knows about ethics in theory, may fall short in his personal life.

A *theory* about values, as Barrett points out, however intoxicating, cannot take the place of concrete action. In modern times,

> philosophers have shifted their inquiry to an analysis of the language of ethics. Such linguistic analysis does not require that the man who makes it himself exist ethically. It is thus perfectly possible—and in fact often happens—that a philosopher who has

---

29   William Barrett, *Irrational Man* (New York: Anchor Books, 1965), pp. 169-70.

30   *Ibid.*, page 170.

> worked out a theory of values in the abstract may
> yet remain in a childish or donnish existence that
> has never felt the bite of the ethical upon it. One's
> values my thus be all down on paper, but one's
> actual life goes on as if the ethical does not exist.[31]

No matter how big his storehouse of ideas, it remains for a man to give life to these ideas in the hard-grained drama of daily life. It is "by an act of courage" that his moral life opens.

There are some, whether in the academic arena or out of it, who fathom this truth more surely than does many a heralded scholar. In every quarter is found wisdom. Be it in a factory or a coal mine, on a battlefield or a modest farm plot in rural Minnesota—and in the academic world itself—one may witness courage, integrity, even sainthood, that gives direction to those of us who encounter it.

Decisive Commitment

Immanuel Kant said famously that his enterprise came down fundamentally to three great questions: What can I know? What must I do? What can I hope?

Inherent limits upon our understanding, he argued, deny us rational certainty about where we stand ultimately regarding such things as God, free will, and life hereafter. But we are not altogether without direction. In our moral experience lies a basis for belief. At the heart of any moral claim, for example, is the belief that I have within me a fundamental capacity to act in one way or another. By the same token, I must see human beings not merely as objects, but essentially as *others like myself*, other instances of "me" with the same needs, the loves and loathings, the freedom and vulnerability, that is present in myself. I must see this and act upon it.

Kant's ethic is grounded in a Moral Law that is sovereign in the realm of decision-making. Its formulation he calls The Categorical Imperative. We must act only on the *maxim*, or behavioral policy, that we can "will" (*i, e.*, rationally choose), for humanity in general. Equivalently, as he saw it, we must always treat others as *ends in themselves*, never merely as a means to our own advantage, thus respecting their innate human dignity.

An act of deceit, he maintained, failed to pass his test—a

---

31   *Ibid.*, page 165.

world in which everyone practiced it would be a world in which the act itself made no sense. (A false promise to pay back borrowed money, to cite one of his own examples, would not be taken seriously by anyone there, since the words "I promise" would now signify nothing beyond selfish desire.) And so, in this world, if I make such a promise, I will one way of life—essentially a way of deceit—for myself, and another for humanity in general. This inconsistency of the will marks my behavior as immoral.

A frequent tendency of texts and course content, in my experience, is to present a theory, seek out counterexamples to it, and decide that the theory is thus inadequate. At UW, for example, there was little celebration of the insight, the life-affirming vibrancy, say, of a Plato, a Kant, or a William James. If, on the other hand, one could find somewhere in his corpus of work a questionable inference, or an assumption that was open (what assumption wasn't?) to doubt, and use it to erode his argument, here was something worth pursuit.

Landmark ideas, in this setting, became grist for a mill that generated little except sharp-shooting objections demonstrating their imperfection. Kant's ethic, for one, is at odds with the fact that there seem to exist extraordinary cases where deceit is justified. (He himself did acknowledge such cases, though refusing to budge on his position.) The ethic of utility, which arose also in the latter 18th century, held that we should act to make the world a happier, less painful place. But this ethic, too, seems open to cases that show its imperfection.

And so, it was on from one theory to another, this next one too lacking somewhere. Rarely was a moral system acknowledged for its merit rather than its imperfection. But one needn't think that a viewpoint is perfect to see value in it. An ethic that celebrates justice and innate human dignity, things upon which Kant insists, has in it something indispensable to a genuine conduct of life. By the same token, one that moves us to promote human welfare, as voiced by pioneering utilitarians like Jeremy Bentham and John Stuart Mill, has in it a message worth adoption. So perhaps, even if neither ethic is perfect, there is something valuable in each.

While it may be hard to give morality an exact formulation, there are times, it seems, when its demand in unmistakable. For now and again, life does present us with a moment, be it in commerce, in a classroom, or on a battlefield, where we know the right course and the wrong one, and know that we have failed grievously if we do not rise to the occasion.

Again, it helps to think in terms of concrete cases. Suppose that I am selling an automobile—should I misrepresent the condition of this car, in order to encourage the buyer to spend more? Conversely, if I am purchasing a car, should I take advantage of the seller's position? I remember years ago, hearing a world-savvy acquaintance remark that an automobile ad featuring the word "sacrifice" was great news, indicating that the owner did not have time to bargain.

"Hell," he said, "you can Jew 'em down to *nothin'*."

Many a reader, of course, will be dismayed by his use of the word "Jew" in this manner. Whether this fellow meant to imply anything derogatory about a whole religion or ethnicity of people I do not know. But what attitude, in any case, does it express toward humanity in general? Was it simply good fortune to come across a situation like this and extort a sale from some poor soul who was uprooting, say, to enter military service, or who needed money to bear an unforeseen expense for a family member who needed it?

My mother was never far from my thinking when I reflected on issues of this kind. I would remember the time, for example, that we were selling a bicycle I had outgrown. A family called and agreed to come by that evening. Later there was a knock, and a father with four or five children standing outside, all excited at the prospect of a "new" bicycle.

I don't recall what we sold it for—certainly not a lot. Yet I remember Mama remarking to me afterward that she'd felt some reluctance in taking money from a family of that size, even if only a few dollars. Her words were lost on me then—after all, I said, the size was not *our* doing.

Such was the thinking of a child, ten or eleven years of age, raised alone and never saddled, as she had been, with tending young siblings, or with raising a family of his own. But when thinking of that exchange between us, in years to come, I would see it in a different light. While no one, I am sure, got cheated on that bike deal, the image of that family, even if a mite vague, stirs in me now a feeling very different from what it did then.

The Universe and the Individual

Toward the end of Kant's *Critique of Practical Reason* is a passage that expresses his amazement at the immensity of the universe and an amazement no less at something that is disclosed within his own heart.

"Two things," he writes, "fill the mind with ever new and increasing admiration and awe, the oftener and…more steadily we reflect upon them: the starry heavens above…and the moral law within."[32]

The former, he says, "begins from the place I occupy in the external world of sense," and takes me outward into "worlds upon worlds." To feel the impact of this statement, one might think, for a moment, of what it is like to behold the heavens on a clear night, away from the atmospheric clutter of an urban center. The sight is outrageous, hardly bearable in its expanse and majesty. And yet there it is.

This phenomenon, which "annihilates…my importance as an animal creature," shows me as infinitesimal amid all of time and space.

Yet still, amid this dark infinity I have it within me to act (for better or worse), in response to a truth that is unconditional. As I am diminished outwardly by the vastness of the universe, so I am raised up in dignity as a being who can act on the basis of principle.

An Incandescent Spaniard

Born in 1864 in the city of Bilbao, Miguel de Unamuno studied classics and philosophy at Madrid and came to Salamanca in 1891 to teach Greek at the local university. He was appointed Rector there ten years later, and Rector for life in 1934. In 1924 he was deported for some time to the Canary Islands for his attacks upon the totalitarian policies of General Primo de Rivera.

He was an odd specimen, this long-limbed Basque, and a formidable one, judging from what is said by those acquainted with him. A voracious scholar of European languages classical and modern, he was remarkably well-read in several. Unamuno was tall and bony, recalls Salvador de Madariaga, eying his friend's portrait, his eyes deep set,

> under the high aggressive forehead prolonged
> by short iron-grey hair…eyes like gimlets eagerly
> watching the world through spectacles which
> seem to be purposely pointed at the object like

32	Immanuel Kant, *The Critique of Practical Reason*, (Chicago: The University of Chicago Press, 1949), page 168. Lewis White Beck, translator.

> microscopes; a fighting expression, but of noble
> fighting, above the prizes of the passing world...[33]

In a subsequent commentary, he refers to the man as being taut and unsmiling, "a challenge on legs" who made you feel, on meeting him, "that he had begun to contradict you before you had spoken."[34]

I first came onto this man from a passing quote in a book by John Macquarrie on existentialism. It came from Unamuno's *magnum opus The Tragic Sense of Life*, an outpouring of the inner warfare of heart and head wherein he seeks to reconcile his need for eternal life with the failure of his reason to grant it.

The vanity of the passing world and love, he insists, are the fundamental and heart-penetrating notes of true poetry, neither of which can be sounded without causing the other to vibrate. This haphazard world occasions in us love, something that triumphs over the vain and the transitory, "the only thing that fills life again and eternalizes it." And love, "above all when it struggles against destiny, overwhelms us with the feeling of the vanity of this world of appearances and gives us a glimpse of another world, in which destiny is overcome and liberty is law."[35]

It sensed to me, when coming onto this passage, that Unamuno had in mind romantic love, but surely what he says applies to other loves, as well. It struck a chord, drawing me to the volume from which it had come. Here was someone who spoke from depths unfathomed by most of the people who had shaped my education to this point. In coming years, *The Tragic Sense of Life* would figure into some of my own courses, and I would devote a chapter to this man in one of my own books. I will note him again in later chapters.

The Greatest Loss of All

My mother's feet, as I have noted, bore a cruel mark of her early life, each bent outward by shoes that had not kept pace with her growth. What a relief it was to see her go in for surgery, at

---

33   The quote is taken from an introductory essay by Salvador de Madariaga, page x, in Miguel de Unamuno's *The Tragic Sense of Life* (New York: Dover Publications, 1956).

34   See his introduction to Anthony Kerrigan's 1972 translation of the same work.

35   *The Tragic Sense of Life*, page 136.

long last, to have this problem corrected. I waited uneasily for her to waken from the anesthetic, so glad when she and I could speak to each other again.

I had always harbored a fear where she was concerned, knowing of her physical frailty. At times this fear had given me moments of virtual paranoia, as when at Harney, two or three times I felt a stab of anxiety hearing the phone ring in the classroom, thinking it might involve an emergency for me at home. Now, in the summer of 1981, Mama confided to me that she had felt an irregularity in her heartbeat. She insisted that she would be all right, and that the problem would go away soon. I cannot fathom, looking back, why I did not take her that minute to the hospital.

Meanwhile, I was making another investment in my career development, taking advantage of the freedom I had been given at Clark. I offered a trio of new courses ranging over practical ethics, theory of knowledge, and philosophy of religion.

The last of these was a "Topics" entry devoted to ideas about a future life using sources that included John Hick's voluminous *Death and Eternal Life*. I was surprised to see noted on the back cover that Hick, whom I had admired for some time, was now at the Claremont Graduate School after his years in the UK and later at the Princeton Theological Seminary. It struck me that I might one day actually meet him.

Then, one afternoon when I was leaving class—it was a Wednesday—our Admin assistant Paula walked up and handed me a note with the words *YOUR MOTHER* and a phone number. A minute later, I was wheeling out of the Clark parking lot, out Mill Plain east to St. Joseph's.

I arrived to learn that Mama had suffered a devastating heart attack—an *acute myocardial infarction,* as one attendee smartly termed it. He didn't elaborate, but no matter—obviously it was severe and involved her heart, even if I had not heard the exact phrase before.

When I got to her room, she was sitting up and looking worn. Still, she was resilient in spirit—"They said it was serious, but I guess I'm a tough old bird."

I took her hand—"Oh," she said, "your hands are cold!"

I continued to meet classes the next day, going in and out of the hospital when hours allowed. Over the next couple of days, we spoke as intimately as we ever had as I saw in her face the pain she tried not to show. On Saturday, I came into the ER room and her pale hand reached out to meet mine.

"Oh, your hands are *warm.*"

The American philosopher and theologian Paul Tillich once said that people are apt to see *doubt* and *faith* as opposites, one essentially as the enemy of the other. But doubt, he said, is integral to faith, each tendency residing within the religious life.

By Saturday reality lay heavy in the hospital room. All my deftly worded philosophy now counted for little as I began to feel the approach of a loss unspeakable.

I said to her, my voice half-shattered, that if this was the end, I would look for a sign in my life somewhere to tell me that all was well.

At one point, she told me that this situation was in God's hands. Thirty years old, lost as a child, I answered, "I don't know, Mama, I'm not even sure there is a God any more."

She paused for a second. She knew something.

"Oh, yes, there is."

There was joy and assurance in her face. God was present, she told me, and all of this would come to pass.

This moment, while a skeptic might not understand it, would have more effect on me than all the words, pro and con, I would ever hear uttered from a podium. While I did not feel its impact altogether right then, and might later waver, now and again, in my convictions, I would always find in this moment cause for reassurance. I know now that as she lay there, her mortal life ebbing, she spoke with certainty. In some way, perhaps while unconscious of this world, she had seen this situation from another vantage point.

At around 5:00 Sunday morning, I was awakened by the scream of the telephone. I heard my father say, "Yes, do whatever you think is necessary."

I shot east on Mill Plain in a panic.

A short while later I saw her asleep. The doctor, who was a credit to his calling, had been able to perform an invasive procedure and he was satisfied, for the moment, with the result. With the sun outside rising blood red in the sky, I allowed myself one last moment of hope and threw myself into work on my classes for the next day.

Later I went back to the hospital, somehow hoping to see her recovering.

"It's just about over," said my father, turning to me, half-crying as I entered the emergency room. I didn't quite absorb the words, even when he said them again.

Then I stood over her bed and beheld her snoring, wires everywhere as hospital staff strained to keep her alive. Her skin was white, her eyes red and half-open.

She would not survive the trip, said the doctor, to the nearest facility where she might get a transplant.

She regained consciousness briefly. I took her hand, frightened as I would have been at the age of five. Closing my eyes, I willed my own life force, as best I could, into her body. I could tell that she understood.

We waited one hour, and another. I finally had to go home, before I collapsed, and rest a short while. I did not wake up until early in the morning. When I got to the hospital my father was gone. I sat in a foyer and the attending Pastor remarked on how much better I looked from the night before.

Robert Kunz was one of those special souls who provide support to all manner of stricken folk in situations of this kind. A minister for fifteen years with the St. Matthew Lutheran Church in nearby Washougal, he had become, in 1973, the chaplain for the Southwest Washington Hospitals and hospice program.

Approaching her bed, I was in a kind of limbo, still holding to the idea that she would pull through as the inevitable pressed upon me. Yet I had lost the terror that ravaged me the night before.

She was radiant with good feeling, telling Kunz (he would say to me later that people near the end occasionally feel the rush of endorphins), she felt "wonderful." I sat at her bedside, trying to tell her what she meant to me. He asked her if she recognized me. She said, "Yes, he's the man who pulled me through."

She looked at me and asked, "Who are you?"

For a moment, the floor went out from under me. The woman who had been my mother and best friend, protector and confidante, whom I had known from the moment of my birth—the one who had bathed me, swathed me with calamine, cut corn off my cob, and sewed thread around annoying metal ringlets in my hooded sweatshirts, now saw me as a stranger.

I was seeing her, too, at this moment in a new way, from the outside, across her whole life, forty years of which she had lived before I was born. Her journey in this world was nearly over.

"I'm your son."

She looked at me, eyes dim, and said something like "*F Q E E Z.*"

I asked her what it meant, and she said, "It means our prayers were answered."

This exchange repeated. Kunz said that I should let her rest. I went out and waited as they moved her into another room, and sat until hearing one nurse say frantically "Nicholson!" and another came running. I was told to leave the area.

I waited a few minutes outside. The nurse—an amazing soul whose name was Ann Tomich—approached me with soundless steps and said, "I'm sorry, she's gone."

My hand flew to my mouth.

"Oh, my God."

Ann retreated for a moment to speak with someone.

Then it struck—a thing unlike any I expected. From down deep, issuing from a source older and greater than mortal life, came a surge that swept away all anxiety.

Ann asked if I was able to maintain myself.

"This may sound odd, but I'm all right. I feel *strong*."

She led me into the room where Mama lay. Nothing had been done to alter her appearance. Her eyes were open and her mouth agape. The sight might have horrified anyone who had not seen such a thing before. But not so at this moment.

I reached out, strength surging, and put my hand on her head. There was no panic or sorrow, but only a relief that she was done with this vessel, irreparably broken five days ago, that had sustained her for more than sixty-nine years. She needed it no longer.

Ann understood what was happening. She knew, from her experience in situations like this, that souls who depart this world may extend their protective influence to those they leave behind. I had occasion to see her again, once or twice, in coming days. Her words of encouragement were appreciated more than she may have known.

She told me I would feel Mama's influence, now and again, in the years to come. How right she was. And in the days that followed, the strength I felt, in the moments after Mama departed, never left me.

The funeral—how little I care, even now, for that word—was attended by many, including neighbors, family, and students who had taken classes with me at Clark, several from the one this term that focused on human destiny.

Pastor Kunz had asked me if I had anything I wanted to include in the service. I put together a few quotes from the New Testament, Unamuno's Tragic Sense of Life, and the Holmes sermon on immortality. Then I poured out my soul in a letter to my mother. Kunz read it at the end of the service.

July 30, 1981

Dear Mama,

There are a lot of people here who have come to pay their respects at this ceremony, and I want to try to tell them, in some brief way, what you really mean to me.

There is no doubt that every good thing that has been said by Chaplain Kunz, and by those here today who have talked among themselves, is deserved countless times, but if only they had known you as I do.

Shall I tell them about the light prance of your step on the basement stairs, as you went about the housework, and the way that your eyes lit up in girlish excitement when I handed you some little present I had found that day in a bookstore or a seaside market shop? I hardly know how to describe your quiet strength and what it told me about the real world, and all its great mansions, while you were giving all you had each day of your life as you walked through this one.

You were always willing to take the jobs that no one wanted, and to do them better than anyone else. There are some present today who have much reason to be here, and to say the things they have said. But how many others, given the chance, might speak of the way that you touched their lives, if only for a moment? I think of the ones who never knew your name, like the ones who died in a nursing home after they had soiled themselves and could now understand little except the kindness in your hands as you went through the night tending to their needs.

I want to tell them that you were a revelation, Mama. There are some things that can never be known in this world except when they are given to us in love. Those are the things you gave me.

You and I were quite a pair, the two of us, sharing things together for 30 years as no one else could have understood. There were other people in our lives, of course, some of them very special, but in the end, we always knew that it was you and me. But it was the one thing that secretly frightened me, all that time, knowing you couldn't be here forever, and feeling that I couldn't face the world without you.

And so I pleaded with you, in those last hours, telling you in every way I could that I loved you forever and that I hoped you would never be far away – never so far that you couldn't let me know that you were all right. And so you've gone Home now, to a world from which you came, and to which you have joyfully returned, but it wasn't before you told me that everything was going to be all right. And you kept your promise.

You've gone Home to a world brighter and softer and kinder than anything you ever found here, and if I feel tempted to think, for just one minute, that my loss is something to anguish about, I can remember that the dreaded thing is now past, never to be again, and that I wouldn't want things to be another way. You need to know in this very minute that my tears, most of them, have been emptied, and I am happy for you, even if I can't have you here and say it in the flesh.

I'll have more to say, before long, but it's time to end this letter with things as they are. Something funny happened a couple of days ago when a friend brought me out to his cabin, just to have a plunge in the cold river and to sit and relax in the sun. He had an Irish Setter that wanted attention for a moment, and he told the animal to go and play by herself awhile. Somehow, though the comparison may be silly, the words kept drifting through my mind.

A mother doesn't leave her small son, but tells him to run along on his own adventure, until she can be with him again. She is always there and able to listen. The son goes out the door, and into the world, and neither has been abandoned.

Now it is you who have moved on, Mama. But neither of us need worry. There is no way to know the time that is involved, not from down here. But one thing is for sure. We are not meant to stay in this world forever, and I'll be coming along soon enough. Until then, I am yours always. Your loving son, Kelly

A Road Trip

It was mid-way in the term, and classes continued. I immersed myself in them and finished the summer with scarcely a stumble. When classes were done, I embarked on a road trip, heading first north from Vancouver to Seattle and then east across the state. I continued all the way to Minnesota to see Mama's relatives, some of whom had been planning to come west before she suffered the heart attack.

I went down through Des Moines and west into Denver, feeling the thrill of approaching the "Mile High" city at night, climbing in the cold air alongside crevasses dotted with houses below along the way. I continued on to southern California—

this run would total seven thousand miles when finished—to see Cousin Jean and Carl in Alhambra. I remember one moment when walking back into a room where Jean and I were having a talk, and she marveled at my noiseless steps.

"You walk like your *mother*," she said. In hearing the words I took pride and comfort.

Chapter 9
Claremont—and John Hick

...man, created as a personal being in the image of God, is only the raw material for a further and more difficult stage of God's creative work. This is the leading of men as relatively free and autonomous persons, though their own dealing with life in the world in which He has placed them, towards that quality of personal existence that is the finite likeness of God.

John Hick, *Evil and the God of Love*

My reading acquaintance with John Hick began near the end of the BA program in Seattle. It happened when I came across *Philosophy of Religion*, a volume he had contributed to a Prentice-Hall series called Foundations of Philosophy.

Hick was an exception to much of what I had encountered in the field, to this point—while a distinguished scholar and keen analyst, to be sure, he was also a man of religious depth with a forthrightness that made him accessible even to a novice reader. By now, I had used several of his books and anthology collections at Clark, the most recent being *Death and Eternal Life*.

Like me, Hick had been briefly involved in his adolescence with evangelical Christianity. With time his outlook became more liberal. As he continued to explore comparative religion, he became an outright pluralist, advocating a "Copernican Revolution" that recognized the legitimacy of faith traditions the world over. His writing deals with many issues in philosophy, among them the problem of evil, the interpretation of religious experience, life hereafter, and the structure of human knowledge.

The Summer of 1983

After my mother's passing, I continued to teach around Portland and Vancouver, tending to my father's needs and applying new reading to my courses. In the spring of 1983, I was admitted to the doctoral program at Claremont.

Over the years, I had never quite let go of boxing, dipping into it now and again in gyms around Seattle and Portland. I began now to work out at the Vancouver Eagles Club Gym under the eye of Clyde Queensberry, a venerable senior gentleman, long a fixture in Portland area amateur boxing. Clyde and I had first met when he stepped over to give me advice about working one of the *rat-a-tat* speed bags at the old Vancouver Boxing Club.

Now, seventeen years later on a Sunday forenoon in July, several of us drove south to Salem for a show at the Oregon State Penitentiary. It had never set well with me that I'd lost two of my three fights, back in high school and college—figuring, at thirty-two, that this might be a chance to pick up another trophy, I agreed to take part.

"Get that old man outta the ring," yelled one dusky resident, drawing laughs when my opponent and I stood facing each other before the bell. My foe, shorter and wider than I, maybe ten years younger, stung me hard in the first exchange. Several times he beat me to the punch, nearly cutting me in half, late in the round, with a right hand under the heart that prompted a "standing" eight-count. I recovered and wobbled him in the next frame with a right of my own that reversed the damages.

"You got him high on the head," said John, a burly hand from our gym, in what seemed like a moment out of celluloid drama from the '30s. "If you'd hit him on the chin, he would'a been *gone.*"

I sucked in air as the buzzer sounded and we readied for round three. The room was hot and the pace unforgiving. Near the end, we wavered, each of us with nose bloodied on the brink of exhaustion. We traded blows and he stumbled, hands down. I hit him flush with a left that snapped back his head, then a right that felled him over the lower ring rope, the bell interrupting the count. When we were called to ring center and I heard my name announced, I felt I could move on with what awaited in California.

Meanwhile, my posting with the Housing Department at

Claremont had been spotted by Patricia Kimball, a local landlady who contacted me with the offer of a room. In late August, my summer teaching done, I set out on the huge drive on Interstate 5 south to this nexus of colleges—an Oxford of the West, some fancied— community sitting amid tree-lined streets like an oasis in the great Los Angeles sprawl. I arrived as scheduled and took up residence at Tish's house just off campus.

A thousand miles from home, I sat stripping wires for my little Sony speakers and tightening them to the backs with screws. Soon after I was lying back and hearing the lilt of Michael Jackson's "Human Nature" as a new era dawned.

The Claremont Curriculum

The heat took getting used to—on some days it was unmerciful, and every so often the rust-red LA cloud would drift east to envelop us. Even so, I loved this bright venue. And the program, drawing from CGS, Pomona, and the School of Theology, fit hand-in-glove with my needs.

For those entering with Master's degrees, the requirements included two years of further study with an ongoing tutorial in Attic Greek and a year-long course in formal logic and logic metatheory. Each of these put us through our paces. My teaching experience served me well on every front.

And I was in the company of people who took seriously the religious dimension of life. John was brilliant, his classroom guidance assiduous and amazing. His weekly seminars had a couple of us reading aloud our short papers on chosen topics from the readings, fielding at any moment impromptu questions from our classmates. I had never felt more alive, more fulfilled, in any academic setting in my life.

I was also pleased to find here a fight fan among the faculty— Charles Young, whose expertise included logic and ancient philosophy, and who mentored, in painstaking fashion, our progress with the Greek. Charles loved my boxing writeups, and he hosted an occasional fight party when major bouts were being carried on TV.

Sight, Sound, and Mystery

John Hick was a striking blend of mystic and analyst. Profoundly religious, he was ingenious in his replies to materialist skeptics; at the same time, he tended not to put stock in reasoned "proofs" of God's existence—his acuity was never on better display, in fact, than in showing where these efforts were at fault. Still he found them, as he said to me once in his office, strangely interesting. And much like Paul Dietrichson, he was spiritually alive.

There is, he observes in his first major work, "an element of mystery" at the heart of all human experience.[36] Our plain common sense has in it a knowledge that in some way underlies and precedes all that we see.

Perhaps the first example that comes to mind is our awareness of an external world apart from our conscious experience of it. While it may sound odd, this private theater of sight and sound could be taken as a reality on its own, like unto a dream, with no world of space outside as we normally imagine. And though there may exist reasons to discourage such a reading, we do not seem to need them. With or without argument, we know that we are a part of something greater than ourselves.

Other minds, too, seem implicit in this drama. We do not have direct confirmation of them, and consciousness, for all we know, could be an anomaly, residing with some bodies and not others, or even with just our own.

Indeed, it may be worth noting, if we are the molecular accidents that theoreticians sometimes make of us, all that has ever happened in human civilization—invention, fine art, warfare, religion, and everything else—would have come about even were conscious activity not a part of it. Might human bodies, then, be akin to plant life, albeit markedly different in their arrangement? It seems theoretically possible, and yet again, by some means I do not fully understand, I seem to know better.

Hick cites the curious drawing, mentioned by Ludwig Wittgenstein in one of his later works, that will seem to one viewer like a duck, and to another like a rabbit, or perhaps first one and then the other in the mind of a single viewer.

---

36   John Hick, *Faith and Knowledge* (Ithaca, New York: Cornell University Press, 1957), page 118.

All that we see and hear, when one thinks about it, has something in common with this experience. It is interpretive, open to reading—it is never bare experience, but *experiencing-as*, invested not only with sensory content, but with meaning. So, for example, I see a rectangular red object lying nearby and I take it not merely as a datum of sensation, but as an independently existing object. Moreover, if I am familiar with such things, I experience it (as someone from a remotely different culture might not), as a book.

This interpretive process extends to our moral experience. I see someone—say, a stranger lying injured by a pathway in need of assistance. I experience this situation not merely as an event in space and time, but as one that issues to me a practical *demand*. This dimension of my experience incorporates what I presuppose already and adds to it.

Were someone lacking in this moral capacity, there is nothing we could offer to persuade him otherwise. But to us this demand is inseparable from the wider experience of which it is a part. Likewise, my sense of life as an ongoing spiritual event presupposes these other readings and goes further again. In this way our religious framework, while it cannot be proved, has what Hick calls a structural continuity with belief of other kinds.

A Cosmic Ambiguity

The universe taken as a whole, is open likewise to reading. Seen on a grand scale, as Kant declared, these starry heavens are majestic. Yet they do not tell us from where they have come, or what purpose, if any, they might serve.

If the universe excites in us a sense of wonder, it may give rise, as well, to one of terror. "The silence of these infinite spaces frightens me," says the 17th century philosopher scientist Blaise Pascal, reflecting on the vast darkness of time and space that the new science reveals to him, and the oddness of the place he occupies within it.[37] The great cosmic spectacle has a different feel in this emerging modern era, notes William Barrett, than it had a few centuries prior.

The great processes by which worlds are conceived and destroyed gives no evidence, as best one can tell, of special purpose: I see no decipherable plan in the great sprawl of matter, stark and monstrous in its feel, that greets my eyes when looking out upon the Milky Way galaxy and beyond. While this scene is amazing, I discern no reason for the remote planets and veritable oceans of rock particles that lie cold and empty within it.

Some people find in this spectacle evidence of intelligent design—the complexity of organic life, for example, that seems to resist explanation in terms of chance. Some find evidence in the very laws by which the world is governed, and which bestow upon it a visible coherence and beauty. Yet to what end? Life, as best we can tell, is an extreme rarity in this drama, and no special concern is shown for its welfare within the narrow range of conditions that house it. Our own biosphere is subject essentially to the law of force, continuously feeding in terrible fashion upon itself. The great majority of life species ever to appear in this world have gone into extinction, as presumably one day will our own.

Hour by hour, the human drama pours out likewise in haphazard fashion. There is no guarantee that a life will play out aptly as it might, say, in a neatly crafted film or work of literature. A chance plane crash may abruptly take the lives of all on board, individuals of every age and kind, with no regard for their personal histories and ambitions. Historically, a high percentage of human life has ended, whether by natural accident or human conflict, before adolescence. Mishap and atrocity abound.

The Problem of Evil

For this reason, I think, any belief about the meaning of life—the idea, as Hick says, that the universe serves some purpose for consciousness—must admit also that this drama is embedded in a reality containing genuine chaos.

In fact, this grim spectacle is enough to annihilate religious belief in the minds of many who take stock of it. It is said that the revered St. Teresa of Avila, one day making her way to the

37   Noted by Barret in *Irrational Man*, pages 110 ff.

convent during a rainstorm, slipped down an embankment into the mud. Looking to the sky, succumbing to her aggravation, she announced, "It's no wonder you have so few friends, the way you treat them."

While Teresa's chiding of her Maker has a jocular feel, it calls to mind a heart-rending difficulty.

The world, according to much of religious tradition, issues from a creative source that is sovereign and benevolent. Yet before us lies this crushing reality—"Nature red in tooth and claw," in the famous phrase of Alfred Tennyson when grieving at the loss of a close friend.

In fact, nowhere in philosophy does one encounter an issue as agonizing as this longstanding *problem of evil*. It is the problem of how to reconcile belief in a loving Providence with the suffering that afflicts the great mass of sentient life in the world.

Religious believers, notes Bertrand Russell, atheist *par excellence* of the 20th century, often see in nature a mark of creative intelligence. But to what end? Sheer accident, he says, makes more sense of our situation. It is also more comforting. For if indeed the world has purpose, it must have been "the purpose of a fiend."[38]

Traditionally this problem cites two sources of difficulty— *natural* evil, inherent in the structure of the world (in the case, say, of earthquake or flood), and *moral* evil that proceeds from willful human agency. It finds different modes of expression according to the outlook and temperament of each author. Some of this discussion addresses suffering on a global scale, such as mass poverty, famine, and political atrocity around the world. Some focuses instead upon the concrete drama of daily life. This latter, conveyed in "up close" fashion, is especially poignant. Particularly disturbing is the evil that is willfully inflicted upon children.

Thus Feodor Dostoevsky describes, in the historically inspired pages of *The Brothers Karamazov*, young victims preyed upon by adults who take hellish enjoyment in their work. In a section called "Rebellion", Ivan Karamazov, older and more world-wise than devout younger brother, Alyosha, confesses his inability to accept the teaching of the Church.

He tells Alyosha of a small boy who accidentally injures, with the casual toss of a stone, the favorite hound of a land-owning General some years earlier in 19th century Russia. The

---

38   Bertrand Russell, "Do We Survive Death?", contained in *Why I Am Not a Christian* and other essays (New York: Touchstone, 1957), page 93.

boy is taken away. The next morning, naked and shivering, he is brought out to serve as a lesson to serfs and administrators residing on the estate. He is commanded to run. As all watch, he is torn to pieces before his mother's eyes by the General's hunting dogs.

The Church, says Ivan, tells us that events like this one shall in time be rectified in the unfolding of God's great plan. Yet how can this happen? One line of thought holds that an offender of this kind will suffer terrible punishment in return for what he has done here. But his suffering will not undo the pain of the boy and his mother. And at some point, does not even his own pain, when it has reached fantastic length, seem absurd?

Alternatively, we might imagine boy, mother, and General happy and embracing in the next world with all forgiven. But this, too, is travesty. Let the mother forgive him, if she can, for what he has done to her. As to her child, says Ivan, she *dare* not forgive.

There is nothing smug or taunting in his words. Ivan confesses his doubt with sadness, wishing yet unable to share his brother's faith. Perhaps one day he will see with greater understanding. But here and now, he refuses to give assent to something that seems contrary to reason. Once the universe has been stained by such outrage, it cannot be redeemed.

Ivan describes a five-year-old girl, tortured by her parents, locked in an outhouse one night in the dead of winter, who prays with her failing strength to "dear, kind God" to save her.

"Would you, Alyosha," he asks, "consent to be the architect [of a world]," were it necessary to build but one instance of such suffering into it?

The younger Karamazov replies, "No, I wouldn't."

Irenaeus and "Soul-Making"

My own thinking about the problem of evil, and about life in general, was strongly influenced by Hick's *Evil and the God of Love*. Traditional Christianity, he says, has offered two broad lines of theodicy (*theos*, god, and *dike*, justice)—two ways of reconciling present suffering in this world with an unerring divine will.

From the time of St. Augustine, in the fourth and fifth centuries of the Common Era, it has seen human misfortune mainly as something rooted in the willful and grievous disobedience of our first parents. Yet prior to this, another conception was put forth by Irenaeus, a church father who found in the scriptures a different point of emphasis.

Augustine, says Hick, explains our present condition in terms of a disastrous "fall from grace" long past. Irenaeus, by contrast, sees this life in forward-looking fashion as a soul-forging process through which human beings, conceived in the bare *image* of God, are made furthermore into His finite *likeness*. This transformation comes about in gradual fashion not merely by way of divine agency but through active human venture.

"Now it was necessary," says Irenaeus,

> that man should in the first instance be created; and having been created, should receive growth; and having received growth, should be strengthened; and having been strengthened, should abound; and having abounded, should recover [from the disease of sin]; and having recovered, should be glorified...[39]

Man in his present state is nourished and increased by the Spirit, "making progress day by day, and ascending towards the perfect...approximating to the uncreated One." Our creation is an extended process in which we are given a measure of freedom regarding both action and thought, our belief uncompelled. "Not merely in works, says Irenaeus, "but also in faith, has God preserved the will of man free and under his own control."[40] Our odyssey here is undertaken without rational certainty regarding its origin and end.

Irenaeus, says Hick, offers a conception of human origins that would become influential in the Greek branch of Christian thought, starting from scratch, as it were, with traditions as we know them still in process. He pictures our first parents essentially as children, "their sin...not presented as a damnable revolt, but rather as calling forth God's compassion on account of their weakness and vulnerability." While today, of course, human origins are understood within a different intellectual landscape, Irenaeus' outlook may still have something to offer.

At the same time, it might be noted, this soul-making view is prone to misunderstanding. Such a view does not suppose, as it is

---

39   See Irenaeus, *Against Heresies* (Beloved Publishing, printed in USA, 2015), IV.38.3, page 417.

40   *Against Heresies* IV.37.5.

sometimes imagined, that God condemns us to some pre-measured amount of difficulty, then buys it back (rather, one might think, in the way of an abusive spouse or parent), with reward after. He does not make of us *creditors*, as Hick puts it, in a *hedonic bank*, accumulating merit through our difficulties. What we have in this world is not mere quantitative investment, foisted upon us as payment for our happiness, but an opportunity for active growth. Our life in this world is not written in advance, but takes shape "through a hazardous adventure in individual freedom." What comes of this situation depends in some measure upon our own willing participation.

Nor, I think, does this view suppose that difficulty here automatically "makes better persons" of us. A stressful period of life may indeed purge us of immaturity, or it may precipitate instead a fall into embitterment and self-enclosure. Which of these comes about depends upon the way in which we react to the challenge. We contribute by our own willing effort to an end—strange as it may sound—that even omnipotence cannot achieve, namely our own freely won liberation.

No two men, I have always thought, live in quite the same world or speak quite the same language. I was reminded by one encounter, some years ago, that perhaps no two read a book in the same fashion. When researching material for a writing project of my own, I spoke with the Chair of a department at a local university. He remarked to me, in passing, that *Evil and the God of Love* was a rather trifling project, establishing at most the possible co-existence of God and evil without providing the least reason to adopt a religious frame of mind in the first place.

While I agreed that this book did not provide (nor sought to provide) knockdown evidence of God's existence, it struck me that this scholar had never read the book himself—or at least, had not read it as I had. For me, its worth lay in large part in the spirit in which it was written. It awakened in me a stronger sense of what it means likewise to experience life as a spiritual event.

Hick returns to the subject of theodicy in *Death and Eternal Life,* where he takes up that heart-wrenching exchange between Ivan and Alyosha. The events in this story, surely realistic ones, are enough to challenge even the greatest faith. Perhaps we cannot find an answer to the question of the boy and the General in the way that Ivan poses it. But given time, and human potential, we might imagine this meeting in a way different from what he imagines.

Ivan seems to envision this reunion with all three parties as essentially the same beings they were at the time of the murder. But maybe, with time and new opportunity opened to him, the General can make himself worthy of forgiveness; perhaps good ultimately can be wrought out of even the most terrible things that happen in this world.

A good of this kind, as Hick stresses, cannot be found in this world. No social reform or cultural progress can speak to the bygone suffering of those who have lived and died along the way. Such tragedy can be redeemed only in a greater scheme that involves the individuals, precious and irreplaceable, who have trod the soil here in this world.

Forgiveness: A Recollection from Youth

Some will balk at the idea of the General being reconciled with his victims after the pain he has caused them. Ask someone if they could forgive a man who killed their child, and their first reaction (which I well understand), is apt to be an emphatic no. Some things, they will say, can be forgiven, and some things not.

How far, in principle, does the possibility of forgiveness extend? In reflecting on this question, I am reminded of an instance from my own childhood. While laughably small in comparison with the things of which Ivan Karamazov speaks, it provided me with insight into wrongdoing and its resolution.

Late in life, C. S. Lewis recalled time spent with his brother Warren, older by three years, in a wonderful setting of Northern Ireland where the distant sight of the Castlereagh Hills filled him with special longing. One day, he notes,

> my brother brought into the nursery the lid of a biscuit tin which he had covered with moss and garnished with twigs and flowers so as to make it a toy garden or a toy forest. That was the first real beauty I ever knew. What [our] real garden had failed to do, the toy garden did. It made me aware of nature—not...as a storehouse of forms and colours but as something cool, dewy, fresh, exuberant.[41]

This feeling, which would seize him again when it returned

41   C. S. Lewis, *Surprised by Joy: The Shape of My Early Life* (New York: HarperOne, from 1955 original edition), page 6.

suddenly in memory years after, Lewis cites as a moment that shaped his early development. "As long as I live," he relates, "my imagination of Paradise will retain something of my brother's toy garden."

I do not know to what extent this venerated scholar, a deacon of both Oxford and Cambridge Universities, would assent to a comparison of his experience with mine, far removed and half a century later. But when first seeing his mention of this garden, I thought of the time, perhaps around Christmas in the mid-1950s, when my parents and I visited the 10th floor toy section at the downtown Portland Meier and Frank. I stopped in amazement when seeing displayed there a miniature log-style fort, with opening gate in front and blockhouses on its corners, a stunning little drama with crude stepladders and attacking Indians pulling me into its realm.

In those days, most of the homes on our street were owned by men who had made purchases shortly after their time in the Armed Forces. On the rise across from us stood a faded brown unit into which would tumble, over the years, many a brief inhabitant. When I was aged maybe five to seven, there lived under that roof Tommy and his mother, struggling by herself to maintain a life for the two of them.

My favorite possession at that time was likely a Fort Apache set similar to the one that had enraptured me that night at Meier and Frank. There came a day, however, when one of the "little men" from my set disappeared, and another shortly after.

Since these vanishings had followed visits from Tommy, there could be little doubt as to what had happened. Still, fresh as a stumbling fawn, I was slow to suspect him. When I spied a little blue cavalryman on the floor of his living room, he said that he had come across a supplier "at a little place in California."

Rather than cause an uproar, my folks implemented a reward system—one nickel per soldier to anyone who turned up what was missing. Soon one lost troop member was found, then more. Tommy professed his amazement at finding them strewn around his house—"You'll never believe," he said, "where I found one of them, Kelly—right next to *my BB gun!*"

A BB gun no doubt was one more thing poor Tommy wanted and didn't have. In a year or so, he and his mother were gone, and I scarcely gave him a thought. It was maybe a year again before we happened to meet at the birthday party of a mutual friend. He came up and handed me, when it was time to leave, a bag of toy figures similar to the ones he had taken, telling me how glad he was to give them to me, and how ashamed he had felt all this time.

I scarcely knew what to say, and thanked him, saying I would return the favor one day. He insisted not. No matter that he'd had scarcely any playthings of this kind, and I had been surfeited with them—in fact, I would not have raised the issue, and would have born him no animosity over it, had he not brought it up now. Yet it mattered to him, and he was adamant that I give him nothing.

Young Tommy's conviction, though it concerns only a trifling episode from childhood life, stands out sharply in my mind as I recall it more than six decades later. Through it I understand something about forgiveness, and something, as well, about *restitution*, a subject that may deserve more attention in our moral thought than we give it. It strikes me that if the offense had been greater, forgiveness would still have been possible, albeit more difficult, and the restitution perhaps greater.

It strikes me that in principle, even very great offenses might allow forgiveness with time and relevant changes in victim and perpetrator. When people hear of Dostoevsky's General, they may say that his action is unforgiveable. Yet what they mean in their hearts, I think, is not that he can *never be forgiven*, but that they will *never cease to regard his action as evil*.

Nor should they. But as to forgiveness, maybe there is room for optimism. Given time and opportunity, we might imagine that genuine harmony is possible between perpetrator and victim, and between even the staunchest enemies who now inhabit this mortal arena.

The Issue of Future Life

Death and Eternal Life is an amazing work, massive in its scholarship and daring as any I have seen in the arena of religious philosophy. By the time I had gone halfway through it, I was convinced that Hick was the most interesting philosopher of his time. It seems fitting, as I look back, that I was using this volume at Clark during that fateful summer of 1981.

There is an old Buddhist story, notes Hick in the preface, about a mother who has just lost her son. She goes to the revered Gautama, asking for a miracle. He asks her to return first to her village and collect mustard seeds, but only from houses that have not suffered a death. She comes back to him in time, her cup empty, realizing that her loss is not unique.

With this image in mind, Hick undertakes what he calls a

global theology of death, one that employs an "openness to all data," drawing widely from the world's traditions and from each human voice as it may warrant. What he explores in this book is not so much death, however, as this present life and the direction in which it is headed. Herein he seeks to penetrate longstanding pictures of human destiny—heavens, hells, rebirth, annihilation—moving beyond their metaphorical images toward a philosophically meaningful account.

Might it be, Hick asks, that these pictures contain some inkling of our destiny, even if they are not literally true? The idea of judgment, for one, reminds us of our limited time in this world, and the pressing need to make something of this life that has been allowed to us. The idea of multiple lives, running deep in some traditions, holds out the hope of continued chances to rectify even our greatest failures.

Traditional doctrines regarding human destiny, if one thinks about them, are appallingly limited in their scope. Some churches still hold to the idea that our earthly career—which may be a very brief one—is followed by an eternity in one place or another, happy or wretched, depending upon our standing at the end of this venture.

The idea of hell, maintains Hick, is without moral sense, and popular ideas of heaven offer little prospect for the growth that is involved in the soul-making process. For this reason, he finds the idea of multiple lives more plausible. This need not mean that we recycle here, time and again, as some notions have it. But our continued growth may involve multiple endeavors, each bounded as a life is bounded here. With our progress may come passage to higher worlds—an upward journey, as one might envision it, rather than ongoing return to the world we have known.

This idea of a future life is a daunting one, carrying with it the implication of a destiny far removed from anything that we know here. The problems and interests that have absorbed me for these past several decades have defined in large part who I am today, but what will I be, say, in double or triple this lifetime, or many times more?

For this reason, Hick distinguishes between eschatology, the branch of religious thought that deals with the *eschaton*, or final things, and the question of how we may progress, for the time being, in our finite development. Thus he deals, in large part, not with the very last things, but with the *par*-eschaton, or what is on the way.

While this journey may hold much that we cannot yet see,

our moral development in this world, he imagines, may offer us direction. The tendency of this development is a movement from self-enclosure to involvement with others. Our entrance into person-hood, it seems, requires an involvement that transcends ourselves. Perhaps this trajectory allows us some sense of where we are headed. I will note again Hick's thought on this topic in a later chapter.

The Postulate of Rationality

As I have said, one of the favorite enterprises in the UW program (and I doubt that much has changed in years since), was the reduction of all reality to events in the material world.

This effort concerned chiefly the analysis of human beings. The old "dualism" of classical philosophy, alleging that mind and body are fundamentally different from each other, was a quaint notion not worth serious thought. Consciousness, in the eyes of most there, was essentially a material process, analogous to that of computing machinery. Our thoughts, feelings, volitions—at bottom, our very being—were constituted of our neural chemistry, or were an incidental byproduct of it, reducible in the end to brain events and behavioral dispositions.

This enthusiasm, I would learn in time, was not shared by some scholars who were eminent in the field of brain science, among them Sir John Eccles, who saw the brain, much in the way of William James decades earlier, not as generating consciousness, but as providing it, in transmissive fashion, with a means through which to work.

Still, the mainstream outlook in recent decades has been the reductionist one, providing many a theorist with a place in the academic arena. This account, I notice, has been re-chiseled in recent decades, giving rise to offshoot "property" and "predicate" dualisms, conceding that consciousness perhaps is not the very same thing as the material events with which it is associated. But the change is incidental. The implication of this modified view, always and with deadening regularity, is that human beings in last analysis are a perishing outgrowth of the natural order.

Such a view received memorable expression in the 20th century from philosopher and celebrated defense attorney Clarence Darrow.

"We are," he writes, "like a body of shipwrecked sailors clutching to a raft and desperately engaged in holding on." Men, he concludes, have built faith not from facts, but from pathetic hopes.

> They have struggled and fought in despair. They have frantically clung to life because of the will to live. The best that we can do is to be kindly and helpful toward our friends and fellow passengers who are clinging to the same speck of dirt while we are drifting side by side to our common doom.[42]

For this reason, the mind-body issue was to me not, as many in the program seemed to find it, an entertaining conceptual puzzle, but far more. The materialist answer struck me as being a sheer tragedy.

Of course, reality can be tragic. It could be that we are destined to vanish at death as materialism decrees. But I could never find this account of mind and body to be persuasive. For one thing, no matter how it was formulated, it was madly counter-intuitive. Do I understand, say, *being in love* by knowing about the biochemical events associated with it? I grasp it not by neurological study, or observation of how people behave when in its throes, but by way of lived reality.

In general, Hick says, conscious events and neural events seem like realities of utterly different kinds. My consciousness, for example, of the night sky, "as a visual field consisting of millions of points of light against a dark blue background does not seem in the least like a bit of grey matter" or a cellular process therein.[43]

Not only is materialism counter-intuitive, he contends—its rejection is warranted by belief in our own rationality. Take, for one, the epiphenomenalist view, a modified account which holds that consciousness, even if it is not exactly made of brain processes, is an incidental by-product of them. If so, then all that we think, deduce, choose, and imagine is the helpless and accidental result, at bottom, of events at the molecular level. Yet *these* events have no allegiance to such things as reason, evidence, value, and validity. And so, we have no logical right to trust the

---

42   Clarence Darrow, "The Delusion of Design and Purpose", contained in Paul Edwards and Arthur Pap, eds. *A Modern Introduction to Philosophy,* page 438. This election was originally Chapter 44 of Darrow's *The Story of My Life,* published in 1932.

43   *Death and Eternal Life* (Louisville, Kentucky: Westminster / John Knox Press, 1984), page 114.

experiences to which they give rise.

Thus, even if materialism, in some version, should be true, we cannot claim to *know* that it is, since any conclusion we reach on this point is but one more result of the wayward accidents that give rise to it. To reason consistently, then, we must begin with the assumption that mind is "a reality of a different kind from matter." We must suppose that we are essentially self-governing beings, able to perceive and act in accord with such things as rationality and obligation.

A Copernican Revolution

The seven proverbial blind men who described the elephant, said Mahatma Gandhi, were onto something, each according to his own point of view. They were also wrong from the viewpoints of the others, and both right and wrong according to the man who viewed the entire animal. The story has import for those who study world religion.

Raised in the orthodox Indian tradition, Gandhi undertook in his later years a quest for truth that led him examine other faiths, an exercise that gave him an insight complementing that of his own. While his native Hinduism would always be special to him, he saw what lay at the heart of every faith, something that "binds one indissolubly to the truth within and…ever purifies."

Historically, some faiths—principally Christianity and Islam—have seen it otherwise, proclaiming that a great many of the world's inhabitants outside the fold, at life's end, are lost forever. Christianity, in both its Catholic and Protestant branches (each at times condemning the other), has made this picture a part of its doctrine.

In his anthology *God Has Many Names*, Hick cites examples. It was declared during the early to middle years of the 15th century at the Council of Florence (with reference to the Book of Revelation), that no one remaining outside the Catholic Church,

> not just pagans, but also Jews or heretics or schismatics, can become partakers of eternal life; but they will [instead] go to the 'everlasting fire which was prepared for the devil and his angels,' unless before the end of life they are joined to the Church.[44]

---

44   John Hick, *God Has Many Names* (Philadelphia: Westminster Press,

More recently, professed one speaker at the 1960 World Congress on Mission in Chicago,

> In the years since the war, more than one billion souls have passed into eternity and more than half of these went to the torment of hell fire without even hearing of Jesus Christ, who He was, or why he died on the cross of Calvary.[45]

Thankfully, as Hick notes, this outlook has given way in the past century to saner ones. The old conception of salvation has been reworked to provide alternatives to the notion that formal church membership, or given ritualistic rites, or acceptance of key religious doctrines, separate humanity for all time into the saved and the damned.

No doubt the doctrinal cruelty of this older view has generated much of the antagonism toward religion one sees in some quarters. As noted earlier, some thinkers have advocated the abandonment of religion altogether. Hick's pluralism, which would become a source of tension in his longtime relationship with the Presbyterian Church, is an alternative to both religious skepticism and the hard exclusivist doctrine of human destiny just cited.

He is unsatisfied, however, with limited attempts in this direction, which seek to retain the old exclusivism while amending it enough to make it tenable. (Some have said, for example, that individuals outside the bounds may in some cases be "anonymous" Christians who *would have* chosen salvation if given the chance, and so will be spared in the end.) He likens such effort to that of old-style observers during the rise of astronomy, acknowledging new evidence of planetary motions while retaining their belief in an Earth-centered cosmos.

In place of this compromise, Hick advocates wholesale revolution. Just as the old astronomy gave way, in time, to observation, taking Earth out of its central and stationary position, so must Christianity, and other faith traditions, as well, become like unto satellites subordinate to a single Reality.

1980), page 30.
45   *Ibid.*

Religious Pluralism

"The thing known," declares St. Thomas Aquinas, "is in the knower according to the mode of the knower."[46] Our knowledge, in every case, is determined not merely by the thing itself, but by our own conscious structure. What holds true of knowledge in general holds true in our experience of the Divine, which is shaped and qualified by the limits of our present condition. Each religious tradition, by the same token, bears the impress of its setting—its history, temperament, scientific culture, and the like—in human civilization. Always, of course, it owes something to human activity, and as such it is finite and fallible, prone to error. Yet each, in some measure, reflects an encounter with ultimate reality.

Our condemnation of other faiths, Hick notes, is strongly correlated with our ignorance of them. As old caricatures and comic distortions give way to responsible inquiry, there comes new understanding. Attend, he says, a religious gathering and witness its poems, it hymns, its testimonials. You will find a deep likeness of one faith with another in the raw content of its experience.[47] (Take one of these expressions out of context, in fact, and you may have a hard time deciding its origin.) Observe, by the same token, those men and women who have achieved eminence in their respective traditions—their depth and forbearance, their regard for justice, their profound kindness. It seems that something similar is happening within each setting.

A commitment to one's own faith, it seems, does not necessitate the condemnation of others. Indeed, as Gandhi's own exploration of faith traditions would lead him to say, "a friendly study of the world's religions is a sacred duty."[48] His study of these traditions, he would say in looking back, had not diminished

---

46   This statement, contained in Aquinas' *Summa Theologica*, II, Part II, Question 2, Article 1, is cited by Hick in the titular Essay III of *God has Many Names* (Philadelphia: The Westminster Press, 1982).

47   See, for example, Essay IV, "By Whatever path ..." in this same volume.

48   https://www.ncbi.nlm.nih.gov/pmc/articles/PMC3400300/
For an excellent summary of Gandhi's thinking about religion, see Ajai R. and Shakuntala A. Singh, Gandhi on Religion, Faith, and Conversion: [A] Secular Blueprint Relevant Today. This quote first appeared in the native journal Young India, a publication begun in 1922 and overseen by Gandhi himself in later years.

his reverence for his own. Yet they had left their deep mark upon him and broadened his view of life. As he saw it, all religions had truth in them. "All proceed from the same God, but all are imperfect because they have come down to us through imperfect human instrumentality." In a way, he imagined, "there are as many religions as there are individuals."

My own mother provides me with an example. Her faith was a quiet one, yet as strong as any I have seen. She would have loved to explore the academic literature associated with religion, and many other things, had circumstances permitted. She knew, at some level of her being, that Providence was real, and that this life led Home to a greater life awaiting. She also understood, with a wisdom exceeding that of many a religious proselytizer, that the soul might draw breath within a tradition separate from her own.

She was, by the same token, constitutionally incapable of believing that anyone was lost forever owing to mistakes they had made in this life. Her own father, Axel, to whom she had gone often during the trials of her young life, had puzzled over this as well, finding it implausible by any stretch of humane thought.

This is the only image of Axel in his youth that I have in my possession, showing him here on the right, with his brother Fred, when they were young men.

My own thought took me in a similar direction. As to hell, should someone today ask if I believe in it, I would say yes—for I have seen it firsthand in my own life and in the lives of others. But I have never been able to understand it as a *destination*. I could never imagine that anyone might be punished without end for what they have done in this life, much less their beliefs, or refusal to believe, as seems right to them.

Religious Belief and the Moral Voice

Like Kant and other philosophers influenced by him, John was impressed with the connection of ethics with religion. He gives eloquent expression to this tie in one of his anthologies.

Our moral experience, as noted earlier, is open to more than one theoretical reading. David Hume, for example, thought it was grounded in nothing more than our own peculiarity, as have a number of prominent thinkers in the time since.

Certainly this outlook is possible. But imagine that I am, say, a French underground fighter in the Second World War who must risk his life if he is to save others. Does it make sense for me to sacrifice myself if I believe that "there is nothing more to human morality than group compulsions…basically akin to those of an ant-hill?"

"It may be said," Hick writes,

> that self-sacrificial action is not usually based upon rational calculation at all, but expresses some altruistic impulse of our nature. But why, from a naturalistic point of view, should we not try to suppress such an impulse? Why should we respect it? The answer of the moral consciousness itself seems to be that in the call of…duty we are aware of a valid claim upon our lives, a transcendent demand that is authoritative and absolute.[49]

---

49   John Hick, Appendix to *Classical and Contemporary Readings in the Philosophy of Religion* (Englewood Cliffs, New Jersey: Prentice-Hall, Inc., 1970), page 532.

We cannot get outside ourselves, so to speak, and assess this inner voice that bids us to help others. Its cry, however piercing, does not reveal to us the nature of its origin. But suppose I decide to act as this freedom fighter has done. Have I done rightly, or have I merely been duped, as it were, by my own chemistry?

I cannot know with rational certainty, here and now, which is true. But to the extent that I trust this voice, and abide by it, I believe that it connects me with a truth that issues from a spiritual source. And it makes little sense to accept this claim in practice, yet refuse to accept it in my philosophical outlook.

A Brief Crisis

In the spring of 1985, I wrapped up the remaining coursework and received approval from my committee on the qualifying exams. This meant that a candidate was allowed to begin work on the dissertation once its topic was approved.

I received also a thumbs-up from Charles on the Greek, which required passing an exam on Plato's *Crito*, an early dialogue depicting Socrates after his conviction in the Athenian jail cell. Third, I aced the exam in the year-long logic, requiring proof of various "meta-theorems" of logic as a formal system.

With this "hat trick," I ended the year feeling that I had launched a veritable walk-off home run. Relieved and happy, I returned to work that summer at Clark, feeling optimism a few months later when heading south to California.

Yet as days passed, I suffered from a procrastination that kept me from launching full-force into the writing. My topic—the prospect of a future life—had been given the green light, and the runway seemed open. Surely I had never been in a better position to undertake a project of this kind.

There is a phenomenon oft-witnessed in graduate school, one common enough to have earned a label. It is ABD—"all but dissertation"—referring to the tendency of students, even promising ones, to stall, sometimes to quit, after they have laid the groundwork in courses, foreign language, and qualifying exams.

I think that doctoral students at times conceive their task in a way that makes it more difficult than need be. After a couple of years of coursework, they feel as if they have done a vigorous walk across flat terrain, only to face now a harrowing climb—or in literary terms, the first white page, cold and empty, of what will be perhaps one or two hundred.

In truth, the dissertation can be a lively exercise, shaped by the writer's own personality, realizing his or her creative energies like nothing prior. Day by day, it is no more challenging than what has been required up to now. Once fully engaged, a writer may find it to be the most rewarding part of the program.

I must have known this by now, or should have. But whatever the reason, I found myself day upon day without traction, telling myself that tomorrow would be different. There came a stretch when I would lie awake, in the wee hours, wrenched with doubt, briefly falling asleep before starting the day again. Soon depression was part of my every waking hour, leading me at last to feel I could not go further. For the second time in my life, I thought I was beaten.

Not until much later did I look back, finding it odd that I never spoke with John while in this turmoil.   In fact, I had scarcely thought of contacting him, a reflection maybe of my own solitary frame of mind, at that time, and his own aloofness toward students—oddly, it seemed, an aloofness especially toward those of us who were most strongly inclined toward his own outlook.

Another Life Transition

More weeks passed. In November my father turned 80. I was home for the holidays soon after, still stymied on my writing. At around this time, he was doing therapy sessions with clinical psychologists.

After my mother's passing, he hired a succession of people to keep house. One of these was Anna Brown, the same age as he, living where her son John had raised a family a few houses up from us on the knoll across the street. Though she did not last long at that job (no one did), she and I developed a friendship after I sent her a Christmas card in the wake of her departure, and often she would invite me in for coffee on my return from morning runs out toward the east end of town. In coming years I would provide her with frequent shopping rides to the local Fred Meyer and the old downtown.

One day she and I and her daughter Billie, paying a visit, sat and enjoyed Anna's amazing coffee—strong, with thick cream—and began trading family "war stories". There was a bit of sadness in this talk, but mostly we laughed. I mentioned at one point how severely hunched over my father had become as I grew from childhood to adolescence. "Maybe," I said, "he didn't think much of himself." With my own words came insight into the cringing habit that must have been obvious at first glance to some people when they met him.

Now, days before hitting the road south to have another go with the dissertation, I was there at the clinic when he went past me in the hallway and I was greeted with the surreal sight of him walking upright, a sight I should have acknowledged, though surprise and inhibition kept me from it.

It was January, and as I started the engine out front, readying to head up the curving road and hooking down the hill toward the I-5 freeway, he was looking out the kitchen window. We waved to each other when I pulled away, starting the journey south. My mother and I had exchanged that wave years earlier each time I left for Seattle. He was weeping.

A couple of weeks later, near the end of January, I received a call late at night from Anna. She said that a small ambulance had picked him up, taking him to St. Joseph's, and she gave me the number of his doctor.

I called, and he and I talked briefly about what had happened—a heart failure had left my father slumped on the floor in front of the living room couch. His housekeeper had called for help and he was rushed away soon after.

I asked if he would be returning home soon. "Oh, no," replied the doctor. "He is not expected to live through the night."

I was able to book a flight out of Ontario, California, for the next morning. Around 9 AM I sat awaiting the plane in the airport lounge. I went to the bar, despite the early hour, to savor an Irish Coffee and ponder where life might now lead. I must confess, at this moment there was no sense of loss or sorrow, but only of entrance into a new stage of life.

A couple of hours later we landed and were sitting on the plane at the Portland airport. We were waiting to deboard when words came bright and clear over the speaker from a popular tune by Jim Croce years prior.

"Well, I know it's kind of late…"

How significant these words now did seem—"Every time the time was right, all the words just came out wrong, so I'll have to say I love you in a song." I was met outside the plane by an obliging neighbor who clasped me behind the neck as we walked toward the entrance and told me what I already knew: My father was no longer with us.

Chapter 10

Home—and Continuing Discovery

> *I believe that we live after death and again and again, not in the memory of our children or as a mulch for trees and flowers, but looking passionately and egocentrically out of our eyes.*
>
> Brenda Ueland, *Strength to Your Sword Arm*
> ("What Do I Believe?")

He had told me, awhile back, that he wanted no funeral, asking only that his ashes join those of his mother in the old Tacoma Mausoleum. After complying with this wish, I flew back to Claremont, lingering awhile before packing happily for the long drive north.

Once home, I enjoyed peace and solitude, picking up with old friends and renewing favorite haunts. I put money into refurbishing the house and taught at a few of the local colleges and universities, putting aside the dissertation for awhile to enjoy being in the place I had been raised.

I continued to find authors akin to men like Holmes and John Hick, vibrant examples of life and spirit who spoke to my heart and to the writing project that lay ahead. Powell's Books, a massive block-sized establishment on the outskirts of Old Town Portland, became a haven. Late at night, one could cruise down the Interstate when traffic had waned, parking near the store to wander The City of Books, each great room housing literary neighborhoods in beautiful array.

Another source of treasure was Shorey's Bookstore in Seattle. Founded by newspaperman Sam Shorey in 1890, it had begun as a magazine and cigar shop downtown at Third and James. In 1939, a young fellow named John W. Todd, Jr., having spent rough time in the Dust Bowl of the Dakotas, ventured west and bought it,

158

turning it into something on a larger scale.[50]

Now in its third incarnation, the place stood at First and Union near Pike Place Market, down near Puget Sound on the west side of town. While not the size of Powell's, the store had incredible charm. It abounded, like something out of *noir* Hollywood, in weathered hard-bound material, with shelves requiring a ladder if you wanted to see it all. In some places volumes were double-stacked, making you pull out some to find others.

In the years since, Shorey's has had other moves, retaining each time something of its soul. "It's a business that constantly stretches the mind," said co-entrepreneur Bill Todd in a 1990 article for the *Seattle Times*, "and it challenges you beyond belief...I wish I had another 70 years to do it. I would redeem the world tomorrow, if I could, with literature and books."[51]

Maryhill

The Oregon Coast, sweet venues of old Portland, and to the east Multnomah Falls—each place seemed to beckon. The Falls, though it had given me in childhood always an eerie feeling, had filled me also with a sense of belonging. About 90 miles east of Portland on the Washington side lay the Maryhill Museum of Fine Art.

---

50   John W. Todd Jr. built Shorey's into a bookstore legend (seattlepi. com) This article by John Marshall of the Seattle Post-Intelligencer was written in 2007.

51   Shorey's Used And Rare -- Seattle's Oldest Bookstore Is Poised On The Brink Of The Computer-Search Age | The Seattle Times. This 1990 article by Donn Fry, written on the cusp of the new computer age, recounts the store's history and describes its commitment to finding difficult items for inquiring customers.

Around 1962, I had seen it with the England family, cousins on my father's side who lived in his birth area of Tacoma. Naming the estate for his wife and daughter, entrepreneur Sam Hill had intended it to be his main residence, seeing here in mind's eye a rural community where eastern desert and coastal rain forest had their meeting.[52] A massive compound of steel and concrete, it stands high above the Columbia near Goldendale, Washington. Sam thought, as it was being built, that the house might stand for a thousand years.

Perhaps centuries from now it will turn out he was right. When construction stalled, however, during the First World War, owing to a labor shortage and Hill's financial setbacks, a change in plans came regarding its purpose. An earthy bundle of drive and genius, little Loie Fuller had risen from humble origin to prominence in the theater late in the 19th century. Maryhill, she insisted, should be a museum.

While Loie had little sense of how to plan events or handle money (she made it fast and spent it the same way), her stage productions became a sensation in Paris, where she made the acquaintance of Queen Marie of Romania. Though from different worlds, the two became fast friends, and soon Loie was a confidante, helping Marie through the loss of a child from typhoid fever in 1916. She would help also to arrange aid for Romanians during the Great War when famine was ravaging the country and Marie herself was in hospital tents tending the sick and wounded.

In 1919, Loie introduced Hill and the Queen, and the relationship grew with Sam's frequent trips to Europe. In 1926, though the timing was not ideal, Marie made a much-publicized trip to America. She brought with her $1.5 million in paintings and statuary, along with carved furniture, journal manuscripts from her own hand, and a cloth-of-gold gown she had worn to the 1896 coronation of her cousins Tsar Nicholas and Tsarina Alexandra of Russia. Marie spoke to a crowd of 2,000 gathered at the east ramp entrance of the building, one that included 400 children from Goldendale and an auto caravan from Portland.

It was a strange event, drawing widespread curiosity as well as jaded suspicion in some quarters (though Marie's own journal comments would tell against it), regarding the actual relationship between her and Samuel. While the estate at that time had a somber

---

52   A splendid summary of the Maryhill story and the people active in its conception is provided in *Maryhill Museum of Art* (Beaverton, Oregon, 2017), text by Linda Tesner and photographs by Robert M. Reynolds

look, Marie saw in it something deeper. She complimented Hill on his vision and expressed her profound thanks to Loie.

In her later diary comments, the Queen would recall

> ...that strange uncouth cement building erected by the just as strange old Samuel Hill... I knew when I set out that morning to consecrate that queer freak of a building that no one would understand why; I knew it was empty and in no wise ready to house objects for a museum. I knew there were scoffers about me, even hostilities, but a spirit of understanding was strong in me that day and I managed by my own personality, by my word, by my spirit, to move all the hearts beating there this morning ... I knew that a dream had been built into this house, a dream beyond the everyday comprehension of the everyday man. [53]

A Vague Longing

Now back in the Northwest, I began to think of this place we had visited many years ago. Though unable to recall the name, I could not shake the feeling that I needed to be there again. It lay, if memory was right, a couple of hours east, in the direction of the Tri-Cities (Kennewick, Pasco, and West Richland), on the Washington side.

Today, of course, the information could have been found in seconds by way of a laptop search entry. Poking around, I came to think that Maryhill might be the place we had visited. One morning I set out, arriving at last at the entrance slope off the old river highway.

My heart stirred when I looked down, seeing the mansion as we had first come onto it. Now and again, over the next few years, I would make a retreat to those grounds, an idyllic place set in regal solitude above the water, its lush green courtyard and multitude of shrubs and trees, towering East Coast Elms and Ponderosa Pines aplenty, creating a fresh mosaic amid untouched surroundings that lay in each direction.

Maryhill was a strange enterprise, marked by uncertainty

---

53   Queen Marie of Romania dedicates Maryhill Museum of Art on November 3, 1926. - HistoryLink.org

from the outset, garnering mixed reviews for the next few decades while plagued now and again with gritty problems of administrative blunder and instability.   Yet always it gave rise in me some sense of the otherworldly, as if forged under a special influence.

Near the entrance, off to the right, was a plaque bearing the words of Marie, words reminiscent of her dedication statement and taken perhaps from that same time.[54]

"Sam Hill," reads this statement,

> is building not only for today but for tomorrow. There is much more in this building made of concrete than we see. There is a dream built into this place. Some may smile and scoff, for they do not understand. But I came in understanding of his dream. For these dreamers I would say good things are not only for this life but beyond. [55]

To all who visit this place and share this vision is given peace away from the passing world below.

One More Go in the Ring

Being in the old house, the place where I was conceived, brought a restoration of life and purpose. In late afternoon the Columbia sometimes turned an unearthly red, and at night I heard the call of trains that ran along it.

Over the years, as mentioned earlier, I had flirted with boxing now and again, toiling in gyms around the Northwest. I began to work out now at the Vancouver Elks Club.

Meanwhile, over the past decade, the "Tough Man" craze had developed at small arenas around the country. It started off as a lark, pitting men with little experience against each other, whether to satisfy curiosity or to settle some private beef. With time, it developed into serious competition, a respectable minor league, as it were, of pro boxing.

---

54   For a detailed account of Maryhill and the people who were involved in its development, see Steve Wiegand's *The Dancer, The Dreamers, and the Queen of Romania* (Baltimore: Bancroft Press, 2019

55   Again, I give thanks to Maryhill's Tabitha McCoard, who provided me with help on this research and sent a photograph of the inscription outside the museum entrance.

In the Northwest, shows were frequent, and some of the fighters were now parlaying their experience into full-fledged professional activity. In May of 1987, I was persuaded to have a try on a show promoted by a wonderful free spirit named Bob Oleson, a keen matchmaker whom I had met a decade earlier when covering one of his pro cards for *The Ring* in Hillsboro, Oregon.

Now 36, I still had fast hands, my staying power increased by lengthy runs, in recent years, taking me at times ten or fifteen miles on a morning jaunt. I found myself matched with a glowering young tough, twenty-two-year-old, who outweighed me by about ten pounds. Like a number of these competitors, though he lacked polish, he hit like a crashing boulder.

He had also earned quite a rep, I gathered later, in scraps outside the ring. Though I was able to outhustle him most of the way, a right hand late in the second round sent a shock to my soles.

At the end, I had won by a handy margin. I shook hands afterward with eight or ten guys from the crowd, most about my age, several of whom had thought I was doomed (a couple of them admitting they had lost money on that hunch), when they saw us face off before the opening bell.

Final Orals

At last I was done with fighting, though gym workouts would continue for another decade. I set myself to work now full-time on the dissertation. Additional readings tardily recommended by one committee member caused a delay in the schedule, but by Christmas I had a solid draft.

A couple of months later came a call from the Philosophy Department at Claremont, saying that Hick wanted to convene a meeting for the final oral exam. I ticketed a flight to California.

Shortly after arriving in town, I found myself thinking repeatedly of how great it would be to run into Clarence, a splendid old fellow who had spent much of his life in the ministry. During my time there, he and I had become acquainted when he was auditing classes.

A bit later, standing on the lot at a car rental, I was startled to find him there a few feet in front of me. Later that day we talked at length about our time on the campus—he shared my sense that John had been oddly aloof, on a personal level, to some of us who had felt the deepest kinship with him as a philosopher. John, he thought, had leaned this way because he would find it too hard to be objective in his academic role otherwise. So it may have been—still, I would always treasure the influence of this great and daring scholar during my time on that campus. And my encounter that day with Clarence, though a small event, seemed significant to me, as did every encounter he and I had during our time at Claremont.

Tish, at whose house I had roomed off-campus during the time in residence at the school, arranged for me to stay overnight at the home of a nearby acquaintance.

I still remember an odd dream that had visited me that morning, in which I fielded questions on my dissertation for an hour or so, then wandered down the street and fell asleep under a tree, missing the remainder of the session. This mishap aroused the ire of the committee members, who now spent their time devising doubly hard questions for an extra meeting now planned. I woke up with the realization that the meeting hadn't happened yet—one of those moments when you reenter the world feeling you have been given a reprieve.

A couple of hours later, the stage was set for real. The exam session was intense, yet friendly all the while and filled toward the end with laughter and good feeling. A couple of classmates were on hand to lend moral support, and to get a sense, no doubt, of what they would be facing in time.

There was a short session behind closed doors afterward. Charles Young came out and extended his hand. "*Congratulations,*" he said, "you're a success in life." Hick got out champagne, lifting his glass and saying, "Here's to Doctor Nicholson." I flew home feeling on top of the world.

A Wild Leap

It is a marvel, the path-changing moments that come in this life. A passing thought or impulse, while it may seem like little at the time, can trigger a choice that swings life in an entire new direction.

Around the winter of 1989, I was working part-time at Portland State University. I'd had idle thoughts, of late, about teaching overseas. One Friday afternoon, I decided to take a different route from the classroom to the parking lot and have a peek at an office connected with international study.

On one shelf sat a volume listing ministries of education around the world. Jotting down a few addresses, I went off to enjoy the weekend, later sending out a CV and cover letter to a few of them. One was on the Chinese mainland.

Some time after—I did not, at first, even make the connection—came a letter from the Aero-Tech Institute in Nanchang with a contract, offering a year of full-time teaching. I sent back an agreeable response, figuring that this proposition might yield both a wild ride and a career investment.

Shortly after came a moment of doubt, when the Tiananmen Square tragedy triggered news broadcasts that had China verging upon chaos. I sent the Institute a regretful telegram, saying I didn't think I could join them at this time. In coming days I wavered, thinking that perhaps the reports were exaggerated, and that the Institute might be doubly appreciative of anyone braving the trip at this time. (I was right, it did seem later, on both counts.) I wired my acceptance.

"Strongest in your weakest area"? Peale's phrase comes to mind when I think of how we let fear, at times, have its way with us. I remembered the trepidation I'd had at twenty when heading north to Seattle, not three hours up the I-5 from home. Now, moving was an adventure. I boarded the plane in late August without apprehension.

Jiangxi had seen few western visitors until recent years. The only other people I would meet in Nanchang from America, as it turned out, were those in a small group that resided downtown and were bound by a church affiliation.

On occasion friends would ask, in coming years, if I wasn't frightened when hopping that flight across the ocean. Maybe fear would have been reasonable. But I could not feel it. "When this plane lands," I thought, "I will be in the middle of *Communist China*." However daunting this idea, the amazement outweighed all else. In later years, when boarding planes for destinations in Europe and Asia, the same wide-open excitement churned within me.

The year in Nanchang gave me the sparsest lifestyle I'd ever seen, yet it provided precious life lessons. Fulfillment, I learned, could be found away from comforts and amusements we have come to think essential. The photo above was taken by my beautiful young friend Zou Lixue—Rosy—when we visited her home town of Beijing at summer's end.

In this setting, I found myself thinking at times of Lao Tzu's *Tao Te Ching*, and the simile of water present in early Chinese philosophy. Water, endlessly giving, conforming to its place, yet in time cutting the hardest rock—I found that we ourselves have in us something of that quality.

While that year indeed was a challenge, it paid back several times over. The universe, I would discover from leaps like this, seems to step up to meet the effort of the soul who takes them. If it does not always grant favors, it does reward courage.

During the year in Nanchang, I rented the house to a fellow named Jeff Handran, who had taken a couple of classes with me at Clark. He kindly sent this image in two halves, showing the view from the back yard, looking out onto the Columbia Gorge in the distance. This is the view (though it is actually wider), I treasured from earliest years, our "big tree" marking a dividing line with the lot next door. In the far distance, Portland glows wondrously at night.

I might add, another amazing thing happened prior to the departure to Nanchang. Not long before the twenty-year Hudson's Bay reunion I became acquainted again with that girl who had left town nineteen years prior. Over the course of time, by letter and phone call, we came to know each other far better than we had during our time in school.

I thought back to the time she was leaving Vancouver, and to that odd feeling I'd had, wondering if she and I had come into the world related in some way to each other, intending to share some portion of our lives to learn something together. That sense came over me again.

We discovered, in any case, that we'd had a lot more in common, back then, than we had imagined. She bolstered me during those twelve months at the Aero-Tech Institute, and looking back after, we each felt that we had reached back, in some way, into those old days and cast them in a redeeming light. (Maybe, who can say, this turnabout had been presaged by that soul-cleansing moment in the prayer room at Lighthouse Mission, when I received the assurance that all would be well. At any rate, she and I forged during that year a bond everlasting.)

Writing and the Soul

Another discovery during this time was Brenda Ueland, whose 1938 volume *If You Want to Write: A Book About Art, Independence, and Spirit* may be the greatest book on its subject ever authored. Born in 1891 in Minneapolis, she would spend years in New York's Greenwich Village community before returning to Minnesota during the 1930s. A live wire of spirit and intellect, she brought to her every endeavor a will to test assumptions about what was proper and possible.

Photo supplied by Minnesota Historical Society.

Like Lewis, whose *Abolition of Man* would appear a few years later at the height of battle on the WW II European front, Ueland saw the freeing up of emotion, rather than its inhibition, as crucial in the development of a writer. Her enthusiasm flows over, at times, into veritable mysticism.

"I think love," she states in her memoir in 1939,

> is an actual thing—not just an emotion, a pleasant warm feeling in my chest, but a stream of power that you can send out to people without speaking and across great distances...[a] translucent stream of pure golden power which turns every molecule of the person you send it to...into a two-hundred-watt electric light bulb.[56]

If You Want to Write contains a chapter called *Be careless, reckless! Be a lion, be a pirate, when you write; and Keep a slovenly, headlong, impulsive, honest diary.* Another is *Why women who do too much housework should neglect it for their writing.*

An *honest* diary: There is no real writing without forthrightness. We need to trust what is within us, not stopping to contrive something else. On this point she is in harmony with sources, ancient and modern, that insist upon genuineness in every human endeavor.

"He who stands on tiptoe," said Lao Tzu, "does not stand firm."

Thefts, as Ralph Waldo Emerson famously contended, never enrich. Alms never impoverish. "The least admixture of a lie," he notes in his address to the graduating class at Harvard Divinity School in 1838,

> —for example, the taint of vanity, any attempt to make a good impression, a favourable appearance—will instantly vitiate the effect. But speak the truth, and all things alive and brute are vouchers, and the very roots of the grass underground...seem to stir and move to bear your witness.[57]

Our effort to embellish, in every arena, will sap an effort of

---

56   Brenda Ueland, *Me: A Memoir* (Duluth, Minnesota, 2016), page 357.

57   Ralph Waldo Emerson, quoted by William James in *The Varieties of Religious Experience*, page 32.

its force. When we try unnaturally to seem better in the eyes of others, we are out of accord with truth. The universe works out continually, in each venue of activity, a profound *compensation*, enriching our lives with each positive effort—each effort that involves honesty, courage, fairness, and compassion—regardless of whether the world may credit us for it.

The spirit in which an author writes, notes the celebrated mystic, scholar, and Trappist monk Thomas Merton, may be worth more than his dexterity. "The world," he says,

> values books, and thinks that in so doing it is valuing Tao. But books contain words only. And yet there is something else which gives value to the books. Not the words only, nor the thought in the words, but something else within the thought, swinging it in a certain direction that words cannot apprehend.[58]

"Study them all," said the great Tyrus Raymond Cobb, "but imitate none." Late in his career, Ty penned a series of articles for the *New York Evening Journal* recalling his education as a ballplayer. Sam Crawford, Shoeless Joe Jackson, and many others – Ty had learned something from watching each man who excelled in the art of hitting. But he never sought to duplicate one. No individual could ever achieve greatness, he maintained, without some element of originality.

Reading Ueland's book, I was reminded of my own fledgling efforts as a sportswriter with *The Ring*. Early in 1978, about a year and a half after the first success, I crafted the story mentioned earlier on one of my favorites, Argentine world middleweight champion Carlos Monzon. Much taken with Mark Kram, the *oh, so hip* fight beat *maestro* at *Sports Illustrated*, I had tried to adopt his tone. I showed a draft to my old friend and mentor Lee Partain.

He gave it back soon after, visibly dissatisfied, as he had been with one of my 101 compositions in the fall of '69. He had that same odd look in his nostrils.

"Look at how the great ones do it," he said, making me feel eighteen all over again. "They make it look easy." He had the feeling that my scholarly mindset was getting in the way of what I was trying to do.

------

58   Thomas Merton, *The Way of Chuang Tzu* (New York: New Directions Books, 1997), page 82.

"It *smells*," he said, "like an academic bias."

I got to work. Months later, the story was published, photos included, a generous check arriving in return. In later years, Lee was thrilled when I published books on philosophy and the history of boxing. (At risk of self-flattery, I remember also the words of Jack Vickers, a key member of our Claremont faculty, in his letter of recommendation: "He is incapable of writing with subterfuge." They were worth a thousand times any I could have gained with pretense.)

Ueland, too, had a low threshold for "tip-toe" effort. When she put a sample of insincere writing next to an honest one, the contrast was striking—and comical. But her dominant tone was success, not failure. She stressed the need, when helping a novice writer, for *positive* criticism. And to the reader, as well, she gives encouragement:

"You do not know what is in you," heads Chapter XV, "—an inexhaustible fountain of ideas". The writer who trusts himself, in this regard, may find depths he or she has not imagined, depths that genuine effort can bring to the surface.

> We are apt to think of ourselves as a stomach with arms and legs and a skein of nerves in the skull, which sometimes, when we have plenty of sleep and some hot coffee, seems to give off a few ideas.
>
> But to write happily and with self-trust you must discover what there is in you, this bottomless fountain of imagination and knowledge.[59]

She cites the passage in Plato's dialogue *Meno*, familiar to students of philosophy, where Socrates' titular young friend sees him sketching in the dirt to show a young slave boy the properties of geometric figures.

Here, says Socrates, is a *square*, two units on a side in length. Imagine another that is twice the size. How long, on each side, would that one be?

All through the exchange, it is Socrates who asks questions. He does not pour answers *into* the learner, but draws out what is in him already. Might the sought-after square be the same length on each side as the original? (No, of course not.) Might the length be double? This, too, would be wrong. Nor could the

---

59   Brenda Ueland, *If You Want to Write* (St. Paul: Greywolf Press, 1987), page 146.

square, the boy sees, be three units on a side, though that would be closer.

If they hit an impasse, Socrates backs up and goes again, each time relying upon the learner's own insight. At last, the answer is deduced. (The side of the square will be the length of the first one's *diagonal*.) It is a picture, says Socrates, of how we gain real knowledge. Our sensory contact with the passing world gives rise in us to knowledge of something more. With our intelligence we grasp not just particular truths, but such things as numbers, geometric entities, beauty, courage, justice—the things of eternity. Our souls are wellsprings tapped by this "Socratic" method.

In poetry, says Ueland, we find truth that has lain dormant until this moment. Repeatedly she quotes William Blake, a writer and poet of strong mystical leaning, on what is involved in creative activity. Near the end she heads a chapter with his own words: "He whose face gives no light shall never become a star." It is a fundamental law of life. We give in order to receive.

A book, she insists, is not measured by what it may reap in critical acclaim or sales figures. Its worth lies in the genuineness of its content. If her own work expressed honestly what was in her to give, and it gave hope and inspiration to ten people, it was worth writing.

Ueland practiced what she preached, in her writing and in her life. A joyful spirit bursts forth in her memoir, and in the book for which she is most famous. So does her pride, a surprising contrast to the way in which some writers approach the things of the spirit. While recognizing the greatness of Leo Tolstoy, she laments the drab modesty of this sage that could make her want "to give all I have to the poor, wind straw around my legs with crisscrossed clothesline, and live on a frozen raw carrot a day." Each one of us, she insists, should have "a reckless, indomitable, arrogant, joyful self-esteem," a self-trust and a self-belief.

And still she pays respect to the old wisdom. You cannot ever have too much pride, energy, or bravery. You cannot have even too much ego. But it must be "centrifugal"—generous—rather than the in-pulling kind. The enclosed self tends toward conceit and obtuseness. The Divine self, on the other hand,

> is a liquid eternally-moving-onward stream which says, "I have a god in me, and this is what I think and believe and care about, and tomorrow it will be something different and better, I hope. And

now tell me what is in you, for that will help me to
understand everything better."[60]

Active in teaching, writing, and radio broadcast, outspoken
always, Ueland gave much of herself to social causes. Possessed
all her life of a spiritual intimacy with her generations of pet cats
(in this respect she was like the mysterious Dr. Rampa), she would
devote time to improving the treatment of non-human animals.
In 1946, while covering the trials of accused war traitor Vidkun
Quisling, she was awarded a knighthood in the Royal Norwegian
Order of Saint Olaf. Physically active into her advanced years,
often hiking several miles a day, she set a swim record for
participants over the age of eighty. Exuberant and lovable, she
lived to be ninety-three.

(I cannot help thinking that Brenda and my mother would
have enjoyed sharing their Scandinavian family dramas, and
would have gotten along famously—or perhaps, by now, they
have.)

The Exploration of Human Potential

Here and there, whether in dreams, prayer meetings, or
moments of stress, or out of the mid-day blue, we may feel that
we have received an influence of a special kind. Ueland ventures
into this territory when bidding the reader to trust what lies within.
She has a kinship, in this regard, with writers during her lifetime
who explored the depths of human potential.

Certain features of human experience, declared classicist
scholar Frederick Myers late in the 19th century in his massive
two-volume work *Human Personality,* give evidence of a
subliminal mind (i. e., beneath the conscious threshold), that has
wider reach than the one studied by conventional psychology.

Myers, says Aldous Huxley in an introduction to an amended
edition of the book, had a different orientation than Sigmund
Freud, an analyst concerned largely with treating illness. Freud's
notion of the unconscious Huxley likens to a dirt basement,
to which undesirable impulses might be relegated. Myers, by
contrast, was interested in positive content.

"He knew," says Huxley,

that the cellar stinks and is alive with vermin, but

---

60   *Me: A Memoir* (published in Duluth, Minnesota), page 358.

> he was more interested in what goes on in the
> rooms (ordinarily locked) above street level—in
> the treasures of the *piano nobile,* in the far-ranging
> birds (and perhaps even angels) that come and go
> between the rafters of a roofless attic that is open
> to the sky.[61]

Telepathy, mediumship, out-of-body and near-death visions—late in the 19th century, a shared interest brought together Myers and others who wondered if it were possible to apply standards of science to these alleged episodes. It was no easy task—such episodes, it seemed, were rather like meteors, coming without warning and hard to observe, yet still seen now and again. So began in London the enterprise of the Society for Psychical Research.

Despite the inherent difficulty of its subject, this movement, in time, would yield an interesting chapter in the investigation of human nature. The founding members of this effort were men of high aptitude and upright character. One was G. N. M. Tyrrell, an engineer and mathematician who joined the Society in 1908 and became its President in 1945. Much like Myers, he was impressed with this seeming reservoir of potential beneath the conscious threshold.

It is a significant fact, notes Tyrrell, "that those creations of the human mind, which have borne pre-eminently the stamp of originality and greatness, have not come from within the region of consciousness." Rather they have come from beyond that region, "knocking at its door for admittance," bursting forth at times with amazing power.[62]

He offers an array of testimony, citing such composers as John Keats and Percy Shelley, each of whom attests to the spontaneity of the creative process. His description of Apollo in the third book of his poetic work *Hyperion,* says Keats, came to him essentially as a gift, as if by chance or magic.

Similar examples abound: "The songs," insists Johan Goethe, "made me, not I them." Wordsworth had times when "the world around him seemed unreal and [he] had occasionally

---

61   F. W. H. Myers, *Human Personality and its Survival of Bodily Death* (New Hyde Park: University Books, Inc., 1961), page 7. For a lengthier discussion of Myers and psychical research, see Chapter 4 of my book *The Prospect of Immortality.*

62   G. N. M. Tyrrell, *The Personality of Man* (Middlesex, Pelican Books, 1947), page 30.

to use his strength against an object, such as a gatepost, to reassure himself." Dickens admitted that he owed much when writing to some beneficent power that showed him the way. Kipling, Dostoevsky, George Eliot—all say kindred things.

Minot Savage

What a precious find was this Harvard Divinity graduate—a mentor, I would later find out, of the young John Haynes Holmes. Minot Judson Savage was born in June of 1841, in Norridgewock, Maine, joining the Congregational Church when he was thirteen. He enrolled at Bangor Theological Seminary and served in the Civil War with the Christian Commission, which provided supplies, medical service, and religious literature to men in combat. He graduated in 1864, and four years after the war's end became minister of the Congregational Church in Hannibal, Missouri.

Powerfully religious, yet dissatisfied with much of religious thought, Savage joined the Unitarian Fellowship, a liberal movement with roots in 16th century Europe. After serving in the ministry in Chicago, he was called to the Church of the Unity in Boston. In 1896, he began a ten-year residency as Associate Minister of the Church of the Messiah in New York City.

Savage, like Holmes, was freethinking, comfortable with the emerging theory of life's evolution and with faith traditions outside his own. He was receptive also to the emerging literature of psychical research, though aware of how often paranormal claims were the product of delusion or trickery. He wrote extensively on a variety of topics, publishing *Life Beyond Death* in 1901 and dedicating it to his beloved son Philip Henry, who had died at age thirty-one, three years earlier. He lived until May of 1918.

Like Sir William Barrett, whose 1926 volume *Death-Bed Visions* became a classic of this era, Savage was impressed with the experiences of the dying, and particularly those of children. He cites the case of two young girls, eight or nine years of age, close personal friends who lived in Massachusetts and were taken mortally ill at the same time with diphtheria.

One, whom he identifies as Jennie, died on a Wednesday, and much care was taken to keep the fact from her playmate for fear that the news might put added strain upon her. On Saturday morning, notes Savage, the dying girl made out "her little will," specifying things that should go to her friends, including items for Jennie.

"A little while later," he explains,

> She seemed to be between the two worlds, seeing the friends that were about the bed, and also seeing those [on the other side] who are ordinarily invisible. She spoke of her grandfather and grandmother, and of others, expressing her delight to see them. And then she turned to her father, with face and voice expressing the greatest surprise, and exclaimed, "Why, Papa, why didn't you tell me that Jennie had gone? Jennie is here with the rest! Why didn't you tell me of it?"[63]

Had the girl known of her friend's death, notes Savage, this vision might be chalked up to hallucination, but she had not. He cites another case involving a very young boy, perhaps three years of age, who saw in a dream his older friend, a prominent judge, telling him that he had gone to the next world. The experience was vivid and powerful, and the boy was heard crying as a result, prompting friends to enter his room, where the little one told them that he had lost his dear companion.

Such cases, it is true, are only anecdotal. Yet they come, oft times, from highly estimable people, honest and lucid, and seem credible to those who hear of them. Those involving children, Savage points out, are especially interesting, young subjects who have not, like adults, "come to possess certain theories, ideas and prepossessions in regard to them, which might produce or determine the nature of these visions."

There are some who suppose that science and religious belief are antithetical to each other. Yet to the contrary, insists Norman Vincent Peale, the advances of the past century are quite compatible with spirituality. His own experience leads him toward a reconciliation of these things, toward the view of "a dynamic universe, surcharged with mystic, electric…atomic forces," all so wonderful that we continue to be amazed by them. The universe, he senses, "is a great spiritual sounding house, alive and vital."

He mentions, toward the end of his most famous work, several incidents involving people who feel the presence of a departed loved one, or who lay at death's door, finding revelation in their final moments. One, similar to that noted by Minot Savage, was

---

63   Minot Savage, *Life Beyond Death* (New York: G. P. Putnam's Sons, 1902), page 310.

described to him by Natalie Kalmus, a scientist and industry executive involved in the development of film technicolor, whose dying sister asked her to make sure she received no drugs, in her last hours, so that she might be fully lucid at the end.

The woman's request was granted, though it caused Natalie a good deal of anguish as the time neared. After a lengthy conversation, the sister grew tired and was beginning to fall asleep, at which point Natalie and the nurse left the room. Some time after, Natalie heard her name called. She took her place beside the bed and listened as her sister described seeing those on the other side. One of those, to the dying woman's surprise, was her cousin Ruth, who herself had died a week earlier, though she had not been told of it.

"Chill after chill," said Natalie in recounting this moment, "shot up and down my spine. I felt on the verge of some powerful, almost frightening knowledge." Her sister remained clear in thought and voice, even as she came to mortal end, saying to Natalie with a last euphoric embrace, "I'm going up!"

Over the years, Peale was privy, firsthand or through trusted friends, to many unusual episodes involving those who were departing. Whether or not they involved extraordinary knowledge like the one described by Kalmus, their impact was lasting. Such experiences had left him with no doubt about the life that awaits. "I firmly believe," he writes,

> in the continuation of life after that which we call death takes place. I believe there are two sides to the phenomenon known as death—this side where we now live and the other side where we shall continue to live. Eternity does not start with death. We are in eternity now. We are citizens of eternity. We merely change the form of the experience called life, and that change, I am persuaded, is for the better.[64]

---

64   *The Power of Positive Thinking,* pp. 205 – 06.

Chapter 11
Human Progress and Human Potential

And if it is nothingness that awaits us, let us so act that it shall be an unjust fate ...
          Miguel de Unamuno, *The Tragic Sense of Life*

[I kept] busy staying away from the truant officer and it got to be like a game, me all the time running away and hiding out and coming home by the rooftops...I learned a lot, wandering around the city. I learned that if you're fast enough you can pick up pennies, sometimes nickels, off the stack of papers at newsstands. But you got to be ready to run.
          Rocky Graziano, *Somebody Up There Likes Me*

"Worn-out garments," declares the Lord Krishna, "are shed by the body. Worn-out bodies are shed by the dweller."

To this point I have recalled a fair part of my life, and the impact of my mother upon me through our thirty years together and beyond. In this chapter and the ones following, I describe further an outlook that has taken shape owing in large part to this relationship.

The above quotation comes from Book II of an Indian classic entitled *The Bhagavad Gita*, or Song of God. Its story, originally part of a much wider epic compiled over several hundred years, took its present form around the fourth century of the Common Era. The story concerns Arjuna, a *kshatriya* caste warrior who looks out upon the battlefield where two armies are arrayed against each other. As mortal combat looms, he loses heart, telling himself that the task is senseless.

Though Arjuna's reasons seem plausible, they betray a deep failure. He is rebuked by Krishna, his charioteer, who dispels his confusion and tells him to arise and fight. As the story unfolds, the lessons continue and Krishna reveals at last his divine nature—a glory like unto "a thousand suns" rising in the sky. While this story is grounded in a tradition that understands warfare in spiritual terms, it describes also the battlefield present daily within each individual soul. In this way it transcends time and culture.

I will return to this source toward the end of this chapter. In the chapter following I will propose an alternative framing of this subject in place of the *all or nothing* tendency, simplistic and at times vindictive, that long has held sway in the mainstream. Following the example of authors I have noted, I offer what I believe is a more constructive line of thought.

An Idea That Spawns Many Questions

My interest in a future life, which began in my late teens and was given impetus by things I experienced after, has figured into much that I have taught and written.

Is such a life, one might ask, important in the first place? Some people manage well with no such expectation—we do better, they say, to concern ourselves with opportunities given to us here. In contrast to this view is another, expressed memorably by Miguel de Unamuno, who believes that immortality is the greatest question in all of life.

In this chapter I contrast these views, after which I address an inadequacy in much of Western religious tradition concerning human destiny. I make a related plea for restraint in our estimate of individuals in their present earthly condition. Human science in the past century has shed light upon the dynamics of human agency, light giving rise to more responsible judgment in many quarters. We have begun, for example, to fathom criminal behavior in relation to human chemistry and the environmental setting in which it is embedded. I believe that such insight should bear, as well, upon our spiritual outlook.

Insight into these dynamics, I think, is found also in plain firsthand testimony: In the homely stories of men reared in difficult surroundings, I find truth regarding human nature and the deep reservoir of human potential. I propose, too, that we seek out insight that has long existed within certain religious traditions— for one, that of Vedic India, which has long recognized the complex nature of human constitution and its endless possibility.

Whatever we may be, here and now, there is no limit to what we may yet become, whether in this world or the next.

Two Attitudes Regarding Survival

As I say, not everyone shares my sense regarding these "worn-out garments" and what happens when we shed them. Some, in fact, seem not to need it. For this present life, they imagine, is sufficient unto itself.

Some people find the notion of a future life inherently flawed, supposing that such a life, sooner or later, would prove dreadful whatever its content. Should death never come, they imagine, the very satisfaction of our wants, were it granted, would in time become tedious.

Some, by the same token, take comfort in their own mortal limit. Life, writes Walter Kaufmann in *The Faith of a Heretic*, may be likened to a book with a fixed number of pages. Within this limit resides its meaning. As sleep is welcome at day's end, so might death be welcome after a life of striving and commitment. He cites the poet and scholar Johann Friedrich Holderlin, who desires but a *single summer*—a mortal span in which he lives "like the gods," beyond which more is not needed.

"The life I want," says Kaufmann, "is a life I could not endure in eternity. It is a life of love and intensity, suffering and creation, that makes life worth living, and death welcome. There is no other life I should prefer. Neither should I like not to die."[65] A frank acceptance of life's end, he believes, is liberating, and can make our existence here and now all the richer. How many of us, when we stop to think, make good use of the time we are presently given? How many hours do we fritter away on things of little consequence?

Some people, though they may doubt that anything awaits us beyond, rest content with figurative versions of survival—even should there await nothing, their efforts here, they suppose, will benefit those who come after. Now and again, one hears it said, too, that a departed loved one "lives on," carried in memory by those who have known this one along the way.

Some find hope in the coming of a new social order that may one day overturn longstanding injustice. Perhaps humanity, <u>building upon</u> its past, will undo its tragic errors and achieve an

65   Walter Kaufmann, *The Faith of a Heretic* (Princeton, NJ: Princeton University Press), page 375.

earthly harmony. ("Imagine there's no heaven," John Lennon bid his listeners, and only this life. Our abandonment of religious hope and of present day competition will perhaps one day allow the world to "live as one.")

On occasion, our conscious end is embraced even by a theist. We are known by God, declares philosopher theologian Charles Hartshorne, and so reside ever present to His loving omniscience. Herein we are eternal, though our own activity concludes with this life. God will not "insult" those who have found satisfaction in virtuous conduct by bestowing on them reward in addition.

Granted, these qualified versions of survival, like them or not, may be all we ever shall have. Perhaps at life's end we sink back into the earth that has spawned us. And perhaps, as some say, it is no cause for sorrow. But I was always of a different mind.

True, I have frittered away time on things that did not matter—things, even, that were to my detriment. But I have spent time also on things that have given me fulfillment, and hopefully have enriched others in the process. And I feel, amid this exertion, that there is more in me than will find expression within this current life span.

"For half a century," says novelist Victor Hugo, "I have been writing my thoughts in prose and verse…but I feel that I have not said a thousandth part of what is in me." This sense of unrealized potential gives rise in him to a sense of adventure awaiting. British philosopher James Martineau, when turning eighty, voiced kindred feeling, noting how few of his plans he has been able to carry out. He takes this limit not as cause for lament, but as reason to believe that this life is only a fragment of what lies in store.[66]

It is a sense I share, and one in which I trust. In any case, I think, no real consolation can be found in these versions of survival just cited. Should present injustice, for example, give way in time to social reform, so much the better. But it will not speak to the suffering of those who have endured it, a suffering that cannot be arithmetically bought back by the good fortune of those who come later.

Such victims, as Kant reminds us, are *ends in themselves*, precious in their own right, rather than mere cannon fodder contributing to the good of someone else. No rectification of their enslavement and violation can be found in a social scheme to be enjoyed one day by a coming generation. Thus any real hope, as John Hick emphasizes in his discussion of "soul-making," must

---

66   Each quote is contained in Holmes' immortality sermon.

involve the participation of those who have tread this path.

Granted, it is pleasing to think that my actions have some continuing effect—that the tree I plant, so to speak, may shade someone when I am gone. But it pleases me endlessly more to think that I might one day be reunited with those with whom I have shared this journey—to engage in activity anew and make amends where needed for things I have done, or left undone, in this earthly span. (And if it is true, as Hartshorne says, that some noble types find virtue here to be its own reward—*all the more reason*, I say, to count them worthy of preservation.)

Whether this hope is destined for fulfillment, I cannot yet know. But without it, I feel, my own life has little meaning. So, as noted earlier, was I gratified when coming onto Unamuno's *Tragic Sense of Life*. While his head, this man confesses, cannot establish immortality, neither can his heart live without it. And whatever may come, he will have none of the compromised versions of a hereafter in which some take satisfaction.

"All this talk," he maintains, "of a man surviving in his children, or in his works, or in the universal consciousness, is but vague verbiage which satisfies only those who suffer from affective stupidity." A single soul "is worth all the universe." A *soul*, he emphasizes, and not just a fleeting *life span*—seen under the aspect of eternity, one solitary being is of more importance than the mortal life of every man who roams the Earth. (By the same token, as his subsequent words make clear, Unamuno is no pacifist—he does not shrink from the thought of mortal combat when a worthy cause demands it.)

And if consciousness is, "as some inhuman thinker has said, nothing more than a flash of life between two eternities of darkness…there is nothing more execrable than existence." Indeed, so terrible was his own fear of annihilation, even in youth, that Unamuno was immune to the efforts of Church educators to instill in him a proper fear. As a child, he recalls, "I remained unmoved when shown even the most moving pictures of hell, for even then nothing appeared to me quite so horrible as nothingness itself. It was a furious hunger of being that possessed me…"[67]

And so, he says, "I do not want to die…nor do I want to want to die; I want to live for ever and ever." While this desire may seem to some egocentric, Unamuno sees it otherwise. "*Nullum hominem a me alienum puto*," he declares, modifying a phrase of

---

67   *The Tragic Sense of Life*, page 9. For a lengthier discussion, see Chapter 4 of my book *The Prospect of Immortality* (Salt Lake City: Homeward Bound Publishing, 2001, second edition).

the Latin playwright Terence, who held that nothing human was alien to himself. Rather, Unamuno calls no man a stranger—not humanity, but the human being, concrete and irreplaceable, who stands before him. This love of existence is a love that spreads outward.

Like Blaise Pascal in the 17th century, who declared famously that the heart has reasons the head does not fathom, Unamuno too knows, at some level, that this life is not all. "When I contemplate the green serenity of the fields," he says, "or look into the depths of clear eyes through which shines a fellow soul, my consciousness dilates…[I am] bathed in the flood of life…about me, and I believe in my future." Should he hear it whispered within *Thou shalt cease to be,* "the angel of Death touches me with his wing, [flooding] the depths of my spirit with the blood of divinity."

The Inadequacy of Traditional Belief

If we allow that a future life is real, or possible, the question remains whether we can have any sense of its content. Even writers inclined toward such a belief have acknowledged the strangeness of this task.

Let it be said first, a remarkable amount of space regarding a future life has been devoted to *condemnation.* Typically, in such accounts, our fate hereafter hinges upon some single criterion, such as immersion in water, a self-surrendering act of faith, or participation in some set of ritual sacraments. Failure, in this regard, comes with infinite penalty.

At times this belief has fueled gruesome expression, on canvas and in print, of what awaits the great majority outside the fold. A good deal of oil painting, much of it during the Renaissance, depicted the calamity of hell and loss of hope therein. So has many a word from the pulpit.

In *A Portrait of the Artist* as a Young Man, a novel inspired by his own youth, James Joyce recalls teachers who bid their students to dwell upon what it will mean to be lost forever. His protagonist Stephen Dedalus, attending a three-day academic retreat in Dublin, receives a series of sermons on Last Things from his former schoolmaster Father Arnall.

"Now let us try for a moment to imagine," intones this revered speaker, "as far as we can, the nature of that abode of the damned which the justice of an offended God has called into existence for the eternal punishment of sinners." Hell, he proclaims, "is a strait and dark and foul-smelling prison, an abode of demons and lost souls, filled with fire and smoke."

The great number of condemned souls in this prison allows not even the limited mobility of an earthly confine, and the fire casts no light.

> All the filth of the world, all the offal and scum of the world… shall run there as to a vast reeking sewer… The brimstone too which burns there in such prodigious quantity fills all hell with its intolerable stench; and the bodies of the damned themselves exhale such a pestilential odour that… one of them alone would suffice to infect the whole world.[68]

This assault, promises the orator, will be compounded by its sound, wherein the damned will "howl and scream at one another, their torture and rage intensified by the presence of beings tortured and raging like themselves." If this pain is not adequate, another feature of God's dungeon shall add to it. This will be the presence of devils who torment the lost, visiting rebuke upon them for choices made in this life.

While some effort of thought goes into this soot-caked drama, there is no justice in the picture it creates, and that has informed Christianity, in one modification or another, in several of its branches. The wide literature of human destiny, in fact, is strewn with assertions that defy logic. There is a special and designedly awful hell, I was once told by a member of an offshoot Christian ecclesia, for murderers. An act of suicide, according to one murky spiritualist treatise, requires "at least two" added earthly incarnations as payment for its cosmic breach.

Such assertions are moral nonsense. For one, not all murders are alike. Every such action, indeed every transgression, and every noble action, as well, must be seen in its context if we are to understand it. Its good or evil cannot be read off, in formulaic fashion, according to the heading under which it falls. A man who kills one of his fellows, though he may commit a great wrong, may also have endured—perhaps from infancy—a trauma that would have inclined each of us in a similar direction. This truth, I believe, should qualify our judgment with respect not only to this life, but to any that may await.

The killing of oneself, by the same token, is not the same in

---

68 James Joyce, *A Portrait of the Artist as a Young Man* (New York: Signet Classic, 1991), page 127.

every case. First off, not every suicide has even the same motive. Those who end their lives, whether alone or in the "assisted" fashion now available to the terminally ill in some quarters, make this choice often on grounds of personal dignity, believing that the prolongation of their suffering serves no purpose for themselves or their loved ones. And whatever its motive, how do we know that a suicide, in some given case, has not endured in this earthly round enough to consume us twice over?

I do not mean to say that the killing of another, or oneself, is justified in the typical case where it happens. But its context, in every case, must be kept in mind. A criminal act, in any responsible legal system, is defined in large part by the circumstance in which it occurs. It is for this reason that our statutes have in them enough "give" to accommodate a range of possibilities. (Not all homicides, for example, are classed as offenses of the same kind, and not all murders villainous in the same "degree".) So should our religious thinking have in it a restraint in deference to justice and compassion.

Perseverance in life, I have come to believe, is indeed better than resignation. My own crisis, which began in late teens and lasted more than two years, brought me as close to defeat as a young man may come. In the years that followed, in fact, death would remain a quiet companion, standing by in the shadows, surfacing momentarily now and again as the end-point of a "worst-case" scenario should all come to naught.

Each time looking back, I might add, I was struck by how misguided my train of thought had been. Always it owed to a distortion of my reality at that moment. The world, as it turned out, contained more possibility than I had thought; the thing I wanted was not as valuable as it seemed; I had underestimated my own capacity to meet the challenge—whatever the case, there existed choices better than self-destruction.

And just the same, this experience taught me to temper my judgment with understanding. The trite notion that suicide is mere cowardice, or that it is unforgiveable, or (as I have heard a time or two) "the worst" of all possible sins, expresses little sense of what brings an individual to the point of it.

Whatever its doctrinal origin, the idea that our fate is decided with finality by what we do or what we believe, in this one mortal round, is strange beyond measure. In the natural history of our kind, death has befallen many an individual in early childhood. By what toss of the coin might this fledgling creature be transported to a good place, for all of time, or to a bad one?

Imagine, by the same token, that one soul achieves right standing at the age of seventy-five, and another, potentially capable of the same spiritual turn, is cut down in puberty. Is the second lost? (Serious argument, I gather, has taken place in some religious quarters over the question of whether *an aborted fetus* is subject to this ineradicable judgment.) It is with good reason that the concept of salvation has been rethought, over the past century, in some venues of Christian belief.

Another disturbing facet of this yes or no conception of human destiny is the continuing relationship that may obtain between those in one place and those in the other. Now and again, Christians have imagined that witnessing the torments of the damned will be an actual part of their reward. This has been supposed, on a few occasions, by thinkers otherwise quite estimable.

In some cases, the sentiment is understandable. Carthaginian Church Father Quintus Tertullianus, writing late in the first century, describes the Roman styled entertainment of his day as a violation, a cruel and raucous exhibit that paled before the heroism of the Christian community. While at present the overturning of this social order was available to him only in mind's eye, he looked forward to witnessing hereafter the enemies of the Church writhing "in fires more fierce than those…they [have visited upon] the followers of Christ."[69]

In fairness, it might be added, this flight of imagination did not reflect Tertullian's whole outlook. For he maintained, too, that the innocent find no pleasure in another's suffering, and so will mourn the fact that a fellow man has sinned so grievously as to warrant an ultimate punishment. The idea of witnessing the torment of the damned has a more decided expression, perhaps, in the writing of Thomas Aquinas.

"The blessed in the kingdom of heaven," declares St. Thomas in a less traumatic setting a thousand years later, "will see the punishments of the damned, in order that their bliss be more delightful for them."

Granted, he admits, it may seem odd that delight will arise from this sight when pity would be more apt. Yet pity, reasons Aquinas, would diminish the happiness of those souls who feel it. Hence it will be absent. In seeing this suffering, however, the saved will understand better the magnitude of their own good. And while they will not enjoy the suffering *per se*, they will take

---

69   See Tertulian's *De Spectaculis* (Savage, Minnesota: Lighthouse Christian Publishing, date uncited

satisfaction in the enactment of divine justice.

Father Arnall's oration notwithstanding, I wonder how many of those who believe in final damnation have ever stopped to imagine what this doctrine entails. Consider, I once said to a class, the pain that results from brushing your hand against a hot stove burner. How would it feel if you planted your hand on it, say, for two or three full seconds?

Have you ever done anything in your life, I asked, that would warrant being kept in this experiential state for a week? Or even for one minute? No one, on serious reflection, seemed to think that he had.

What, then, of a year, or ten thousand? Once or twice, when feeling provocative, I asked students in a World Religions class to imagine that we now resided, here in this room, in the abode of the blessed. Across the hall were the damned—among them perhaps some who were friends and family in mortal life. Suppose, I said, that we had all we wanted here, except that we would hear, now and again, the anguished wail of those others. Would this sound have an impact upon our own condition?

No one in the class seemed to doubt that it would—and for the worse.

If so, would it help if these sounds were moved further down the way, so that they were not as loud? Before long, it seemed, they would weigh just as hard.

Maybe the suffering could be moved across town, where it would be known about, but would not impinge upon us as it had. Yet in time, it seemed again, this knowledge alone—even did these lost souls include among them *our worst mortal enemies*— would make our own condition less desirable. Yet again, such knowledge might be removed from our knowledge altogether, but the question remained, *was this state of affairs desirable*, in mind's eye, here and now? It struck me that the keenest, more sensitive students were the first to declare it was not.

Whether witnessed or not, such suffering seems horrific— and nonsensical. What insanity, to suppose that these same beings whom we are bid to love, here and now, beings who are loved immeasurably by God from their first moment, should be forsaken in this manner. Does God's love somehow vanish the moment this life has ended? Imagine, say, a five-year-old child, loved by his parents and by God, being cast into a fate of the kind that Joyce's orator describes. Indeed, think of a man or woman of any age, perhaps not even equipped in mortal life with a means of salvation, being subjected to this fate.

The unlimited majesty of God, I have heard it said, makes rejection of Him an infinite evil. While an odder conflation of "infinites," I think, would be hard to find, let us imagine that this rejection occurs, a naysaying that is willful and not atoned for in mortal life. Still, I ask, can such a man be fully aware of what he does? Or is he better likened to a small child who momentarily "hates" his parent? (Did some man reject God in full awareness, I should think, he would be not so much evil as infinitely *masochistic*.)

Those who think that our status is decided by belief in some doctrine, or public declaration of such a belief, or kindred membership in some given religious organization, are guilty of colossal absent-mindedness where justice is concerned. Suppose, for example, that I and my sibling are raised in a cultural backwater where some doctrine is preached and salvation promised to all and only those who accept it. She, let us imagine, travels the world, her thought expanding with each new experience. In time, by way of reflection, she grows away from the mindset we had once shared. I, on the other hand, lacking the nerve for this venture, never challenge what I have been taught. When we come to the end, which of us has lived with greater integrity? If we suppose that I have, we embrace a sheer inversion of what moral intelligence declares.

Spiritual Failure

In rejecting conventional thought regarding a future life, I do not mean to say that every life should be looked upon as an unqualified success. I believe that our actions in this life have impact—for better and for worse—upon us hereafter. There may well be sorrows awaiting those who inflict wanton sorrow in this earthly round. But I have never been able to imagine that a man could do anything, no matter the extent of his hatred and his rage, that would separate him from the love of his Creator for all of time.

Alternatives to this notion of endless condemnation can be found in literature both East and West. Vedic tradition, for one, speaks of various states hereafter of blessedness, and of wretchedness, depending on the life that has been lived. But it allows opportunities anew, even for those who have done miserably this time around. Some Christian authors, too, recognize the need for revision of traditional doctrine concerning the next life.

Longstanding ideas regarding punishment, notes Richard Purtill in his book *Thinking About Religion*, are particularly inadequate in their conception.

A truly benevolent God, says Purtill, can make use of suffering only as a means to our own development. Take, for example, the doctrine of *purgatory*, introduced by the Roman Catholic church as a modification of the idea of damnation. This idea, as he notes, meets with resistance in some quarters, owing to its lack of scriptural confirmation and the abuses to which it was historically prone—the practice, for example, of believers paying money to relieve their departed loved ones of difficulty on the other side. But in principle, thinks Purtill, it may have some value.

Were purgatory merely a kind of prison or torture chamber, it would lack constructive meaning. But seeing our own evil—to experience it perhaps as *our victims felt it*, with ourselves as the perpetrators, might provide insight enabling us to move forward.[70]

I think that Purtill's discussion is an admirable one, far more humane in its spirit than many others in this arena. At the same time, I say again, my own instincts require some element of restitution from perpetrator to victim, if justice is to be done. While the exact means of this atonement may be unclear, from our present vantage point, I trust that future meetings, if they are destined to occur, will afford this possibility.

Personal Growth Amid Adversity

Our thinking about human behavior has benefited, as I say, in the past century from insight gained in the arenas of social science and human biology. With this insight has come a tempering of our thought about what people do and how we make sense of it.

We know today that certain features of our makeup—our tendency, say, to be outgoing or withdrawn—are powerfully correlated with factors present in early environment and possibly at conception. Likewise with criminal behavior: To cite a case, and surely a heinous one, let us take the sexual abuse of children, which has a statistical tie with the perpetrator's own abuse at a similar age. While this prior misfortune does not excuse the offense, neither can we imagine in good faith that such tragedy is irrelevant to understanding it.

70   See, for example, discussion in Chapter 9, "Life After Death" in Richard Purtill, *Thinking About Religion* (Englewood Cliffs, New Jersey: Prentice-Hall, Inc., 1978).

All told, our outward behavior is never the whole story regarding our present life and our spiritual unfolding within it. I do not deny that human beings are capable of profound evil, and that some offenses may warrant the full penalty of existing civil law—perhaps, in rare cases, even when this law allows execution. But I do not believe that any offender can be understood solely in terms of the crime he has committed. The wholesale condemnation of this individual fails to acknowledge the conditions that weigh at present upon his choices, conditions that may not afflict most of us.

Suppose, for example, that I have never committed, in all my years, a serious physical assault upon another human being. My sibling, on the other hand, afflicted with a chronic impulse in this direction, by now has committed actions that designate him as a violent offender. When we look at this situation in terms of what kind of men we are—how evolved we are in spirit, "how far we have come"—has my attainment been altogether greater?

Perhaps, too, I am harder driven than he to worldly accomplishment. Am I to be judged as superior in this regard, apart from factors, innate or acquired, that have contributed to the difference? Similarly with other qualities of character, such as generosity and compassion: Such qualities, I believe, are real and prizeworthy. But I do not think that they can be gauged apart from the situation in which they develop. If some man seems to have made less progress than I in this life, it might owe to the fact that he has, in a sense, waded in deeper water. And even if not, given time and opportunity, he may remake himself in ways that we can scarcely foresee. (Could it be, I wonder, that we come to this world, in some cases, taking on certain challenges of our own accord for the sake of our development?)

An example might be found regarding my earlier noted aversion to theft. Though I take some satisfaction in it, this feature of my makeup, if I am to be honest, arose out of an environment that encouraged it. What if I had been raised elsewhere, and subject to different influences?

My delving, of late, into earthy memoirs from the literature of the prize ring provides vivid anecdote as to this varying mesh of environment with human nature. Let us note, for one, the life of Barnet Rasofsky, better known as Barney Ross, a multi-division boxing champion, later a hero of the Second World War—a youngster who grew up in a Chicago ghetto crowded and teeming with trouble during the era of Prohibition.

"Petty thievery," he notes, "was such a common habit among

the kid gangs that I just couldn't have been accepted if I didn't go along with it." He and his accomplices would routinely grab from pushcarts small items—gloves, ties, and socks, along with fruits and vegetables—when a peddler was too tired to notice. A basket of coal, which could bring them a nickel, "used to get three of us into the movies for a triple feature, providing we were willing to squeeze three into a seat."

Some may see in situations like this one merely youth who are morally vacant and unable to grasp the precepts of right and wrong. Others may see in them confirmation of the earlier noted determinism that swallows up moral agency, in cause and effect fashion, as an outmoded illusion.

This latter view may be theoretically possible. Yet young Barnet himself, for what it is worth, would not have endorsed it.

"I used to have," he recalls,

> the most terrible guilt feelings whenever I went out with the boys for a 'snatch.' Stealing, no matter how petty, was ten times worse than fighting—it was a violation of one of the Ten Commandments, and every time I picked up a penny in a milk box, my hand would burn as if I'd touched a live coal...[71]

In reading his words, I am struck by the difference between his life and mine. While circumstance did not justify Barnet's theft, neither can this theft be understood apart from it. Our gauging of such acts should be tempered, in each case, with the realization that we do not know all that is true with others—or even with ourselves.

As to violent behavior, a similar recollection from the ring offers insight. I think of my own upbringing, that of an only child never needing to fight for attention or basic life comforts. Contrast this with the experience of Thomas Rocco Barbella, born shortly after the First World War, his early years divided between Brooklyn and New York City. He came of age in a crowded cold-water flat on the Lower East Side of Manhattan, scarcely conscious of a world outlying.

Powerfully extroverted, craving interaction, he could scarcely endure a day-long stint in a public classroom. His mother spent time, in part of his childhood, in a hospital for the insane. His father Nick, an embittered, hard drinking ex-pug often out of

---

71   Barney Ross and Martin Abramson, *No Man Stands Alone* (Philadelphia: J. B. Lippincott Company, 1957), page 42.

work, had hopes for Rocco's older brother Joe as a prizefighter.

Time and again, starting when he was hardly out of infancy, the younger boy was made to put on gloves and have it out with Joe in the living room. Tears flowing, mouth bloodied, he would recall,

> I would get so mad I couldn't see. I would start lunging with my whole body. I wanted to break him in half. I wanted to kick him and stomp on him and mash his head. But the more I punched, the more he ducked and danced and the more I missed and the madder I got. My father would roar with laughter...[72]

Rocco, as he got older, would turn on the old man after this ugly scene was finished. Finding no more success there, he would later sneak outside to wander the city all night. (But for my ignominious count-out on Big Blanket, I have little to compare with such an episode, which repeated itself many times in this man's formative years.)

A dominant strong-arm figure among his peers, Barbella would spend much of his youth in jails and reformatories. One night he became, on the spur of the moment, *Rocky Graziano* to fight on a local boxing card while AWOL from the US Army. In time he would challenge middleweight champion Tony Zale, the two engaging in wars that some call the greatest trilogy in ring history. He would escape, as well, from the frame of mind that had dominated his young life, awakening to the feel of honest accomplishment and loving relationships more valuable than all the ill-gotten gain in the world.

Spiritual Progress in the Vedic Tradition

Stories like these, I think, and our exploration overall of human behavior, reveal to us the powerful shaping influence of human circumstance upon human behavior. Yet their lesson, I think, is not that human beings are helpless in this regard. Indeed the lives of men like Ross and Graziano provide inspiring examples of the potential that resides within each human individual.

In fact, no amount of acquired data concerning human

---

72   Rocky Graziano and Roland Barber, *Somebody Up There Likes Me* ((New York: Simon and Schuster, 1955), page 18.

behavior, it seems to me, can in principle ever bring us to deny this freedom. For always, no matter how many new facts we acquire, we will be confronted with the question of what we must now *do with them*. And this choice involves value judgment.

Our thought regarding human potential, as I see it, concerns not just this life. It is relevant, as well, to our thinking about a life beyond. Perhaps we should consider what has been said on this topic of human agency by religious sources themselves.

"If I were asked under what sky," declares Max Muller, an extraordinary 19th Century scholar of comparative language and philosophy, "the human mind…has most deeply pondered over the greatest problems of life, and has found solutions…[that] well deserve the attention even of those who have studied Plato and Kant—I should point to India."

While no religious tradition has a monopoly on insight, I am inclined to agree with Muller that there is something special in this one. On matters of the soul and its progression, its subtlety is remarkable. Muller's statement begins Huston Smith's chapter on Hinduism, in which Smith describes the paths of classical yoga, the "yoke" (to use a cognate English word) by which the soul is brought into harmony with ultimate reality. Each path is fitted to the temperamental makeup of the one who embarks upon it. One of these, *karma* yoga, emphasizes the importance of outward effort in the world.

This word 'karma', which gained Western currency with a mid-20th century rise of interest in Far Eastern religion, means actions or deeds, referring not merely to their outward result, but to intentions underlying them. In related use, it refers to cosmic law. Karma, in the sphere of moral action, is a little like *action* and *reaction* in classical physics. My effort, for good or ill, rebounds upon me with the same force, whether it be in this life or in the life to come.

According to Vedic doctrine, says Smith,

> Every action performed upon the external world reacts on the doer. If I chop down a tree that blocks my view, each stroke of the ax unsettles the tree; but it leaves its mark on me as well, driving deeper into my being my determination to have my way in the world.[73]

This notion of moral balance, supposes Indian historian and

---

73   Huston Smith, *The World's Religions,* page 38.

political leader Sarvepalli Radhakrishnan, could have had its first stirring in early observation of the sun, moon, and stars, and the cyclical alteration of the seasons. In time, it would figure deeply into Vedic religion as a principle of cosmic justice. This law concerns not only external appearance, but the quality of the will. Varuna, the god most closely associated with it, cares not only about external conduct, but purity of intention.

"Where law is," states Radhakrishnan, "disorder and injustice are only provisional…The triumph of the wicked is not absolute. The shipwreck of the good need not cause despair."[74]

Religious thought both East and West, John Hick notes in *Death and Eternal Life*, envisions a distant good that exceeds our present imagination. Vedic philosophy conceives of salvation as a oneness with *Brahman*—a realization that Brahman and Self (*Atman*) are ultimately in some sense one and the same. The man who seeks after fleeting scraps of enjoyment in this world is like unto an unhappy soul who wanders after riches without knowing of gold that lies all the while beneath his feet.

No constructive effort, in this life, is ever wasted. When Arjuna, noted at the start of this chapter, is told of the eternal prize that awaits his fulfillment of his warrior duty, he wonders if his effort will be enough. If he strives and falls short, where does it leave him? He forsakes his own security in mortal life, yet does not win liberation. Perhaps, then, he loses out both in this life and the next.

"No, my son," answers Krishna. "That man is not lost, either in this world or the next. No man who seeks Brahman ever comes to an evil end." Such a man, in return for his striving, "will still win the heaven of the doers of good deeds and dwell there many long years." The universe will meet his effort by giving him birth thereafter into circumstances that favor his completion of the task.

As to our progress along the way, there is insightful commentary along this line in a book by Swami Prabhavananda called *The Spiritual Heritage of India*. Actions performed in this life have impact upon us, believes this author, both here and in the life to come. But this impact is finite, according to the energy we have expended within our present span. What heavens or hells await a man after death, says Prabhavananda, "depend entirely upon his moral quality, and…this depends upon his deeds." [75]

---

74   Sarvepalli Radhakrishnan, *Indian Philosophy* (London: George Allen and Unwin Ltd., 1971), Vol. I, page 78.

75   Swami Prabhavananda, *The Spiritual Heritage of India* (Hollywood: Vedanta Press, 1980), page 69.

Such deeds involve not just his observable behavior, but the inward condition out of which they come. This condition, Prabhavananda believes, is a product of his whole life, and even lives before. Each continuing action must be understood in its context—in relation not only to outward circumstance, but the wellspring from which it issues.

"The outward act you perform today, the thought you think, qualify your will of the next moment, your will of tomorrow." Our moral worth at death is determined not merely by the outward record of what we have done, in our present round, but by our inner condition, a "more complex compound" than any chemist can imagine.

Undying Freedom

By the same token, insists Prabhavananda, this causal tie to our past does not make us passive recipients of our fate. The Vedic conception of human destiny, he notes,

> is at no time, or in any sense, fatalistic. The will... has in it an element of complete freedom, a power sufficient to enable a man to act in direct opposition to the... tendency of his accumulated character— and therefore to control his future. [76]

Our makeup—aptitude, temperament, inclination, and more—is shaped and qualified by actions we perform. With habitual debasement, the task of putting life aright becomes ever more difficult. Yet there remains, even in this fallen condition, a deep and undying freedom to move in in a positive direction. Through all of life, in every situation, we have it within us to respond nobly or ignobly to the challenge.

---

76   *Ibid.*, page 70.

Chapter 12

An Awaiting Frontier

*Religion hardens into rigid forms. It is identified by its
devotees with its historic encrustations. It becomes not
a liberator, but a slave-driver to the mind and justifies by
its obscurantisms all that its worst enemies can say about
it. But that is not the true genius of religion as the seers
have known it.*

Harry Emerson Fosdick, Adventurous Religion

It remains to be seen, for those who take seriously the thought
of a life to come, what might be said about that life in positive
terms. Again, it is a strange task, some say a fanciful one,
involving a world as yet unseen, and one that might far exceed
this in its nature and possibilities. Regarding such a world, some
imagine, we cannot have any coherent notion.

Yet perhaps we are not altogether without direction. If this
present life, as religious folk tend to imagine, has a broadly
educative purpose, it must bear some analogy with the next.
Perhaps the next world is not the same for all, but if this life
is relevant to it, in the way that most believers imagine, it is a
world of space and time, of volition and personal interaction,
structurally akin to the one we now inhabit. Truths and ideals
sacred here will hold there, as well. And perhaps things that gave
us fulfillment in this life we will find anew.

Rest—and More

Our thought regarding a future life, notes John Haynes
Holmes, tends often toward *rest*. This is not surprising, perhaps,
given how strenuous are many lives on this side. To want rest,

and to wish our loved ones relief from the strain they endured here, is natural. Yet by itself, I must think, this idea offers little. For we have in us the capacity for so much more.

When I see the hopeful words "rest in peace" (put often as *RIP*) in reaction to the loss of a comrade, I think, even as I share in this hope, that rest is but a small part of what I wish for a man or woman who has thrived in this world. Where, after all, does our present fulfillment reside?

We might do well to think for a moment of what Aristotle maintains in a classic treatise—that our real good lies not just in leisure or pleasant feeling, but in a blessedness of the soul (*eudaemonia*) that involves active *flourishing* in the employment of our human faculties. So do I look back on my most worthwhile times, even into childhood, times I learned, played, taught, and explored—took on challenges and surmounted them. I cannot imagine a meaningful existence apart from this element.

Socrates, as he spoke on his own behalf before the court of Athens at seventy years of age, denied that death, when it comes, merits the fear that so many feel toward it. Our mortal end, he imagined, is apt to be one of two things. In each case, it is a gain.

"Either," he proposed, "it is annihilation, and the dead have no consciousness of anything, or as we are told, it is really a change—a migration of the soul from one place to another."

If the former, "and there is no consciousness but only a dreamless sleep... I call it a gain, because the whole of time, if you look at it in this way, can be regarded as no more than one single night."[77]

A sound night's sleep, as he says, is more welcome than many a day that a man may spend amid the turmoil of this world. Perhaps, then, it is nothing to dread, at least for a man who has lived for seven decades a strong and vigorous life.

But more exciting surely is the latter prospect.

> If... death is a removal from here to some other space, and if what we are told is true, that all the dead are there, what greater blessing could there be than this... Put it this way. How much would one of you give to meet Orpheus and Musaeus, Hesiod and Homer?[78]

---

77   See the Apology, 40c – 41a, Hugh Tredennick, trans. Contained in Edith Hamilton and Huntington Cairns, eds., *The Collected Dialogues of Plato* (Princeton, NJ: Princeton University Press, 1961), page 25.
78   *Ibid.*

Personal Survival and Present Intimation

If there should be, writes H. H. Price in a paper addressing the literature of psychical research, "other worlds than this…who knows whether with some stratum of our personalities we are not living in them now, as well as in this present one which conscious sense perception discloses?"[79]

I think of this passage, now and again, when coming upon lyrical poetry, and ideas that break free of the stagnation afflicting human thought in many arenas. If things should be as Price imagines, Socrates surely would qualify as an archetype. Might it be that some individuals, in every age, are more powerfully attuned than their comrades to a reality that lies beyond?

The mainstream religion of his own day, said Minot Savage, failed to speak meaningfully to anyone possessed of an open heart and mind. Nowhere, he thought, was this failure more prevalent than in its notion of a life to come. We ought to think of the greater life, he insists, not only as a place of rest, or even joy, but one of fulfillment. Rather than a static condition of good feeling, could the next world be a place furthermore of *opportunity* for thought and action that surpasses our present understanding?

He recalls in *Life Beyond Death* a former president of his *alma mater*, prominent in the field of mathematics, who was asked what he hoped to find on the other side. "There are enough problems," replied this old Harvard deacon, "connected with the arc of a circle to keep me busy and happy for at least a thousand years."

Savage notes, in a similar vein, his correspondence with Edward Everett Hale, author, historian, and Unitarian minister, who hoped to see him again on that far shore.

"When we get to heaven," said this kindly soul,

> and have been there a few eons, and had a chance
> to get rested a little and to look around us, I hope
> I shall have an opportunity to get off with you in
> some secluded place and have a leisurely talk

---

79   H. H. Price, "Personal Survival and the Idea of 'Another World'", contained in John Hick's *Classical and Contemporary Readings in the Philosophy of Religion*, page 393. This paper first appeared in Proceedings of the Society for Psychical Research, Vol. I, Part 182 (January 1953).

> about some things that I despair of ever getting
> hold of here.[80]

So, while rest would be welcome, it would hardly suffice to provide our good in the next world, any more than here. Along with rest, concludes Savage,

> this thrilling, throbbing occupation of love and
> service, this thirst of the discovery, of the inventor,
> this genius of the artist, the musician—all that is
> noblest and finest and sweetest here, I believe...
> will find ample scope and unfolding over yonder.[81]

Often, he notes, friends aware of his spiritual bent have asked whether our comrades on the other side are aware of the difficulty we may yet be facing here. If so, are they troubled by it?

Those who have gone ahead, he imagines, will know how we are faring. If they see us, at times, amid trials, it need not diminish their own happiness, for their perspective is different from our own.

> A mother, who sits at home with her little child
> playing at her feet, sometimes has an experience
> like this. The child breaks her doll, or plaything of
> one kind or another; and this is a heartbreaking
> sorrow to the little one; but it does not break the
> heart of the mother... She picks the child up in her
> lap, clasps her to her heart, soothes and comforts
> her. She knows that it is but a passing sorrow, and
> is not going to cloud the child's life forever.[82]

Those who see life from this higher vantage point will not be troubled when "we shed a few tears over a loss [on] Wall Street or...have a pain which may last us for a week. They know what is before us, they know it is to be victory in time..." Perhaps they see that these purging moments are instrumental in readying us for the life that awaits.

Death, agrees Holmes, will not mean an absolute break with the lives we have lived. Nor will we be suddenly transformed into something utterly unlike what we were in our last earthly moments. Rather, "When we open our eyes in the future world,

---

80   *Life Beyond Death*, pp. 292-93.
81   *Ibid.*, 293.
82   *Ibid.*, pp. 281-82.

we shall awake to find ourselves just what we have made of ourselves here."

We will not be what our friends or enemies *think* we are, nor even what we ourselves may think, but only what we have forged daily by the thoughts and deeds, the motives and purposes, that have filled our present lives. Our entry into new life will follow in step with the pervasive *continuity* that characterizes the universe in which we now live—"[it] must begin for each one of us exactly where our present life leaves off."

"I venture to prophecy," he says,

> that life beyond the grave will be in its essence very much like what life is here…namely, a growth or evolution. Heaven is not to be some marvellous wonderland, where growth is to cease in the sudden fulfilment of desire, but [rather will] be a condition in which the soul, at last delivered from the encumbrance of its earthly frame, will continue to unfold and blossom…under more favourable conditions than here are ever known.[83]

Thus we may find this new world to be more generous, more amenable to our efforts than our present one, and our powers heightened in regard to the task. It will pose no limits upon the soul in its voyage of discovery.[84] Rather, it will provide ever further "the chance for labor, growth, and achievement."

Victories, he anticipates, "will be won there beyond all that we had ever dreamed of here," summits gained we have not yet dared. Always will remain "the chance to improve things by our own efforts," to do better, to be more. For that universe, like this one, "is a realm which knows not boundaries, but frontiers."[85]

This notion of a *frontier*—of exploration and discovery in fresh new territory—has always had for me a special resonance. Maybe the feeling is rooted in early childhood, and adventures I saw portrayed (however fancifully, at times) in Golden Age western fare in film and television wherein men and women braved the challenges of an uncharted new world. In Holmes' account this element of adventure is central, as in that of Minot Savage. I think that there is something in this idea, and that our destiny might be best imagined not merely as one of rest, or

---

83   *Is Death the End?*, page 295.
84   *Ibid.*, page 322.
85   *Ibid*

contentment, but also of striving that is consistent with our effort in this present life.

Perhaps we may think of the next life as a varied thing, not a single state, and involving more than a single community. Renowned physicist Oliver Lodge, an early member of the Society for Psychical Research, was much taken by alleged communications that were being investigated by the Society in connection with trans-world mediumship. The picture encouraged by this material, notes Sir Oliver, is not that of a single environment, but a series of places fitted to individual development. We take with us the effects of actions we have committed in this world, and while happiness is abundant on that side, we are not "suddenly transmuted" into new beings on our arrival. There is perhaps likewise "a sorting-out process"[86] whereby we do not enter into company for which we are unready, nor are saddled with company unfitted to ourselves.

Whatever one thinks about such things as séances or automatic writing, such purported revelations are worth consideration, I believe, for their intrinsic content even if we remain unsure of their origin. In some cases, it strikes me, their accounts are more plausible—more in accord with justice and good sense—than those found in mainstream tradition. If so, perhaps their images merit a place in our thinking about this life and where it may lead.

Another Kindred Soul

William James, John Haynes Holmes, Minot Savage—how I loved souls like these, who thrived in a time alive with idea and invention, a time pulsing with interest in the deepest problems of human existence. They were men and women bold and alive with intelligence, ready to uncover truth in every quarter, receptive to new ideas, and to amendment of old ones where warranted.

One more of these, deeply religious and free-thinking, who caught my attention during these years of my own exploration, was Harry Emerson Fosdick. Born in May of 1878 in Buffalo, New York, Fosdick graduated from Colgate University in 1900. He was ordained as a Baptist minister in 1903 in Manhattan and graduated from Union Theological Seminary in 1904.

Unlike Holmes, he supported the war effort in Europe (even if counting himself a "gullible fool" for it afterward). In 1917 he

86   See for example Chapter XII of Oliver Lodge, *Phantom Walls* (London: G. P. Putnam's Sons, 1930).

volunteered as an Army chaplain in France. He became widely known in the following decade during the great controversy involving Modernists and Fundamentalists in American Protestantism.

The latter mindset had gained force in the late 19th and early 20th centuries within various conservative camps. It began as an effort to reaffirm certain tenets of the faith amid changes in the way human beings viewed the world and their own origin within it. The term 'fundamentalist' entered into common parlance with a series of essays called *The Fundamentals* issued in the 1920s by the Testimony Publishing Company of Chicago. These essays stressed biblical inerrancy, the divine nature of Jesus Christ, his virgin birth, his resurrection, and his eventual return to this world as being essential to Christian belief.

In the scriptures Fosdick saw the unfolding of the Divine will, yet unlike these reactionary types he did not insist upon their literal reading, or even their uniform inerrancy. His openness, in this regard, caused him difficulty with the conservative wing. His sermon "Shall the Fundamentalists Win?", delivered on May 21, 1922, at a Presbyterian church, was called by some a brazen heresy.

At the same time, he shared with that element a common ground, upholding the reality of the soul in the face of rising efforts to do away with it, and to reduce human consciousness to events in the natural world. Such accounts, when he investigated them, struck him as being wildly implausible.

Can we really think that selfhood, or moral agency, is a cluster of neural processes? "Was it brain cells," he asks in his 1926 work *Adventurous Religion*,

> [that] by some fortuitous concatenation produced our higher mathematics or [Percy Shelley's] *Ode to a Skylark* or Beethoven's *Fifth Symphony?* Did the cells of the [left frontal brain] convolution move… one happy day to such good effect that they produced the Sermon on the Mount?[87]

Suppose we could rig some device that would allow a subject to examine certain brain processes occurring in his own head. "It would be a curious experience," he points out. *"For who would be doing the watching?"* He finds it odd, if not incredible, that

---

87   Harry Emerson Fosdick, *Adventurous Religion* (New York: Harper and Brothers, 1926), page 192.

these neural entities "could be cleverly looking at themselves."

Adventurous Religion gives lively expression to this spirit of a new and freer faith, embracing the New Testament narrative without the rote adherence that marked much of the Christian mainstream. Need we think, he asks in its opening chapter, that religion must retain its same formulas throughout the whole of human development?

> In all realms, religion included, human life is creative. It spontaneously wells up into new insights and endeavors. It outgrows its old formulations as a child its early clothes. Continuity in any realm of human interest is not to be found in its formulations but in its abiding life.[88]

Thus, for example, health is an ongoing concern, yet medicine, while its aim is constant, is ceaselessly evolving. Beauty, forever prized, finds ever new artistic expression. Perhaps the spiritual life of mankind has room for development, as well. Our relationship with the Eternal, insists Fosdick, will find new expression with the growth of human understanding.

He was mindful, just the same, of how this modernism could empty religion of its content if it lost hold of what inspired its original community. Christianity, he believed, needed to recapture something of its vital origins. Yet this did not mean a rote adherence to tradition. Jesus himself, in fact, did not approach others with a recitation of doctrine, but met each man and woman in spontaneous fashion as the situation required. "He invited each, starting where each was, to begin a spiritual adventure in a hitherto-untried way of living."

Resigning from the First Presbyterian Church a couple of years after his provocative sermon, Fosdick became pastor at the Park Avenue Baptist Church. One quite famous member was the financier and philanthropist John D. Rockefeller, Jr., who would fund the Riverside Church overlooking the Hudson River and Columbia University. Fosdick took the helm when the doors opened in the fall of 1930.

Having antagonized the old guard, Fosdick raised eyebrows, as well, within the news industry. This maverick minister, notes a wry commentary in *Time* magazine,

> proposes to give this educated community a place of greatest beauty for worship. He also proposes

---

88   *Ibid.*, page 6.

Fosdick wrote prolifically during his career on such topics as ethics, prayer, theology and the ministry. Like these other men, he wrote with an urgency and a conviction, and an earthy good sense that is no less impressive a century later. He saw no compromise in the lifting of faith out of its traditional sequestering and its integration into broader life activity. Always he was guided by his conviction regarding the greater scope of human destiny.

Another Shore

Indeed, as noted in the early pages of this book, it must have been cause for joy in those Northern voyagers on the thrashing seas to find new land awaiting. So, too, with the ones who followed. Death, writes Fosdick, is not an end, but an adventure. The believer, he declares, may face it as Columbus faced his first voyage across the great ocean.

"What lies across the sea, he cannot tell; his special expectations may all be mistaken; but his insight into the clear meaning of present facts may persuade him beyond doubt that the sea has another shore."[90]

In reading the words of ministerial authors like Holmes, Fosdick, and Norman Vincent Peale, I am reminded again of Huston Smith's great work. Those who encountered Jesus' early followers, notes Smith, "were as impressed by what they saw as by what they heard."

---

89   *Time* magazine, "Religion: Riverside Church" New York: Time, Inc., October 6, 1930), vol. XVI, no. 14.

90   Fosdick, *The Assurance of Immortality* (New York: The Macmillan Company, 1918), page 141.

simplicity, and cheerfulness that their hearers had nowhere else encountered. Here were people who seemed to be making a success of the enterprise everyone would like to succeed at—that of life itself.[91]

______

91   Smith, *The World's Religions*, page 331.

Chapter 13
The Timeless Philosophy

*Our moral consciousness, when taken in earnest, involves
us in a whole realm of religious truth.*

D. M. Baillie, *Faith in God*

For all that has been said, it must be noted that this notion of
a future life is to many a fanciful thing, one involving a shadowy
existence, as it seems to them, tacked on to the more vivid and
real one they have now. Yet this idea of a future life, as Fosdick
notes, is integral with others that enrich the life we presently live.
"Life beyond the grave," he insists,

> is not an artificial addition to this present existence,
> but a natural continuation of it; if a man is immortal
> at all, he is immortal now. Eternal life is not a
> possession conferred at death, but a present
> endowment, the full appreciation of which
> incalculably deepens, beautifies, and solemnizes
> the meaning of our most common days.[92]

Belief in a future life is part and parcel of a wider view, a
Perennial Philosophy, as noted in the first pages of this book, and
has a connection with beliefs concerning value, agency, and life's
ultimate meaning.

Ideal, Freedom, and Human Potential

I have noted in prior pages the reverence of men like Kant,
Lewis, and John Hick for the moral law. Our embrace of this law,
they imagine, has import moreover for what we believe about the

92   *The Assurance of Immortality* , page 95.

world and our place within it.

Here, as elsewhere, such men may have their differences. They may not think of this law in exactly the same way, or agree upon all points concerning day to day life conduct. Recalling discussion earlier, I doubt likewise that a single *theory* of ethics—Plato, Kant, the utilitarians, and others—each embedded in its own cultural nexus, is apt to give answers satisfactory to all about the nature of good and evil.

What unites these philosophers, and others like them, is a deep and heartfelt sense—a veridical sense, I believe—that this moral dimension of life is a real one; that good and evil are real things, superseding other concerns we have in life, such as material wealth, popularity, and personal standing in the eyes of our fellows.

As Christian scholar D. M. Baillie observes in his 1927 classic *Faith in God*, our moral outlook has implications regarding ourselves and reality.

> Either our moral values tell us something about the nature and purpose of reality…or they are subjective and therefore meaningless. The conviction, 'I ought to do this', if it means anything at all, tells me something not simply about myself or about the action indicated, but about the very meaning of the universe.[93]

In similar fashion, British philosopher Hastings Rashdall, bearing the influence of Kant, takes moral duty as a metaphysical starting point.

> We say that the Moral Law has a real existence, that there is such a thing as an absolute Morality, that there is something absolutely true or false in ethical judgements, where we or any number of human beings at any given time actually think so or not.[94]

If we are subject to this law, says Rashdall, we must suppose that we are not a mere sequence, as some philosophers suppose, of fleeting conscious episodes, but are real and enduring, and

93   D. M. Baillie, *Faith in God and Its Christian Consummation* (London: Faber and Faber, 1964), page 182.

94   Hastings Rashdall, *The Theory of Good and Evil* (Oxford: Clarendon Press, 1907), vol. II, page 211.

are the originating cause of what we do. Our actions must be "the work of a single self which has a definite character of its own, a spiritual character [that] expresses itself in these actions, and which is susceptible of spiritual changes and amenable to spiritual influences."

If we are instead, as materialism would have it, chance entities governed by nature, by-products essentially of material accident, all notion of value and responsibility is illusion. Conversely, if value is real, and our obligations genuine, the self must be a substantial thing, capable of deliberation and responsible, in some measure, for its actions.

As noted earlier, in connection with C. S. Lewis, when it comes to moral law, we are in the realm not of molecules, but of principle. Such a law cannot reside in material things, brute objects that in themselves offer no guideline. It must be a reality of another kind.

While such a reality may seem to some elusive, it is not nothing. Throughout history, and across cultures, it has been acknowledged as the greatest thing of all. Though unseen, it provides the basis for all right living. Sacred in its force, it is sovereign in the realm of practical decision making.

Philosophers have characterized this law in different ways— some see it as an entity on its own, separate from gods of any kind; others (primarily in the Western tradition), as a set of *commandments* expressing a divine will. Rashdall conceives of it (a line of thought somewhat different from "divine command" theory[95]), as *an eternal idea* existing in the mind of God. But however exactly this moral thesis is cashed out, it has import: The bare admission that there is something one *ought to do*—to act, in some given case, in *this* way and not *that*—means that Reality is more than particles and energies in space. It must be understood also in terms of value.

By the same token, if I am obligated, in any given case, to do something, I must have a capacity that lies deeper than material processes. It must be possible for me *to succeed* in this regard or *to fail*—to abide by this demand or to violate it. In which case, the universe has in it, at this moment, more than one potential line of continuation. For I have the capacity to shape its narrative, in some measure, in one direction or another. I must have, in some deep and crucial sense, *moral freedom.*

Further, imagines Rashdall, morality cannot be passive—

---

95   For a current discussion, see for example Chapter 4 of James Rachels, *The Elements of Moral Philosophy* (New York: McGraw Hill LLC, 2023).

it cannot be merely an ideal, but a directive and a revelation concerning the nature of reality. There can be "no meaning in the idea of Morality for a being who is mere Thought and not Will." If our own moral sense reflects the divine will, it tells us something about the way in which reality is moving and the end it will realize.

God, selfhood, freedom, value, life purpose, justice, a continuation of the adventure that has begun here—such things are not isolated notions, but blood-related aspects of a single truth that informs our present existence. Belief in survival, by the same token, has kinship with an earlier noted principle of the moral life, namely the innate and special worth of each human individual. The prospect of a hereafter carries with it the possibility not only of further life, but continued personal evolution. What we see of a human being, recalling the sermon of John Haynes Holmes, is but a hint of what exists in potential.

This connection of religious belief with human potential is captured memorably by Lewis in his essay "The Weight of Glory". It is a serious thing, he observes, to live among "possible gods and goddesses," beings who may one day be vastly more than they are at this present stage of life.

> There are no ordinary people. You have never talked to a mere mortal. Nations, cultures, arts, civilizations—these are mortal, and their life is to ours as the life of a gnat. But it is immortals whom we joke with, work with, marry, snub, and exploit.[96]

A Singular Vision

From Lao-Tzu to Emerson, writes John Haynes Holmes, seers have borne witness to a single truth, a *Perennial Philosophy*, as Aldous Huxley calls it, that gives timeless expression of the human spirit. "It is on the basis of this philosophy," says Holmes,

> that we affirm the existence in the cosmos, and in the heart of man, of a fundamental being which is spirit. In the cosmos, this being is known as God, in the heart of man, it is known as the soul; in relations

---

96   C. S. Lewis, *The Weight of Glory and Other Addresses* (New York: Collier Books, 1990), page 19.

between men, it is known as conscience. [97]

In his Introduction to Swami Prabhavananda's translation of the *Gita*, Huxley summarizes the content of this vision, distilling it into four fundamental and related doctrines:

First, "the phenomenal world of matter and of individualized consciousness…is the manifestation of a Divine Ground within which all partial realities have their being, and apart from which they would be nonexistent."

Second, human beings "are capable not merely of knowing about the Divine Ground by inference; they can also *realize* its existence by a direct intuition, superior to discursive reasoning." This knowledge does not merely add to our store of facts, but further *unites* the knower with what is known.

Third, we possess, in a way, a double nature, "a phenomenal ego and an eternal Self" that is like unto a spark of divinity within the soul. It is possible for us to identify wholly with this greater Self and so with the Divine Ground from which we have issued.

Fourth, our life here on Earth has one ultimate end, which is this union. [98]

This last assertion may give pause to some, who will wonder if it makes our present day-to-day activity—far removed, in most cases, from the cloistered abbey or the Vedic *ashram*—irrelevant to what life is really about. Yet its gist, as I read it, is not that we need abandon our current life's endeavor as builder, planter, educator, or athlete in service to this end. We progress in the spirit when we confront the tasks that stand before us, tasks for which we are presently fitted, advancing with each constructive effort we make. Each effort is indelible, and no such effort is for naught.

This philosophy, as noted in the first pages of this book, is an inversion of the view that reduces all of reality to material accident. It is also perennial—undying—however much or little it is embraced at any time. Always it will return—not merely as style or trend, but of necessity. It lives because it is rooted in human nature, present in each of us even if we are not fully aware of its reality. And it is present not merely by accident, but because it is real.

---

97   John Haynes Holmes, *The Affirmation of Immortality* (New York: The Macmillan Company, 1947), pages 20-21

98   Aldous Huxley, Introduction to Bhagavad-Gita: *The Song of God* (New York: Signet Classic edition, 2002), page 13. Swami Prabhavananda, translator.

This way of understanding, then, is not peculiar to esoteric seers, saints, or scholars. It resides in every human being in some limited fashion. Each glimmer of goodness and inspiration in this life owes to its abiding presence.

And always, it would seem to me, this wisdom was present, in flesh and blood, in the humble example of my mother. Her own open-mindedness—something that proceeded, I believe, from her profoundly giving nature—instilled in me an openness, in turn, to all that life contains. It made me receptive to this philosophy, which unifies all that is positive in our lives, from lofty concern with other worlds to those homely virtues forged in the grind of daily human existence.

From Ego to *Atman*

Here, as elsewhere, culture has a shaping influence. Our notions of who we are and where we are headed bear a conspicuous tie with the world into which we are born and within which we are raised. Observe, he says, the lush hunting ground of many Native Americans, or the great castle scene of Valhalla envisioned by Norsemen. The Islamic picture, expressed in the *Qur'an*, abounds in gardens, fountains, and beautiful maidens.[99] The Christian New Testament speaks in its final book of walls made of jasper, streets of transparent gold.

While some will see in these images merely the quaint limits of human imagination, each has in it, I suspect, some intimation of what awaits an individual according to the world of activity in which for now he is immersed. This life provides many lines of human development, and we might imagine them—as with the pursuit, say, of mathematics noted earlier—continuing beyond.

Still, at some point, we find ourselves asking how far such lines extend.

Some years ago the Reverend Billy Graham remarked that recently he had asked his wife if she thought there would be *golf* in heaven. She replied that golf, were it essential to his happiness, would be there.

While the exchange may have been lighthearted, Mrs. Graham's response, I think, is an apt one. Recalling discussion in the last chapter, our interests in this world are probably not left behind all at once on our departure from it. But such interests,

99   See Chapter VIII of *Is Death the End?* (New York and London: G. P. Putnam's Sons, 1915

by the same token, reflect in each case particular stages in our personal development. Changes may occur hereafter that outstrip anything we can foresee. Thus even if our present activities continue, in some fashion, in the life to come, regarding things in the distant future we have perhaps only the barest inkling.

I am reminded, in this vein, of another case from the rough-hewn lore of the prize ring. Many years ago, a sporting monthly ran a piece on the great middleweight champion Harry Greb, who thrived in the years of the teens and 1920s. A veteran of more than 300 professional contests, Greb ranks high to this day on "all-time" lists within the sport. The author recounted Greb's battles, and ended on a reverential note, saying that Harry would continue to fight them for all eternity.

I shared in the spirit of this statement, which of course was not meant to describe the far reaches of heaven, but to hail the timeless courage that infused Greb's ring career. We can imagine this activity, I think, extending beyond this earthly round should it be essential to Greb's fulfillment. But it is hard to think of ring contests—or mortal contests of any kind, really—resurrected without end, or any man's fulfillment requiring it. Even within this life, our inclinations can change markedly, and our pursuits with them. (To cite an example close at hand, the great Mickey Walker, arch-rival of Harry in the ring, began a career as a canvas oil painter when his ring days were over.)

A more promising line of thought, when we try to envision our remote destiny, may lie at another level. Our moral trajectory, as John Hick notes, takes us always from self-centered existence to something communal—a journey, as he terms it, from *egoity* to *personhood*, or borrowing from the language of the ancient Vedas, "from ego to *Atman*."

Our present life, as noted earlier, bids us to respect human beings, whether others or ourselves, as "ends in themselves." For Kant, this demand was inseparable from religion. For our moral progress, he believed, is coherent only if it extends beyond this brief mortal existence.

Hick sees in this progress likewise an intimation of our destiny. The ego, he states, is "an enclosed entity, constituted and protected by its boundaries." As such, it is *atomic*, excluding and excluded by others of the same sort. Our greater self, by contrast, is essentially *interpersonal* and finds purpose also in the welfare of others. (One upshot of this situation, says Hick, is that there must be two persons, in effect, if one is to exist at all.) Our flourishing as human beings requires that we engage ourselves in the world as more than merely self-interested seekers.

As we move in this direction, he imagines, boundaries between us may diminish and our existence may become "more corporate than individual." The developed personality is essentially outward-looking. Ego is a limit upon this development. A liberated individual, Hick suggests, may be one without "egoity"—"a living consciousness which is transparent to…other consciousnesses…in a full community of love."

He offers, then, "the picture…of personal centres without… peripheries. They will have ceased to be mutually exclusive and will have become…open to one another in a richly shared consciousness." They may "experience an intimacy…which we can at best barely imagine."

Is our progress endlessly temporal, and achieved in an embodied state? Time, as he notes, is the dimension in which change takes place, and so seems essential to development of any kind. Our development here and now involves the interaction of distinct persons within a common and sometimes competitive environment. But in the far distance, it may be different. The world's faith traditions converge in their recognition of a unitive state, far beyond this life and transcending what we presently understand. Perhaps, at some point now remote, a mutual love shall become, Hick imagines,

> the universal principle of life, whilst self-protective egoity withers away, so that the individual's series of lives culminates…in a last life beyond which there is no further embodiment but instead entry into the Common Vision of God, or *nirvana*, or the eternal consciousness of *atman* in its relation to Ultimate Reality.[100]

Here, it seems, we verge upon conceptual limit. Perhaps, at some point, we can only trust in Providence to bring about the end that we cannot yet wholly fathom. Still, I sense that there is something in Hick's line of thought for us here and now. In reading his words, I am reminded, too, of John Haynes Holmes' discussion years earlier.

Our knowledge in this world, maintained Holmes, is a fragmented and largely exterior thing, involving glimpses of each other's habits and interests. It is qualified as well by the present

---

100   John Hick, *Death and Eternal Life* (Louisville, Kentucky: Westminster / John Knox Press, 1984), pages 463-64.

limits of our own comprehension. Might it be that such knowledge is "only the beginning of a knowledge which, in the end, far transcends all the conditions of this material environment?"

In last analysis, "we are not bodies at all, but souls," and any real knowledge we may have of one another, must be knowledge at this level. Perhaps with time, in a freer medium, this knowledge will go deeper. Ultimately, it may be, "Soul will call to soul, and answer from each to each will never fail. Spirit will commune with spirit in that sweet language of mystic intuition which needs no words to speak its meaning."[101]

This photo comes from one of my trips to Minnesota. The night before I left, I took this picture of Bea, Mama's younger sister, whose lifespan would exceed hers by the better part of three decades. Their resemblance is strong, and this image reveals in Bea the same quiet dignity that was present in Etta.

Divine Grace and Daily Diligence

Great and fundamental questions, observes Huston Smith in *The World's Religions*, tend to divide human beings on their relationship to one another and to the universe. To cite one example, is reality, when all is said and done, *friendly* or not? Is it essentially on our side, or are we on our own? Each philosophical

101   *Is Death the End?*, page 305.

tendency can be found in the world's faith traditions, where one may emphasize help from on high, and another the concrete and assiduous task of daily striving.

Original Buddhism, Smith notes, leaned decisively in the latter direction when the rebel saint Gautama, dissatisfied with a currently decaying Vedic system, chose to break with it. To this end he purged his community of certain elements that many think essential to religious life. One of these was *ritual*, which in its current form had become an impediment to spiritual progress. Another was *grace*, the notion that the universe might occasionally reach down, as it were, to lend us a hand when needed.

In time there arose a wider Buddhism—the Mahayana "great raft" that offered salvation to the masses, and that brought back these elements in a healthier, less manipulative form than was the case in the Buddha's own lifetime. Buddhism and Hinduism would each flourish in coming centuries, the latter at last acknowledging, in its fluid and giving fashion, the wisdom of the man who had left it to begin anew.

Does the universe extend itself, now and again, to give us what we cannot manage on our own? Such a belief is essential to Christian life in each of its major branches. The best description of salvation from a Christian perspective, in my experience, came from a man who was now essentially a Hindu. During that period of darkness in my second year at Clark, in 1970-71, I attended an informal weekly session in meditative yoga at a community center in downtown Vancouver.

Our leader George, a tall and gentle soul about thirty years of age, had undergone a very deep spiritual search that began in his adolescence. He once described to a couple of us, when we were talking one night at his apartment, an experience during his time in a Christian commune devoted to the "born again" brand of faith that flourished during those troubled years in American culture.

Imagine yourself, he said, thrashing in a dark storm on the high sea, feeling you had spent your last strength. Then, unexpectedly, a hand reaches down and lifts you free. This was how salvation felt.

I understood this picture well from my time at Lighthouse Mission, the charismatic church in that sector of Old Portland I attended in my Senior year of high school. It was a place of genuine worship, a place wherein surrender of personal will to the divine power had given its members a release from the ego-ridden existence they had known.

George had an acute understanding of this phenomenon, even if he did not share the outlook of the people in that old style commune where he had once resided. I, too, was impressed when seeing this brand of faith, a faith that captured the energy perhaps of the early Christian community described by Huston Smith

One emphasis or another, grace or diligence, will inform religious life wherever it may take root. Perhaps there is wisdom in each. The people at the Mission, for example, were keenly devoted to "getting right with God" in their daily conduct, as are many Christians who feel a divine presence in their lives. The early Buddhist *sangha*, a community rooted in Vedic Indian tradition and predating Christianity by half a millennium, had a different conceptual scheme. The Buddha wanted no reliance on the popular gods, bidding his followers, when he was near his mortal end, to work out their salvation with diligence.

My mother was raised in a tradition that emphasized grace—help from above—in the life of the spirit. Yet, too, as Pastor Kunz noted, her life was one of energetic service. Her faith went deeper than one I would see often in coming years, brandished by sing-song types who enjoyed a special status, they imagined, though this status, I would notice, seemed to have little bearing upon their everyday conduct.

Mama's faith made a mockery of "televangelist" types purportedly filled with the spirit of God while mired off-camera in an array of personal scandal. It was with her to the end as she lay in that bed during those last few days at St. Joseph's Hospital. Ethel Marie did not have the chance, in her youth, to acquaint herself with the fantastic array of viewpoints available to those who live in the academic world. But she understood life more deeply than many of those who publicly expound upon it.

Despite her faith commitment, as I say, she was able to see wisdom in people in traditions removed from her own. It was owing to her, I think, that I found it easy to do the same. Around the time I was teaching philosophy at Clark College, shortly after that fateful summer of 1981, I attended a convention in the Portland area hosted by the leaders of various conservative Christian churches dealing with issues in the faith. Certain points of doctrine, noted one participant, seem to be open to personal reading.

Might it be, he suggested, that God did not intend every point of belief to be explicit in His message to humanity? Perhaps these gray areas gave believers a chance to learn respect for others within the fold whose outlooks differed from theirs. In hearing these words, it occurred to me (though I did not venture to make a point of it), that differences also on a larger scale, between whole faith traditions across the span of human civilization, might provide such a test.

Old Virtues

These high-reaching questions about future worlds and human enlightenment are always connected, in my thought, with concrete examples of personal rectitude one finds in the ground-level drama of daily life.

I am reminded once more, for example, of Mama's response when I came into the orbit of young proselytizers of the Nichiren Buddhist tradition. I think, too, of her modesty. Some today might dismiss this feature of her makeup as mere *naïveté*. Her concern with attire, for example, as shown by her reaction to the Confirmation photo, belongs to an era that will strike many as being less savvy, less acute, than the one that has followed.

Then again, maybe genuine wisdom is sometimes forgotten. My own adolescence saw a driving trend, in popular culture, away from the older sensibility. While I shared, in some measure, in the spirit of this new wave—its casual manner of speech and dress, for one, and its willingness to challenge longstanding institutions of authority—there was a limit to my enthusiasm. In some quarters, its sound, its gloat, its manipulative advocacy of "free love" and knee-jerk resentment of authority, warned me away from it.

One casualty of this movement was a loss of self-restraint. Another and related loss was that of courtesy. It was no longer thought important to maintain a sense of tact or propriety in social discourse. Vulgarity was embraced, and conservatism was seen as mere hangup and false inhibition. Recent decades have shown little reversal of this trend, as insult, embarrassment, and "in your face" confrontation become the stuff of entertainment.

In recent years, *civility* has come under criticism, discounted as a remnant of a European culture concerned merely with superficial appearances. Such concern, it is said, inhibits the expression of those seldom heard folk who have not been accorded a place within present day society. In response to this claim, Alexandra Hudson composed her treatise *The Soul of Civility*.

While acknowledging truth in this criticism, Hudson distinguishes between this virtue and that of mere *politeness*, which involves a smoothing or (to use a cognate word), *polishing* effort in the give and take of personal interaction.[102] Civility, by contrast, its name rooted in Latin discourse regarding the state and its citizens, goes deeper, requiring a sincere and constructive attitude toward others, respecting their innate worth as individuals.

This virtue, as she notes, is timeless. The same may be said for others, whether they are in vogue or not at any given time. A few years before Mama was born, Presbyterian Church leader Robert Elliot Speer published a book called *The Marks of a Man,* which dealt with virtues essential to Christian faith. Among these were purity, patience, and an unflagging adherence to truth.

There are several ways, says Speer, in which we may react to evil, one being indulgence and another being constant indignation. Better than these, he believes, is the innocence that the Apostle Paul recommended to early Christian communities in places like Rome and Corinth. Men are drawn to evil for its diversion, imagining that life is improved by the variety it provides. In so doing they are compromised, and made victim to a life-dulling monotony all its own. In purity, by contrast, they find freedom and power.

My own life, by now, has strayed at times from this purity of which Speer writes. Yet I find something worth note in his discussion of the way in which the qualities of the soul are displayed. To cite a small scale example, one might consider language.

"Men begin to swear," he observes,

> as an enrichment of the vocabulary. But nothing so contracts and impoverishes human speech. After a little while the profane man becomes the slave of a dozen oaths, perhaps of only one or two. All the emotions which his soul feels, all the judgments of his intellect, have to be expressed in these few words.[103]

More than a hundred years later, the situation is worse than it was in his time. At times I see young people with strong potential who have never learned how to exploit the depth and richness of their own language. With this contraction comes not just verbal

---

102   See, for example, the introductory section of Hudson's The Soul of Civility (New York: St. Martin's Press, 2023).

103   Robert Speer, *The Marks of a Man – Or, The Essentials of Christian Character* (New York: Fleming H. Revell Company, 1907), page 63.

atrophy, but a loss of sensibility.

How one uses words is not merely a point of style, but a reflection of inner development. Modesty involves not mere restraint upon natural urge, but an expression of inner decency. In Etta's modesty, and that of others like her, is something timeless.

While virtues may wane, for a time, they remain real. The strength to withstand physical stress, for example, without making a conspicuous show of it, was a virtue largely forgotten, noted William James early in the 20th century. But it was a virtue no less. Tact, modesty, self-containment, the endurance of which James speaks (qualities that would reside in this young woman all her life), are as valuable now as ever.

This concern with language provides a small yet instructive example of that truth Huxley describes. One of the clearest indications of our constitution, says the Stoic philosopher Epictetus, is our use of words. ("Laugh *with*," he cautions, "but never *at*.") When the Buddha laid out his Eightfold Path to *nirvana*—to the great deliverance from all worldly limit—he included "right speech" as a part of it.

These virtues, as the Buddha saw them were not mere checklists that bid us to avoid violations: They were matters for reflection and scrupulous daily effort. Right speech, as I think of it, does not mean mere avoidance of gross insult or profanity. We ought to ask, moreover, are the words we deliver in daily life honest ones? Are they uplifting and constructive? Are they just? (Do they acknowledge, say, the achievement of people for whom we feel no affection, and whose success we do not enjoy?)

Mama, in fact, could be earthy and plain in her words, her tone of voice turning an occasional four-letter utterance to humorous effect. But the words were never brazen, never insulting. Not once in her seven decades, I think, did she take pleasure in the discomfort of another human being. She spoke with encouragement to all who entered her company.

Faith and Action

Divine grace and personal diligence—some traditions emphasize one aspect of salvation, some the other, according to their historical setting. Yet perhaps these two, again, are not antagonistic, but complementary. While a reliance upon Providence is vital to my own religious understanding, I reject the "all or nothing" mentality of believers who suppose that they are made right in their spiritual condition by their faith declarations.

More vital to my own outlook is Smith's passage regarding the impact of the ax on the tree, and the continuous impact likewise of our own willing actions upon our spiritual condition. Each effort in a positive direction ennobles me; each effort the other way moves me back. All day long, we make of ourselves something different, for better or worse, by our concrete choices.

In my mother's homespun wisdom, I find a marvelous distillation of this truth. She and I, as I have recalled throughout these chapters, were always sharing thoughts amid difficulties that arose during our years together. She said to me once, regarding some conundrum that had me troubled, and recalling perhaps what some wise soul said once to her, "Pray as if it all depends on God. Then act as if it all depends on you."

Chapter 14
Reflections

Knowledge can grow to all eternity and yet not exhaust reality. Our direct awareness is only of...aspects... accessible to our animal senses. We see only material things and they are not ultimately satisfying. We are conscious of a yearning to go beyond them; we feel that we are dwellers in an unseen reality of which we catch only occasional glimpses.

Sir Oliver Lodge, *Phantom Walls*

In this chapter, I offer a few thoughts regarding the activity of philosophy and how it may take shape within the heart of one who explores it. In the process, I try to convey something of the conceptual stance that is involved in a spiritual life outlook.

In ancient wisdom East and West, I believe, is insight superseding much that one finds in thought that is current. I believe, too, that philosophy, as Miguel de Unamuno declares, is in each case a product not merely of reason, but of what he calls the *humanity* of each philosopher. Reason, though essential to philosophy, is grounded always in the deeper constitution of the man or woman who practices it.

A Classic Scene

When Socrates was found guilty by the court of Athens, he was allowed by law to propose an alternative sentence for the jury's consideration.

Professing himself to be innocent, proposing that he receive honor in place of punishment, he hears the original sentence reaffirmed. He spends his waning hours in a prison cell consoling his young friends with the idea that death will bring his passage into greater life.

Socrates, Walter Kaufmann once said, might have been the greatest man who ever lived. A warrior cited for bravery in the conflicts of Sparta and his native Athens, an unfailing friend, a philosophical inquirer without an equal, he was unflinching at the verdict of the court.

In that cell, awaiting the hemlock he would lift to his lips, he did not waver. When asked by his friend Crito if he had advice to offer those he was leaving, he told them to act as he had always bid them in their marketplace go-rounds. Virtuous action would benefit each of them, here and hereafter, whatever fortune this passing world might bestow.

How, asked the distraught comrade, should they bury him?

"Any way you like," he replied,"…if you can catch me, and I don't slip through your fingers."[104]

He looked to the others, saying he could not make Crito see that *he* was not the thing they would shortly be tossing away as he departed for the world of the blessed.

Philosophy as a Product of "Humanity"

A benchmark of mainstream philosophy's attitude, where things of the spirit are concerned, might be found in a parallel dialogue by John Perry, first published in the 1970s, that reaches an opposite conclusion.[105]

In this one, a mirror-image reversal of the classic, the central figure is a female philosophy instructor who has suffered mortal injury in a motorcycle accident. As her end nears, still lucid, Gretchen Weirob spends her time listening to close friends, each seeking to console her with hope of a life beyond. With all the cunning of a 20th century analyst, she confounds her visitors with arguments that challenge their beliefs and spell her own annihilation.

To some in the field, I am sure, this dialogue represents two and a half millennia of *progress*: In it, they see a quaint and very old pre-scientific optimism overridden by hard and unrelenting insight. I doubt, however, that the wisdom of Perry's Gretchen

104   *Phaedo* 1154 b-d, contained in *Plato: The Last Days of Socrates* (London: Penguin Classics, 2003), page 195.

105   John Perry, *A Dialogue on Personal identity and Immortality* (Hackett Publishing Company, 1978).

exceeds that of Socrates.

I doubt, too, that philosophy exhibits straightforward progress over the course of its history. Perhaps it does yield with time an advance, of sorts, its principal figures in each era reacting logically to their predecessors and influencing in turn those to come. But its predominant voice, at any given time, need not express altogether greater wisdom than do the voices preceding. Its activity is not a positive stairstep climb.

In a typical history of thought, notes Unamuno at the outset of his most famous work, systems of thought are often presented as a grand logical unfolding, their ideas "growing out of one another spontaneously" with their authors appearing essentially as historical footnotes. Yet it is the inner flesh and blood dramas of these men and women that make sense of what we read. Philosophy, as he reckons it, is the product not merely of rational inference, but of each philosopher's own humanity. Each, in the end,

> is a man of flesh and bone who addresses himself to other men of flesh and bone like himself. And, let him do what he will, he philosophizes not with the reason only, but with the will, with the feelings, with the flesh and with the bones, with the whole soul and the whole body. It is the man who philosophizes.[106]

It may be, as someone once said, that philosophy is best likened not to a set of stairs, but to a range of peaks, varying in height, its wisdom distributed across the centuries. Its prevailing mindset, at any given moment, expresses not so much advancement as cultural mood-swing that may give way to another mood in time.

Materialism and Personal Intuition

Again, as James asks, which world has our allegiance? Rational inquiry does not produce this allegiance, but rather proceeds from it.

This present world, flooding us with impact from our first waking moment, is for some the only one worth concern. Maybe it is no surprise that such a mindset should dominate this present age, where scientific advances of the past few centuries, as Walter

---

106   *The Tragic Sense of Life*, page 28.

Stace notes,[107] have so powerfully shaped human experience that today we see the world habitually in terms of its mechanics, rather than its purpose.

In materialism some find, too, a logical elegance wherein reality, in last analysis, is all neatly of a kind. At times, I detect an emotional element, as well, in this view, a visceral antagonism to religion (one that may owe, as I have noticed on occasion, to early encounter with an abusive religious mindset).

And still, in every age, are some who feel the pull of a world unseen. There are, as James puts it, "tough" and "tender" minds, one concerned fundamentally with what is seen and touched, the other with something more. A fathomless gulf, it seems, separates these types, neither able to sway the other with its argument.

"It is," writes James in the *Varieties* concerning this latter type, "as if a bar of iron, without touch or sight, might nevertheless be...endowed with an inner capacity for magnetic feeling," sensing at times something unseen in its vicinity.[108]

When listening to materialists, I am reminded of how different they are from those of us who feel this inner pull. At times, for example, they speak with disdain for the notion of *having* a soul—some gratuitous wraith, as they seem to imagine it, added on to what is real and primary.

Be there souls or not, I say in turn, this is hardly the way that religious people understand themselves.

"I do not believe for a minute," remarks Minot Savage, "that I have a soul...I believe I am a soul, and have a body."[109]

In these words is expressed the core of my own sensibility.

My aversion to equating selves with bodies extends to common practices that have dominated western culture for many generations. I know not what to make, for example, of persons who "visit" their departed loved ones in graveyards to tell them what they might not hear otherwise.

Nor, I confess, without meaning to antagonize those who earn their living in the funeral industry, do I grasp the ceremony that has as its centerpiece the mortal remnant of one who has passed

---

107   See Stace's article "Man Against Darkness", contained in Steven Sanders and David R. Chaney, eds., *The Meaning of Life* (Englewood Cliffs, New Jersey, Prentice-Hall, Inc., 1980).

108   William James, *The Varieties of Religious Experience* (New York: Penguin Group, Inc., 1982), page 55. This volume, which represents James' Gifford Lectures at the University of Edinburgh, was first published by Longmans, Green, and Co. in 1902.

109   *Life Beyond Death,* page 211.

from this world. (*A life celebration*, filled with recollections of that individual and his time on Earth, seems apt and fitting. But memorial services in the old style, the stiff remains of the departed cosmetically freshened and on display, good land used for its disposal afterward, seem quite different.)

I do not fathom, either, the linguistic mode in which many speak when referring to loved ones who have gone before them. We hear how this friend or family member "would have been" pleased, or flattered, or made proud by something—say, by an apt eulogy, or by the success of her children—if only they had been alive to witness it. Not *would have been*, I say, but *are*. Let others, if they wish, speak of their loved ones in a hypothetical manner—I speak in the actual, saying that such a thing fills them with pride, with joy, with satisfaction now, when they see it from a vantage point better than they had in this life.

Thus I was enlivened, to cite a piece of dialogue from popular film, when seeing the 1992 neo-western motion picture *Thunderheart*, a mystery drama involving governmental corruption on a Sioux reservation. Toward the end, the protagonist Ray (Val Kilmer) wishes that their deceased ally had been with them to see climactic events that have just transpired.

Replies Walter Crow Horse (Graham Greene), a resident police detective who by now has become his friend, "She *was*, Ray."

By the same token, I cannot see kindred souls, in this life, as beings who incidentally share our life for a time and then leave it. True, this intersection of lives may be limited, and circumstance may remove them from this world altogether while we remain. But I cannot see it as a final parting.

As Walter tells Ray, when they go their ways at the close, there is no word in their language for a final *good-bye* to those with whom we have tread the path. I do not know enough about the Lakota language to say if this is true, but I know that there is no such word in mine.

Selfhood in the Vedic Tradition

Whole traditions of thought, one finds when coming onto them, differ fundamentally in their sense of what is real. The student who enters a classroom to explore Vedic Indian philosophy finds himself at once in a world different from the one down the hall that is haunted by Hume, Comte, and Bertrand Russell. Certain things that require argument, in the Western analytical tradition, are so deeply a part of India (in its dominant tradition, at least), that they are implicit in its outlook.

The Vedic tradition of yoga, to note again the discussion of Huston Smith, developed along multiple lines, accommodating the different personal types who wished to pursue it. These lines are like unto paths, varying in angle and terrain, yet leading to a single peak. The verification of this outlook is found not by way of logical proof, but in firsthand realization.

The classic *jnana* path, fitted to a reflective temperament, emphasizes conceptual activity. Its basis, says Smith, "is discrimination, the power to distinguish between the surface self that crowds the foreground of attention and the larger self that is out of sight."

As training unfolds, the student studies the classic scriptures, and is encouraged to reflect upon basic questions regarding human identity. Everyday habits of thought and speech give us opportunity for this exercise. The word "my", for example,

> always implies a distinction between the possessor and what is possessed; when I speak of my book or my jacket, I do not suppose that I am these things. But I also speak of my body, my mind, or my personality, giving evidence thereby that in some sense I consider myself as distinct from them as well. What is this "I" that possesses my body and mind, but is not their equivalent?[110]

By the same token, "science tells me that there is nothing in my body that was there seven years ago, and my mind and my personality have undergone similar changes." Yet throughout these turnovers, I seem to endure. There is something—*someone*—who lasts through them, making me profoundly the same individual across ongoing change.

Such exercises stir in the practitioner a deeper sense of what selfhood involves. They pave the way for effort that in time will drive a wedge between the limited self and the greater reality—*Atman*—that is celebrated in the ancient texts.

---

110   *The World's Religions*, page 30.

An Odd Moment on the Highway

Ancient wisdom is present, as well, in scripture central to our own culture. In the third chapter of Genesis, deceived by the serpent, Adam and Eve partake of fruit that was forbidden to them. Soon after, God calls out to Adam, asking him to give account of himself.

"It is easy," to quote Smith again, "to smile at the anthropomorphism of the early Hebrews, who could imagine ultimate reality…walking in the Garden of Eden in the cool of the morning." But when we make our way through the *poetic concreteness* of this image to its underlying claim, we may decide otherwise.

These ancient people, Smith says, were seeking to comprehend the immense reality by which people everywhere are confronted, a reality whose handiwork the heavens declare. In human beings, they found "greater depth and mystery…than in any of the other wonders at hand." The image found in Genesis expresses a basic conviction: Ultimate Reality "is more like a person than a thing, more like a mind than a machine."

Might it be that these people were in advance of many today, who see in human nature merely a product of blind accident?

Following my return to the Northwest in 1986, I hosted parties each Fourth of July, the hillside providing an ideal spot from which to view the huge annual fireworks display at Pearson Air Park a few miles off.

I remember one occasion when my dear friend Tom Donovan, who had taught Latin years earlier at Hudson's Bay, was on hand. Tom and I had become reacquainted several years prior when a girlfriend and I would see him Friday nights at a pizza parlor a few blocks south of Tom's three-story house on West 29th Street, a magnificent structure that his father had built in the 1920s.

I introduced him to Franz Mayr, a prodigious veteran scholar at the University of Portland with whom I had worked when completing requirements for the Claremont degree. Tom and Franz, each a free-thinking academician raised in the Roman Catholic tradition, felt an immediate kinship. (Through Franz, Tom was able to pick up adjunct work teaching Latin on the UP campus into his late 80s.)

"Some of these analytical types," Franz sighed when we were musing over our profession, "work themselves to death trying to understand *personal identity*." (Though a casual remark, it had me seeing the legendary Sisyphus roll his rock up the hill.) Franz realized that human beings have in them something that resists clinical dissection.

Thinking back, I recall an episode around this time that furnished an end to any doubt I had regarding the legitimacy of my basic life outlook. Strange as it may seem in the telling, it gave me peace.

I was on the I-5 freeway heading south across the Interstate Bridge to downtown Portland. For some reason, running through my mind at that moment were the many things I had heard skeptics say, over the years, about life and value.

There are times, even in the mind of a believer, when all this business of hidden worlds and higher truths does seem fantastic. Do our departed loved ones actually carry on activity right now in some realm invisible to those of us left behind? Perhaps our cherished ideals are what reductionists make of them, mere phantasms grounded in human impulse, our whole existence a fleeting byproduct of happenstance.

I had long harbored, of course, a different view, but maybe the view was grounded more in longing than in logic. Value, love, selfhood, freedom, all that was central to my life—I tried now to step away and see it as accident, as the tenuous pale froth on this great molecular wave that materialism would make of it. Was this the way to real understanding?

Off to my right, as if in reply, passed a weathered transport rig. I saw, as it rolled on into the distance, the words posted on the back:

Don't Worry About It.
So, odd as it may sound, ended my perplexity.

Personal Integrity and the Limits of Reason

Here and there, in these pages, I have expressed dissatisfaction with the going tendency of academic philosophy. I have said things that run contrary to its going mindset, and an episode like the one just noted might suggest that I have taken leave of its enterprise altogether.

Be this as it may, and whatever my success or failure within its arena, my regard for philosophy has grown with the years. I have been enriched by every book, every article, every encounter in the classroom that has filled these past decades. Clarity, formal rigor, inspiration, awakening—new insight, and the crystallization of things that perhaps I knew, at some level, yet could stand to hear again; these are among the things that philosophy may provide. Its enterprise has heightened my sense of intellectual integrity.

As to the last point, the greatest discussion I have found is contained in Kaufmann's *The Faith of a Heretic*. Now and again, when teaching an introductory class, I have used it as an overture.

As Kaufmann notes, there are few things about which we are less honest than honesty itself. Where our own honesty is concerned, our very framing of the question reveals a lack of commitment. We ask *whether* we are honest, supposing maybe that if we have not told a bald-faced lie in recent memory, we pass the test. But this is not enough. Honesty, as Kaufman reminds us, is not a destination, but a quest, something toward which we may strive each day of our lives.

"Instead of asking whether you are honest or a liar,"

> ask how you might become more honest. The answer: by raising your standards and by cultivating the habits of honesty—developing a keen intellectual conscience. And what does that involve? Intellectual imagination, carefulness, conscientiousness, scrupulousness—making one's beliefs and statements matters of conscience. The man who lacks such standards may be honest— but not very. He has low standards of honesty.[111]

One might use an analogy with courage, which can be distinguished in its physical and moral aspects. Old fashioned German education, says Kaufmann, emphasized the former, which forbid outright lying and could move a man to risk his life in battle. It was less concerned with a willingness to buck authority, "pitting integrity against power." We might think of honesty along similar lines, its physical type pertaining to overt behavior, its moral type involving a less conspicuous triumph over self-deceit.

The quest for honesty is not like "a search for a jewel" that ends happily, once and for all, with what is sought after. Rather it is part and parcel of a quest for excellence, an ongoing effort that finds ever new opportunities within the coarse grain of daily existence. Yet this quest, I believe, will vary with the spiritual condition of the one who undertakes it. The man or woman attuned solely to this world will accept only the things that

---

111   *The Faith of a Heretic*, page 24.

outward investigation can establish. For those attuned otherwise, it will be different.

Which attunement, some may ask, is better? Such a question, as I see it, reaches down into territory that cannot be logically settled. An inquiry into the meaning of life asks not merely about particular events in the world, or relations between ideas, but addresses us at the very core of our being. My own way of doing philosophy differs from that of someone who sees it as a discipline grounded entirely in material science.

If two philosophers arrive at different views of reality, it is not because one is decisively more clever than the other, but because each begins with his own sense of what is real and primary in human experience. Where one may find in this world a great receptacle of space and energy, dark and accidental, another sees in it a miracle of sound and light, an occasion for the unfolding of the human spirit.

If this *love of wisdom* is to speak to all who explore it, it will make a radical admission. It will acknowledge the possibility that wisdom is distributed, across eras and individuals, more widely than most of its devotees imagine. It will open itself to the possibility that some people, even if they lack formal training, have a wisdom that is absent in many a trained scholar.

The Fundamental Choice

Early childhood joys, Mr. May's class, bright June days and trampolines, the thrills of the ring and the ballfield, the treasures of downtown Portland and saltwater plunges into the Pacific, every moment I ever spent with my mother—for some, nostalgia has in it a sadness, a longing for something now gone and never to return. But to me, these moments beckon forward. They contain in them a harbinger of what lies ahead, a life that stands to this one as the waking world to a dream.

Which, then, ought to guide a man—the in-fashion pronouncements of the professional skeptic or his own deepest instincts? Suppose, for example, that some analyst produces a cogent treatise denying the reality of free will. Should I now drop my existing outlook and imagine that I am, as this author would have it, an organic machine causally bound by molecular accident? Or should I believe what every red-blooded man (and perhaps down deep, the analyst himself), believes, that now and again there arises a situation requiring of him a free and vital choice?

While it will be scandal to some who ply my trade, that moment crossing the I-5 Bridge dispelled my doubt as to the validity of my lifelong outlook. All at once I saw the vanity of materialism and the effort to fit myself, even momentarily, into its mental compartment. I knew that the saner choice was to trust my instincts, leaning upon special moments and precious souls who have bolstered me in life. I never again felt the need to spend time digesting the treatises of authors blind to the things of the spirit. And I would never feel that my farewell to such an endeavor cost me an ounce of integrity.

As to the claim that human beings are causally bound by their circumstance, we might look to the account provided by philosopher and psychoanalyst Viktor Frankl relating his experience in the World War II era prison camps, where he witnessed human character being forged in the most trying conditions imaginable. Again, this freedom-denying *pan-determinism*, as he calls it, may be theoretically possible. Yet it did not find confirmation in what happened at Dachau.

While some there would betray their fellows for a slight reward, others were heroic to the end. "We who lived in the concentration camps," he declares,

> can remember the men who walked through the huts comforting others, giving away their last piece of bread. They may have been few in number, but they offer sufficient proof that everything can be taken from a man but one thing: the last of the human freedoms—to choose one's attitude in any given set of circumstances, to choose one's own way.[112]

Are values real? Are we here for a reason? In the vital words of William James in his 1895 lecture at Harvard University, "it feels like a real fight—as if there were something really wild in the universe which we, with all our idealities and faithfulnesses, are needed to redeem; and first of all, to redeem our own hearts

---

112   Viktor Frankl, *Man's Search for Meaning* (Boston: Beacon Press, 2017 edition), pp. 68-69.

from atheisms and fears."[113]
Sharing this feeling, I can imagine nothing in the world more wrong-minded than to deny its veracity.

---

113   William James, "Is Life Worth Living?", contained in *The Will to Believe and other essays in popular philosophy* (New York: Cosimo, Inc., 2006), page 61.

Chapter 15
Philosophy and Human Rapport

What men learn in their I—Thou relationships is far more significant than what they learn in the realm of I—It. Knowing persons gives men a sense of what is most real in the universe.

Eugene Borowitz,
A Layman's Introduction to Religious Existentialism

The One remains, the many change and pass;
Heaven's light forever shines, Earth's shadows fly;
Life, like a dome of many-colored glass,
Stains the white radiance of eternity ...

Percy Shelley,
Adonais: An Elegy on the Death of John Keats

"You and Mama," said my father shortly after her passing, crossing his fingers, "were always *just like that.*"

There was a sadness in his voice, a sadness that owed something to her death and something, as well, to his own inability to relate to me.

Maybe there is a downside to this openness I have mentioned, instilled in some early on, to other people. In such a setting a child comes naturally by sincerity, and expects it in turn. This innocence, as my Seattle friend Silver and I each knew, can lead now and again to rude surprises. More often, however, brings sincerity in turn. Most people, whether they admit it or not, want a place in the world where they can speak freely about what is important to them. An openness to others makes it easier for them to say things they aren't used to saying, and to gain some measure of encouragement in the process.

Perhaps these small instances of sharing give us moreover an inkling of our greater direction. In this final chapter, I take note again of human relationship and its bearing upon a general conception of life and destiny.

Hume's "Melancholy"

Hume's questioning of common sense, it may be recalled, led him to negative conclusions regarding beliefs that ground our daily existence: That we have moral connections with others, that life has some deep and genuine meaning, that we are even the same people over the span of our mortal lives, he saw as notions born of our own peculiarity.

Something of this reductionist outlook, as I have noted, figures strongly into mainstream thought today. Yet in the end, I wonder if such an outlook does justice to what is contained in human experience. Hume himself, in fact, seems at moments to doubt its veracity. I am reminded of a passage in a postscript to Book I of his *Treatise*, where he remarks on his own state of mind, having delved into the most fundamental questions of life.

"I am…affrighted and confounded," he admits, "with that forlorn solitude, in which I am plac'd [by] my philosophy, and fancy myself some strange uncouth monster, who not being able to mingle and unite in society, has been expell'd [from] all human commerce."

> Where am I, or what? From what causes do I derive my existence, and to what condition shall I return? Whose favour shall I court, and whose anger must I dread? What beings surround me? and on whom have I any influence, and who have any influence on me?[114]

"I am confounded by these questions," he says, "and begin to imagine myself in the most deplorable condition possible."

Yet fortunately, while reason cannot dispel these clouds, nature herself suffices to the task. From this "philosophical melancholy and delirium" Hume is released by the presence of his comrades: "I dine, I play a game of back-gammon, I converse, and am merry with my friends," after which these earlier ruminations "appear so cold, and strain'd, and ridiculous, that I cannot find in my heart to enter into them any further."

I cite this passage not to disparage Hume or his inquiries,

---

114   *A Treatise on Human Nature*, Selby-Bigge edition, page 269.

which provide a fascinating chapter in the story of modern thought. But I think that this episode in his personal life might say more than he realizes. He seems to regard this restoration of common sense as but a happy accident of his own makeup. I suspect that it involves moreover a fundamental truth about life. For in this communion with our fellows—our friends, our colleagues, our mothers—I believe we find revelation.

Two Ways of Being

In 1922, Hasidic scholar Martin Buber penned a compact volume called *I and Thou*, which explored the ways of being and knowing by which we conduct our lives.

In his early years, Buber was powerfully taken with the mysticism for which this branch of Judaism, grounded in a revivalist movement of the 18th century, is known. Yet his orientation changed as he became more concerned with what happens in the world of human interaction.

Eugene Borowitz, in a concise and splendid book on religious philosophers, recalls an incident that Buber saw as crucial in his own development. One day in the late autumn of 1914, when Europe was falling into a conflict of world proportions, the esteemed teacher emerged from an inward reverie to greet a young visitor soon to enter the army.

The man had come seeking guidance. Buber received him with cordiality, answered his questions, and watched him depart. Yet soon after, he was troubled. For the more he thought about it, the more he realized he had not allowed this fellow to say what was in his heart.

Buber's private joy, as Borowitz says, "had kept him from his brother as he stood before him in all the tribulation and suffering that comes from going to face death." The incident had a lasting effect upon him.

I and Thou is an unusual work. Hailed as a 20th Century classic, it is elusive, refusing to be absorbed in the way of most works of literature. It explores two fundamental ways in which we may encounter the world and explore it.

The relation of *I—It* and the relation of *I—Thou*:

The first of these involves the asymmetrical relationship between myself and an object. Herein I am detached, unsought, alone in my effort. It is the arena in which I employ technique to satisfy some personal want.

"The basic word I—It," Buber says, "can never be spoken with one's whole being."[115] Yet in the modern age, unfortunately, this relation has swelled until it governs practically all of human activity.

The second is the relation between myself and another living being.

This latter relation requires more of me than what is contained in the realm of I—It. In it I am called forth, plunging into an abyss that takes all of me, opening me to risk and vulnerability that were absent in the other case. There is knowledge to be gained here, as well, though knowledge of another kind, gained in another way.

One does not find such knowledge solely in this world, nor in a wholesale flight away from it. Yet in this realm of human relation lies the soul's true path in life and to eternity. "One does not find God," says Buber, "if one remains in the world; one does not find God if one leaves the world. Whoever goes forth to his You with his whole being…finds him whom one cannot seek." While God, as Rudolph Otto said, is the *Mysterium Tremendum* that terrifies and overwhelms, yet also He is a presence "closer to me than my own I."[116]

An Indian Visitor, By Way of England

Near the end of my MA program at the University of Washington, I attended a seminar in philosophy of religion with Ramchandra Gandhi, an Oxford scholar and grandson of Mahatma Gandhi, who was doing a visiting professorship that year.

Ramchandra was something of a curiosity in the department. I remember trading thoughts with Paul Dietrichson about him late one day, shortly before I finished the program in 1978.

"I became quite fond of him," mused Paul—while this odd little fellow, he said, might not have fit neatly into the scene there, "I came to see, in time, that there is something *very deep* in this guy."

Though he could be cryptic, Ghandi intrigued me, as well, with his classroom manner, reclining in his chair at times, exploring the ceiling as he chose his words (I was apprised by one department deacon that this was likely *an Oxford thing*, rather than a product of "the mystic East"), and the way he came at

115   Martin Buber, *I and Thou* (New York: Touchstone, 1996), page 54. Walter Kaufmann, translator.

116   *Ibid.*, page 127.

certain longstanding issues in our trade. He did not understand those who sought to dissolve consciousness into fleeting episodes of experience without a real and enduring subject to *have* them. Granted, we do not introspectively "find" this subject amid the discrete episodes of experience that flow constantly through us. But I—the one who is *called forth* by others—am implicit in this drama.

One afternoon someone mentioned, in passing, the classic problem of how we know that reality exists apart from our experience of it. Rene Descartes, as we all knew, had raised this question in his effort to ground philosophy in unshakable certainty. Of course, none of us really doubted that the world was here and that we were in it. Yet Gandhi was amazed that the problem could exist at all.

"I never understood," he said, "how this could be a real question," he said. "For me the answer was obvious—*other people*."

Though hesitating, I decided later that there was more in his answer than first appeared. In some way, our encounter with others has a primacy that transcends whatever private theories we may concoct. It is a reality by which we are—to use one of Ramchandra's key words, and Buber's—*summoned* to response. My human relations are not mere passing images on my conscious screen, but living encounters. (Maybe I, of all people, should have been the first to see this.)

I think of people I have met in this life, comrades who have deepened my life experience, setting me straight when an occasion called for it and providing encouragement when it was needed. Teachers and colleagues, firefighters and boxing trainers, people of all walks who lived in my neighborhood on the hill and in neighborhoods across the nation and the world: They were sources of inspiration and assurance, giving me fresh insight and reminding me, now and again also, of things I knew yet needed to hear.

Misunderstandings, injustices, and love that went unrequited; moments when things were said in the wrong way, when hostility arose and misfortune seemed to prevail—I have learned that such failures, in some cases, are made right within this present life. So will they be righted in the greater scheme of which this life is a part.

I think yet again of my mother, her kindness vivid now in mind's eye, whether toward family and friends, a stranger at the door, or a stray kitten that needed tending. While she might not have enjoyed the company of everyone she met, her estimate of each was tempered always by what she saw—the scars and fears, as well as the underlying human possibility, that showed in their faces.

I think, too, of her sense of humor, present even in stressful times, a quality she had seen in her own father as they met together the trials of rural Minnesota early in the 20th century. The laughter we shared was a testament to what Viktor Frankl discovered during his time in the concentration camps—that humor is one of the ways we transcend ourselves and find, even amid trying circumstance, a place from which to cope with it.

Plain Advice From Inspired Authors

I mentioned, when recalling a rare bright moment in my high school years, Norman Vincent Peale's classic volume *The Power of Positive Thinking*. When reflecting upon relationships with other people and what they teach us, I think of this book and a related one, rarely noted in recent decades (and then likely in jest), Dale Carnegie's *How to Make Friends and Influence People*.

Such works are timeless, speaking to issues inherent in the human condition. A stream of related works has come in decades since, recasting these issues in terms of new culture and sensibility. At times they occasion breakthroughs for those who read them, at times not.

If a book of this kind does not have its intended effect, it may owe to the writer, who lacks the substance for his own enterprise. But often as not, I think, it will owe something to the reader, who absorbs it only in a passive manner, taking in the words across and down each page without benefit of an added dimension in the process. This extra thing is one that the book itself cannot provide, namely the reader's own willing application of its ideas in the world of lived interaction.

Over the years, I would notice, when these classic works were mentioned, it was sometimes by people who had not read them, much less tested them in the laboratory of life. I remember, for example, one fledgling UW social scientist, fresh out of his doctoral program, who loved to make casual asides, often disdainful, about famous trends and authors—Plato, Aristotle, Freud, the existentialists—having scant acquaintance with any.

He remarked one afternoon about the cheap and "manipulative" way in which writers like Peale and Carnegie instructed their readers to deal with those around them. Here again, this fellow spoke of what he did not understand. The homely stories in these books, if one takes time to reflect upon them, tend in a very different direction.

To cite an example, Carnegie speaks of his time teaching composition classes at the Brooklyn Institute of Arts and Sciences. In one was unhappy fuel salesman C. M. Knaphle, who revealed in a classroom exercise his frustration in trying to break ground with a particular chain store outlet in his neighborhood.

This man, said Carnegie, poured out his wrath on chain stores across the board, deeming them to be a curse upon the nation. Carnegie suggested he try a different approach. He set up a debate within the class regarding the impact of such stores on society.

And now came an interesting twist: To Knaphle he assigned the task of *defending* the stores, rather than attacking them. To prepare for his role in this exercise, the embittered student visited the head of the one that had caused him particular grief. He asked for information that would support the side of the argument to which he had been assigned.

What happened next amazed him. Hoping to receive a few minutes of the man's time, he got far more. He left with all the information he could have wanted—and with new business.

"Here he was," marveled the salesman,

> offering to buy fuel without my even suggesting it. I had made more headway in two hours by becoming genuinely interested in him and his problems than I could have made in ten years trying to get him interested in me and my product.[117]

His attitude toward the stores had undergone a dramatic change, and moreover, he had learned a lesson about life.

Some will disparage such a lesson, saying that it puts success ahead of sincerity. If so, they miss its point. For what it teaches is that success, in any enterprise, requires *an interest outside oneself*—in Peale's words, "a sincere and forthright interest in and love for people."

Cultivation of this trait requires not false flattery or misleading appearance, but integrity. It demands of us the will to find and uproot certain blocks within us that presently impede our progress. So, for example, I must bear in mind the self-esteem of those with

---

117   Dale Carnegie, *How to Make Friends and Influence People*, (New York: Simon and Schuster, 1982), page 17

whom I come in contact in every arena.

"If I deflate your ego and therefore your self-importance," says Peale,

> though you may laugh it off, I have deeply wounded you. In fact, I have shown disrespect for you, and while you may exercise charity toward me, even so, unless you are finely developed spiritually, you are not going to like me very well.[118]

Our real success requires a largeness of mind and soul that will enable us to give to others without need of overt compensation, and to take joy in their own well-being.

"Whomever you help to become a better, stronger person," Peale observes, "will give you his undying devotion." You must extend this help, he believes, not merely as a strategy on your own behalf. Rather, do it because you genuinely like him.

Standing Alone

For all this talk of sharing and communion, I want to add before ending this chapter, there is a sense, too, in which every human being must maintain a basic and solitary independence.

Many people, as noted in the opening pages of this story, take continual refuge in such things as family, faith, social peers and the going political mindset. Yet in the end we cannot default to these sources—rather we must step back, in mind's eye, and decide actively what life will be ours.

"I have never surrendered my mind," said John Haynes Holmes, on the occasion of his retirement in 1949,

> to any church, or party, or individual...and I do not propose to begin now. I have ever counted it my highest duty, as well as my most precious privilege, to do my own thinking, reach my own opinions, stand by my own convictions—and I shall try to remain faithful to that duty to the end.[119]

In these words, I find the spirit of Socrates, who bid his

---

118   *The Power of Positive Thinking*, page 192.

119   This quote, which appeared in the *Christian Register* in September of September 20, 1954, is contained in the Voss anthology, page 222.

friend Crito to "follow the argument where it leads," no matter the consequence. Let each conviction stand or fall as destiny decides. A church doctrine, a family upbringing, an in-fashion view pushed by industries of mass media, the shared view of our inner circle—even the going trend of philosophy itself—all of this involves human endeavor, finite and fallible. For this reason, each of these, in the end, is but one more thing over against which the soul must take its stand.

Unfailing Spirit

    This photo of Mama in the back yard was taken that morning in April of 1954 when we set off for my first day of Sunday School. The Columbia River, rolling to the sea, lies faint in the background.

    "Drag-ass poor people..."

    That remark my father made to me, in the wake of my mother's death, expressed his hope that I would rise above their social tier. He wanted me to have standing in the community, to use *four-bit* words and carry myself in the way of people whom he saw only from a distance. The irony was that the education I received in such abundance, through their generosity, and the many experiences, at home and abroad, that this training made possible, led me to prize unseen things above all.

The door to happiness, remarks one of Kierkegaard's characters in his two-volume work *Either / Or*, opens *outward*. While these words, in their context, are open to reading, I think that they express something of what I learned from the woman who was with me from the beginning.

Years ago, a noted playwright lamented the fact that most of us spend our lives looking for someone who will love us more than they love themselves. Our inevitable failure, in this effort, he saw as life's inherent tragedy.

Could it be that an answer lies in that courage of which William Barrett writes? Perhaps in giving of ourselves, we transcend this egocentric condition of need that brings our habitual disappointment. In giving without need of return, perhaps we find the thing we sought after all.

Here again echoes Mama's influence, this opening of one's own concerns to include others. Such truth, it seems, does not come all at once, but in stages over the course of life. But the impact of these moments is lasting, like unto heat applied to a piece of iron that takes on warmth a little at a time through its length. Her unfailing spirit, buoyant in every situation, glows bright today as ever.

A Philosophy of Life in a Single Sentence

"Much on Earth is hidden from us," writes Feodor Dostoevsky through his character Father Zossima, "but there is given us in recompense the secret conviction of our living bond with another world, a celestial and loftier world: And the very roots of our thoughts and sensations are not here, but there in other worlds."[120]

Five hundred years earlier, in the region of Norfolk, lived a young English peasant girl—her birth, as historian Elizabeth Obbard notes, was an obscure event. She entered this world, it is likely, in crowded and dismal conditions, and we do not have any

---

120   Feodor Dostoevsky, The Brothers Karamazov. These words, which are uttered in the story by Father Zossima, are contained in the *Grail of Life* anthology, page 217.

reliable record of her name. In time she would be called Julian.[121]

We speak today of hard times, but for most of us, life is far less terrifying than it was for her. Between 1315 and 1317, a Great Famine would carry away thirty to sixty percent of the European population. In mid-century the Black Plague, a bacterial nemesis carried by fleas feeding upon rats, brought lethal nightmare to vast regions of Eurasia and North Africa. Spread soon after from human to human in pneumonic form, it would take some 75 to 200 million lives over a period of about seven years.

The Plague entered her area when Julian was perhaps six years of age. During this time, says Obbard, "men and women could rise in the morning and be dead by evening, their faces bloated, their bodies already near decomposition." Scarcely a family was left intact. Priests succumbed even as they ministered to the dying. At night, death carts rattled in the alleys, houses yielding up their bodies. It was a time of sorrow, when loved ones were torn from families and those left behind feared for the spiritual salvation of those who had expired before their eyes.

Julian's childhood, says Obbard, "would have been short as well as sombre." She would have learned quickly the tasks of tending a household. A girl at this time could be married at fifteen.

A second plague struck in 1361, when Julian was nineteen and might have had a family of her own. We do not know when she received her religious instruction—perhaps, if she had the means, she received rudimentary schooling at a convent. From the looks of it, however, she was only "a deeply religious young laywoman, touched early by death and sorrow."

Early in life, Julian had asked God for spiritual gifts that would enable her to grasp His truth. At thirty, lying ill and ready to pass to the next world, she received a series of *shewings*, or visions, that lasted a period of two days. She recovered her health, and retired, in time, to an anchorhold beside the church of St. Julian and St. Edward in Norwich. It does not seem that she had further revelations during her mortal life, but in this brief span she received insight that guided her to the end. Known today as St. Julian of Norwich, she devoted the rest of her life to pondering things she had seen and heard during those hours near death.

---

121   See Elizabeth Ruth Obbard, *Introducing Julian – Woman of Norwich* (Hyde Park: New City Press, 1996

In *A Shewing of God's Love*, she gave a brief account of her experience; about twenty years later, she composed a longer version. She became revered, in time, as a teacher and counselor, though her name, family, and childhood experience would pass into oblivion.

The most famous words contained in this writing come in a passage where Julian, describing her vision, recalls her perplexity at sin. For without it, she imagined, we would all be clean as God might want.

"I mourned and sorrowed over it," recalls Julian, "without reason and discretion."

Whereupon Jesus answered her, saying that sin had its purpose, *but all shall be well, and all shall be well, and all manner of thing shall be well.*"

With these words Julian pours out a message of hope and assurance to fellow souls across the world through all of time. In them is a summation of human destiny wherein she is present to her readers, and they to her, each time her promise is read. Days pass, scenes change. Comedy and tragedy have their time.

Crises pass and recede into distant memory. Yet from all eternity comes assurance. With Julian's words we are beckoned Home with the promise that good shall be wrought out of even the worst moments along the way by a wisdom that surpasses our own.

Words that Beckon

Now and again, I flash on that scene in the hospital when Mama was failing, her eyes red and face ghastly white, surrounded by hospital staff making a last ditch effort to keep her alive.

No sooner do I see this than I see, too, that such an event is not tragedy, but life, working out the great cycle that houses our existence. The signs of mortal age, dreaded by some, cosmetically delayed by those who have the means, are not misfortune, but rites of passage that signal our way Home. This life is part of a greater scheme in which there is resolution, and a vantage point from which all travail makes sense, and sorrow is dissolved in a world whose joys exceed even the greatest moments we presently know.

I think more often of that image of her and me on the sidewalk of East 11th Street, the road opening out into the distance. (A colorized enlargement, matted and framed, stands near as I key these words.) With her help, though every turn and crisis, I walked up that road of life. And now, it seems, the years carry me back to that modest house with yellow shake siding on the edge of the hill.

The message of that birthday horoscope, innocuous as it might appear to a casual reader, encapsulated something she had sought to impart to me so many times in my first thirty years of life. Looking back, I see how often my own anxiety multiplied what difficulty life had to offer. These points of stress, had I the perspective to see it, were part of a wider scheme that would have a favorable end.

"Oh, yes there is." Those words, uttered by my mother when I confessed to her my doubt two days before she left this world, would outweigh all the skepticism I ever saw. Mama never lost her faith, amid any trial, in the final good that we will see one day in its entirety. In her voice, in her image, I feel the call of Home awaiting. Her very last words to me, even as her strength ran out,

were words of comfort. This life is part of something that will redeem, as Julian declares, all that has happened on the way to its realization.

Epilogue

This postcard, *circa* 1910, shows Crown Point and the Vista House along the Columbia River as it rolls on its way to the Pacific Ocean. Multnomah Falls lies a short way in the distance along this road on the same side.

A good many photographs, in coming decades, have captured this vantage point. Always when seeing them (even having driven many times in my later years the I-84 freeway from Portland to Salt Lake City), I am struck by the promise and mystery of this scene as it fades east into the distance.

* * * * *

Plenty more would happen, in the years following the Claremont adventure and the time in Nanchang.

In the fall of 1991, after being home for a year after the China adventure, I flew to Utah to teach at a local college. There I met Maria, and we would be married in 1995. Brief visiting adventures would follow in the Slovak Republic and at the University of Wales, Lampeter. In the summer of 2000, I completed a certification for teaching English as a second language from Cambridge University at the Russian campus in Moscow.

In 2001, nine days before I turned 50, our son Chace McGwire was born, and a new chapter of life would begin. In 2003 Maria and I went our separate ways. In 2011, after five years in New Jersey, I took on a highly rewarding assignment at Shantou University at the southeast end of mainland China, returning in September of 2021 and reuniting with Maria and Chace after a decade working with bright and appreciative students and forging friendships that have not ended.

During these years, I have kept a hand in sportswriting, publishing a dozen extended articles on some of my favorite prizefighters for the IBRO (International Boxing Research Organization) quarterly journal. This book is my seventh, and fifth devoted to issues in philosophy and religion. Two others have centered around boxing at the turn of the century, covering fighters of roughly 1890 to 1910. I have, at this writing, ended my employment with Shantou after a year of on-line teaching, and have happily returned, in semi-retirement, to work again after 20 years with a very engaging group of students once more at Utah Valley State University.

*   *   *   *   *

Again, I express my appreciation to cousins Marcia, Kristin, and Alyssa for their help and encouragement with this project. Thanks are due also to Tabitha McCoard and Mike Clough, who currently work at the Maryhill Museum in Washington, and who leave no doubt in my mind that this treasured hilltop haven is in good hands.

Last, and surely not least, I say *thank you* to my son Chace for his continual help and patience with computer issues during these past eighteen months, often in connection with this book, and to Maria for her painstaking and multiple reviews of the manuscript during its preparation. It is good to be home.

Principal Sources

D. M. Baillie, *Faith in God and Its Christian Consummation*, Faber and Faber, 1964.

William Barrett, *Irrational Man*, Anchor Books, 1965.

Martin Buber, *I and Thou*, Touchstone Books, 1996.

Dale Carnegie, *How to Make Friends and Influence People*, Simon and Schuster, 1982.

Ty Cobb, *My Twenty Years in Baseball*, Dover Publications, 2009. William R. Cobb, editor.

Fyodor Dostoevsky, *The Brothers Karamazov*, The Modern Library, 1950.

Paul Edwards and Arthur Pap, eds., *A Modern Introduction to Philosophy*, Macmillan: The Free Press, 1973.

Harry Emerson Fosdick, *Adventurous Religion*, Harper and Brothers, 1926.

__________, *The Assurance of Immortality*, The Macmillan Company, 1918.

Viktor Frankl, *Man's Search for Meaning*, Beacon Press, 2017.

Rocky Graziano and Roland Barber, *Somebody Up There Likes Me*, Simon and Schuster, 1955.

Edith Hamilton and Huntington Cairns, eds., *The Collected Dialogues of Plato*, Princeton University Press, 1961.

Arthur Herman, *The Viking Heart: How Scandinavians Conquered the World*, Houghton Mifflin Harcourt, 2022.

John Hick, ed., *Classical and Contemporary Readings in the Philosophy of Religion*, Prentice-Hall, Inc., 1970.

__________, *Death and Eternal Life*, Westminster / John Knox Press, 1984.

__________, *Evil and the God of Love*, Harper and Row, 1966.

__________, *Faith and Knowledge*, Cornell University Press, 1957.

__________, *God Has Many Names*, Westminster Press, 1965.

John Haynes Holmes, *The Affirmation of Immortality*, The Macmillan

Principal Sources

Company, 1947.

_______________, *Is Death the End?* G. P. Putnam's Sons, 192.5.

David Hume, *A Treatise of Human Nature*, Selby-Bigge edition, Oxford University Press, 1978.

Aldous Huxley, *The Perennial Philosophy*, Harper Perennial, 2009.

William James, *The Varieties of Religious Experience*, Penguin Group, Inc., 1982.

_____________, *The Will to Believe and other essays in popular philosophy*, Cosimo, Inc., 2006.

James Joyce, *A Portrait of the Artist as a Young Man*, Signet Classic, 1991.

Immanuel Kant, *The Critique of Practical Reason*, The University of Chicago Press, 1949. Lewis White Beck, translator.

Walter Kaufmann, ed., *Existentialism from Dostoevsky to Sartre*, Penguin Group, Inc., 1975.

_______________, *The Faith of a Heretic*, Princeton University Press, 2015.

C. S. Lewis, The Abolition of Man, Touchstone Books, 1996.

_________, *Surprised by Joy: The Shape of My Early Life*, Geoffrey Bles, 1955.

Sir Oliver Lodge, *Phantom Walls*, G. P. Putnam's Sons, 1930.

Norman Mailer, *"King of the Hill"*, New American Library, 1971.

F. W. H. Myers, *Human Personality and Its Survival of Bodily Death*, University Books, 1961.

Kelly Nicholson, *The Prospect of Immortality*, Homeward Bound Publishing, 2002.

Elizabeth Ruth Obbard, *Introducing Julian – Woman of Norwich*, New City Press, 1996.

Norman Vincent Peale, *The Power of Positive Thinking*, Prentice-Hall, 1952.

Swami Prabhavananda, translator, *Bhagavad Gita: The Song of God*, Signet Classic, 2002.

_________________, *The Spiritual Heritage of India*, Hollywood Press, 1980.

Hastings Rashdall, *The Theory of Good and Evil*, Clarendon Press, 1907.

Barney Ross and Martin Abramson, *No Man Stands Alone*, J. B. Lippincott

Company, 1957.

Bertrand Russell, *Why I Am Not a Christian and other essays*, Touchstone Books, 1957.

Steven Sanders and David R. Cheney, eds., *The Meaning of Life*, Prentice-Hall, Inc., 1980.

Minot Savage, *Life Beyond Death*, G. P. Putnam's Son's 1902.

Huston Smith, *The World's Religions*, HarperCollins, 1991.

Robert Speer, *The Marks of a Man – Or, the Essentials of Christian Character*, Fleming H. Revell Company, 1907.

Linda Brady Tesner and Robert M. Reynolds, *Maryhill Museum of Art*, Maryhill Museum of Art, undated.

G. N. M. Tyrrell, *The Personality of Man*, Pelican Books, 1947.

Brenda Ueland, *If You Want to Write*, Graywolf Press, 1987.

_____________, *Me – A Memoir*, published in Duluth, Minnesota, 2016.

Miguel de Unamuno, *The Tragic Sense of Life*, Dover Publications, 1956.

Kelly Nicholson is a much traveled college and university instructor and veteran sportswriter who has taught philosophy and religious studies on three continents for the better part of half a century. He holds degrees and certifications from the University of Washington, the Claremont Graduate School, and Cambridge University in England. A former firefighter and amateur boxer, he currently teaches philosophy part-time at Utah Valley University in Orem.

Other Books by Ozark Mountain Publishing, Inc.

Dolores Cannon
A Soul Remembers Hiroshima
Between Death and Life
Conversations with Nostradamus,
    Volume I, II, III
The Convoluted Universe -Book One,
    Two, Three, Four, Five
The Custodians
Five Lives Remembered
Horns of the Goddess
Jesus and the Essenes
Keepers of the Garden
Legacy from the Stars
The Legend of Starcrash
The Search for Hidden Sacred
    Knowledge
They Walked with Jesus
The Three Waves of Volunteers and the
    New Earth
A Very Special Friend
Aron Abrahamsen
Holiday in Heaven
James Ream Adams
Little Steps
Justine Alessi & M. E. McMillan
Rebirth of the Oracle
Kathryn Andries
Time: The Second Secret
Will Alexander
Call Me Jonah
Cat Baldwin
Divine Gifts of Healing
The Forgiveness Workshop
Penny Barron
The Oracle of UR
The Oracle of UR, Book 2
P.E. Berg & Amanda Hemmingsen
The Birthmark Scar
The Birthmark Scar, Book 2
Dan Bird
Finding Your Way in the Spiritual Age
Waking Up in the Spiritual Age
Julia Cannon
Soul Speak – The Language of Your
    Body
Jack Cauley
Journey for Life
Ronald Chapman
Seeing True
Jack Churchward
Lifting the Veil on the Lost
    Continent of Mu
The Stone Tablets of Mu

Carolyn Greer Daly
Opening to Fullness of Spirit
Patrick De Haan
The Alien Handbook
Paulinne Delcour-Min
Cosmic Crystals!
Divine Fire
Holly Ice
Spiritual Gold
Anthony DeNino
The Power of Giving and Gratitude
Joanne DiMaggio
Edgar Cayce and the Unfulfilled
    Destiny of Thomas Jefferson
    Reborn
Paul Fisher
Like a River to the Sea
Anita Holmes
Twidders
Aaron Hoopes
Reconnecting to the Earth
Edin Huskovic
God is a Woman
Patricia Irvine
In Light and In Shade
Kevin Killen
Ghosts and Me
Susan Linville
Blessings from Agnes
Donna Lynn
From Fear to Love
Curt Melliger
Heaven Here on Earth
Where the Weeds Grow
Henry Michaelson
And Jesus Said – A Conversation
Andy Myers
Not Your Average Angel Book
Holly Nadler
The Hobo Diaries
Guy Needler
The Anne Dialogues
Avoiding Karma
Beyond the Origin
Beyond the Source – Book 1, Book 2
The Curators
The History of God
The OM
The Origin Speaks
Psycho Spiritual Healing
Kelly Nicholson
Ethel Marie

For more information about any of the above titles, soon to be released titles,
or other items in our catalog, write, phone or visit our website:
PO Box 754, Huntsville, AR 72740|479-738-2348/800-935-0045|www.ozarkmt.com